Depression and the Divine

Depression and the Divine

Was Jesus Clinically Depressed?

David C. Wilson

WIPF & STOCK · Eugene, Oregon

DEPRESSION AND THE DIVINE
Was Jesus Clinically Depressed?

Copyright © 2018 David C. Wilson. All rights reserved. Except for brief quotations in critical publications or reviews, no part of this book may be reproduced in any manner without prior written permission from the publisher. Write: Permissions, Wipf and Stock Publishers, 199 W. 8th Ave., Suite 3, Eugene, OR 97401.

Wipf & Stock
An Imprint of Wipf and Stock Publishers
199 W. 8th Ave., Suite 3
Eugene, OR 97401

www.wipfandstock.com

PAPERBACK ISBN: 978-1-5326-6267-6
HARDCOVER ISBN: 978-1-5326-6268-3
EBOOK ISBN: 978-1-5326-6269-0

Manufactured in the U.S.A.

For my longsuffering wife, Charity, and the girls, not forgetting Chris who likewise endured much!

Contents

List of Figures | ix

Acknowledgements | xi

Abbreviations | xii

Introduction | xv

Chapter 1: Genetics | 1
- Speech 2
- Schizophrenia and Bipolar Disorder 4
- The Time before Time 5
- Depression and Psychopathology 8
- Psychosis and Psychopathology 11

Chapter 2: Genesis | 13
- Past Approaches to Genesis 2–3 15
- Dream 26
- A Third Approach 30

Chapter 3: "To Sleep, Perchance to Dream . . . ." | 32
- Depression 35
- Cross-Cultural Psychology 38
- Derived Etic Hypnogram—Abraham 42

Chapter 4: Elijah—A Dreamer Of Dreams! | 50
- 1 Kings 18–19 51
- Elijah's Hypnogram—1 Kings 19:2–21 54
- Spiritual Encounter 61
- Spiritual Encounter within the Dreamform 66

Theophanic Dialogue within the Dreamform   75
Dialogue with other Nepheshim within the Dreamform   81
A Dreamer of Dreams   83

Chapter 5: Dreamtime in the Garden of Eden | 86

"White Man got no Dreaming!"   88
Dreamtime in the Garden   95
The Tree of Life   100
Death in the Garden   105

Chapter 6: "The One Who Was To Come" | 111

The Beatitudes—Matthew 5:3-12   111
The Transfiguration—Luke 9:28-36   120
The Temptation—Matthew 4:1-11   123

Chapter 7: "One Greater Than . . . " | 128

The Sign of Jonah: Luke 11:29-32   129
The Sign   132
The 'Sign of Jesus'   137

Chapter 8: Conclusions: Depression And The Divine | 142

Appendix: The Making Of A Divine Man —The Book Of Jonah | 151

Jonah's First Altered State(s) of Consciousness—Jonah 1:1-2:11   153
Jonah Ben Amittai—Jonah 1:1   154
Fleeing the Presence of the LORD: The Descent from Transcendence—Jonah 1:2-3   162
YHWH Controls "The Horizontal" (The Storm)—Jonah 1:4-16   165
YHWH Controls "The Vertical" (The Psalm)—Jonah 2:1-11   177
Nineveh—Jonah 3:1-4:3   196
The Second Mission—Jonah 3:1-5a   197
The Proclamation of a Fast—Jonah 3:5b-4:3   203
The Dialogue: Altered State of Consciousness (2)—Jonah 4:4-11   210

Bibliography | 217

Index | 233

List of Figures

Fig. 1: The 'Normality'—Psychosis Continuum | 9
Fig. 2: Typical Hypnogram of a Normal Young Adult | 35
Fig. 3: Typical Hypnogram of a Depressive | 36
Fig. 4: Steps in Operationalizing Emics and Etics | 40
Fig. 5: 'Derived Etic' Hypnogram of Genesis 15 | 48
Fig. 6: 'Derived Etic' Hypnogram of 1 Kings 19:2-21 | 59
Fig. 7: 'Derived Etic' Hypnogram of Genesis 2:15—3:24 | 87
Fig. 8: 'Derived Etic' Hypnogram of Luke 9:29-35 | 121
Fig. 9: 'Derived Etic' Hypnogram of Jonah 1:1—2:11 | 194
Fig. 10: Eastern Mediterranean View of the Cosmos | 196
Fig. 11: 'Derived Etic' Hypnogram of Jonah 4:3-11 | 211

Acknowledgements

DURING MY RESEARCH AND the later compilation and writing of this book I have benefited—time without number—from the inspiration, guidance, and teaching of the Holy Spirit, for which I am forever grateful. Special thanks, however, should also go to Professor George J. Brooke for the generous way in which he reviewed and appraised copious amounts of material attached to numerous emails, and the invaluable suggestions he made prior to recommending publication with Wipf and Stock Publishers.

Abbreviations

ABD	Freedman, David Noel, ed. *Anchor Bible Dictionary*. 6 vols. New York: Doubleday, 1992.
Adv Psychiatr Treat	Advances in Psychiatric Treatment
AHRW	Alcohol Health & Research World
Am J Med	American Journal of Medicine
AnOr	Analecta Orientalia
Arch Gen Psychiatry	Archives of general psychiatry
BA	Biblical Archaeologist
BARev	Biblical Archaeology Review
BDB	Francis Brown, S. R. Driver, and Charles A. Briggs, *A Hebrew and English Lexicon of the Old Testament*. Oxford, 1906.
BibInt	Biblical Interpretation
Biol Psychiatry	Biological Psychiatry
BJRL	Bulletin of the John Rylands Library
BSac	Bibliotheca Sacra
BT	Bible Translator
BTB	Biblical Theology Bulletin
BZ	Biblische Zeitschrift
CBQ	Catholic Biblical Quarterly
Chem. Br.	Chemistry in Britain
CJ	Concordia-Journal
DBI	Coggins, R. J., and J. L. Houlden, eds. *Dictionary of Biblical Interpretation*. London: SCM Press, 1990.
DDD	Van der Toorn, K., B. Becking, and P. W. van der Horst, eds. *Dictionary of Deities and Demons in the Bible*. Leiden: Brill, 1995.

DJD	Discoveries in the Judaean Desert
DJG	Green, Joel B., Scot McKnight, and I. Howard Marshall, eds. *Dictionary of Jesus and the Gospels.* Downers Grove, IL: Intervarsity Press, 1992.
DSM	*Diagnostic and Statistical Manual of Mental Disorders*
ErIsr	*Eretz Israel*
HALOT	Koehler, Ludwig, and Walter Baumgartner, eds. *Hebrew and Aramaic Lexicon of the Old Testament.* Leiden: Brill, 2000.
HUCA	*Hebrew Union College Annual*
HTR	*Harvard Theological Review*
J Anal Psychol	*Journal of Analytical Psychology*
JANESCU	*Journal of the Ancient Near Eastern Society of Columbia University*
JASPR	*Journal for the American Society of Psychical Research*
JBL	*Journal of Biblical Literature*
JBQ	*Jewish Bible Quarterly*
JCP	*Journal of Clinical Psychiatry*
JCS	*Journal of Cuneiform Studies*
J Infect	*Journal of Infection*
JNCN	*Journal of Neuropsychiatry and Clinical Neurosciences*
JNES	*Journal of Near Eastern Studies*
JP	*Journal of Parapsychology*
J Psychoactive Drugs	*Journal of Psychoactive Drugs*
J Psychol Judaism	*Journal of Psychology and Judaism*
JQR	*Jewish Quarterly Review*
JRSM	*Journal of the Royal Society of Medicine*
JRH	*Journal of Religion and Health*
JSJ	*Journal for the Study of Judaism*
JSOT	*Journal for the Study of the Old Testament*
JSPR	*Journal of the Society for Psychical Research*
KJV	King James (Authorized) Version
LXX	Septuagint
NEB	New English Bible

NIDOTTE	VanGemeren, Willem A., ed. *New International Dictionary of Old Testament Theology and Exegesis*. 5 vols. Carlisle: Paternoster, 1996.
NRSV	New Revised Standard Version
PEQ	*Palestine Exploration Quarterly*
PNAS	*Proceedings of the National Academy of Sciences*
PR	*Psychiatry Research*
Proc R Soc Lond [Biol]	*Proceedings of the Royal Society of London. Series B: Biological Sciences (London)*
RB	*Revue Biblique*
SGO	*Surgery Gynaecology & Obstetrics*
SJOT	*Scandinavian Journal of the Old Testament*
SBLSP	*Society of Biblical Literature Seminar Papers*
Soc Psych Psych Epid	*Social Psychiatry and Psychiatric Epidemiology*
StudOr	*Studia Orientalia*
Surg Gynecol Obstet	*Surgery, Gynecology & Obstetrics*
SVT	*Supplements to Vetus Testamentum*
TDNT	Kittel, G., and G. Friedrich, eds. *Theological Dictionary of the New Testament*. Grand Rapids, MI: Eerdmans, 1964–1976.
TDOT	Botterweck, G. Johannes, Helmer Ringgren, and Heinz-Josef Fabry, eds. Theological *Dictionary of the Old Testament*. Grand Rapids, MI: Eerdmans, 1977–1999.
TWOT	Harris, R. Laird, Gleason L. Archer Jr., and Bruce K. Waltke, eds. *Theological Wordbook of the Old Testament*. 2 vols. Chicago: Moody, 1980
TynBul	*Tyndale Bulletin*
UF	*Ugarit-Forschungen*
VT	*Vetus Testamentum*
WBC	Word Biblical Commentary
ZAW	*Zeitschrift für die Alttestamentliche Wissenschaft*
ZDPV	*Zeitschrift des Deutschen Palästina-Vereins*

Introduction

WHILE IT HAS LONG been recognized that psychological factors are a feature of the lives of the prophets,[1] attempts to reveal meaningful information by the application of psychological methods to particular texts in the Hebrew Bible have met with only limited acceptance amongst biblical scholars. This is in part due to the difficulties inherent in endeavoring to apply the tenets of what is in essence a modern, empirical, scientific discipline to so-called 'inert' historiographical material. Such an approach amounts to the imposition of a modern, Western, etic perspective onto an alien culture, not least because it attempts to apply the tenets of a single discipline onto that culture, and in so doing is effectively employing reductionist parameters to assess a culture with a much more holistic worldview. Indeed, the sheer complexity of the Ancient Near Eastern cultures under examination suggests that this kind of approach should be widened to include other disciplines, thus applying a more balanced approach intended to better reflect the ancient worldview found in the texts bequeathed by those cultures. This present work has, therefore, from the outset attempted to apply insights from the discipline of psychology—together with its close analogue, psychiatry, simultaneously with other medical disciplines such as physiology and pharmacology. Moreover, a focus on more specific areas (especially cross-cultural psychology) associated with psychology has enabled a more comprehensive methodology to be derived and employed. The resulting amalgam of disciplines becomes capable—especially when admixed with other (more general and sociological) aspects of cross-cultural studies—of producing a much more accurate psychophysiological profile of the 'prophet' than was hitherto possible.

The foundational discipline of the applied methodology is polysomnography (modern sleep research), and this can be validated on the basis of cross-cultural psychology, since the behavior to be identified (overall

---

1. See for example, Wiener, *Elijah*. Also Lacocque and Lacocque, *Jonah: A Psycho-Religious Approach to the Prophet*.

sleep patterns) is found in all cultures everywhere—both ancient and modern. Biblical accounts of nocturnal activity (i.e. overall sleep pattern) can then be compared with modern, laboratory records of nocturnal activity (hypnograms), with the intention of seeking resonance—a demonstrable and significant measure of agreement between the two cultures on sleep as a universal, human activity. In order to produce such a "derived etic"[2] perspective on sleep the speech-action/sleep sequence found in these texts, as represented by the length of text allocated respectively to speech-action vis-à-vis sleep, should be compared with the length (duration) of each component of the dream/sleep sequence found in a modern hypnogram. The result of such a comparison may then be represented graphically, and termed a 'derived etic' hypnogram. It follows that if this operation is successfully performed on selected texts (e.g. 1 Kgs 19:2–21, Gen 2:15–23 and Jonah 1–4), which do not contain any explicit reference to altered states of consciousness (ASCs), then the presence of ASCs in those texts in the form of dreams or visions will have been demonstrated.

It has been affirmed that "methods of literary criticism are more appropriate" to the discussion of dreams in the "Old Testament . . . than a psychological approach,"[3] and this is true insofar as that psychology has usually been solely derived from within the cultural perspectives of the modern West. Given that the latter is an atypical culture—when viewed against a global or historical backdrop—it is important to recognize that the methods of cross-cultural psychology are more appropriate, and when allied to other disciplines can yield significant new insights without diminishing the dream report as a literary creation. Thus, the contention will be defended that many dream reports are not merely deliberate literary devices employed to further the various purposes of the narrator/editor(s), but rather incorporate authentic dream experience as a readily recognizable cultural pattern to authenticate those purposes. It should be acknowledged that ancient observers were capable of recognizing and recording patterns of universal, human behavior in an appropriate manner.

However, and notwithstanding the foregoing, it may be said that in general ancient *writers/editors* of texts recorded the overall sleep pattern in slightly different ways, causing texts to differ perhaps in relation to the date of the final form of a text. Indeed, some foundational texts (e.g. Gen 2:15–23, 15:1–21) contain a relatively complete dream/sleep/dream sequence, whereas others (e.g. Jer 1:4–19) contain few or no references to sleep, despite the sleep sequence remaining punctuated in other ways, as

---

2. Segall et al., *Human Behaviour*, 55.
3. Robinson, "Dreams in the Old Testament," 4.

with Jeremiah where "the word of the Lord" came three times. Moreover, in this passage each period of speech-action still maintains the same relationship (in terms of length) to the others—exactly the same relationship as that found in a depressive hypnogram—where the first period is characteristically elongated relative to the second period. Given that the language and narrative structure used by authors is essentially a dialogue between them and their readers (listeners) where both share the same social world, there would be little need to continually repeat the full dream/sleep sequence in its entirety.[4] Certainly, much later texts such as those found in the New Testament may offer even less complete information, yet they may still carry sufficient material to enable comparison and identification with Old Testament models. Therefore, in pursuit of answers to the central enigma posed in this work, comparisons will be made between the narratives of prophets in the Hebrew bible and passages (principally) about Jesus, yet with the benefit of significantly more information than was hitherto available.

---

4. Pilch, "Transfiguration," 50.

1

Genetics

It is my great hope that this present work remains readable despite having been obliged to introduce technicalities along with their associated jargon, which may be as obscure and esoteric to the reader as they were to me when my more familiar researches led me to them. It is my belief that the biblical story of (modern) man's beginnings in the first three chapters of Genesis, and particularly Gen 2:4b—3:24, are a true and faithful record of a primordial time in the evolution[1] of modern humans. It is my hope that I will be able to demonstrate—at least to the satisfaction of the reader—that during this time human beings were much, much *more* in so many respects than they are now, rather than less as is the common perception, even if my 'technicalities' might fall just a little short of a rigorous scientific proof.

As might be gathered from the title the subject of this present work is very definitely multidisciplinary in nature. Clearly, Genesis might be seen to be connected with Jesus (although that of itself may be disputed in some quarters), but how can a study of genetics possibly inform either the foundational accounts of the Hebrew Bible or the phenomenon that is Jesus? At outset it was stated that the particular account under scrutiny is the second creation (and fall) account, that is, Genesis 2:4b—3:24, hereinafter referred to as Gen 2–3, and it will become clear why both chapters should be considered as a single story. This account is more familiarly known as the story of Adam and Eve in the "Garden of Eden," an account often considered to be little more than myth or even fairy tale (as distinct from a serious historiography of the beginnings of humankind), and this is especially so since the canonical bible itself makes few further references to the story. But what possible defense could there be for considering this 'tale' as serious historiography, and why and how can genetics help in the search for evidence for such a claim?

In order to progress this idea it will be necessary to accept two working premises, the first of which is that the creation story as we have it today is

---

1. I will use the term 'evolution' advisedly throughout this work, but without the seemingly unshakable belief in this theory postulated by some of my sources.

of very great antiquity, and precedes the written biblical account by millennia. Support for understanding the text in this way will be sought from commentaries on the Hebrew text, where terms such as 'pre-history' or 'primeval' are so frequently met. Secondly, reliance will be placed almost exclusively on genetics as the sole determinant of what it means to be a modern human (*homo sapiens*), and when this term is used it will largely exclude so-called behavioral evidence from archaeology (principally artefacts), since the bulk of such evidence may be from glacial periods. This latter point will be significant when it is believed that early modern man may have subsisted by the sea shore[2] for long periods—a sea shore that was much lower during such times, thus leaving physical remains (if any) lying beneath present-day sea levels. Genetics will, moreover, be relied upon to determine as accurately as possible the approximate time when 'modernity' could be authentically attributed to humankind.

Speech

The genetics, or rather the specific genes of interest here, are those related to speech. They include the genes responsible for the development of anatomical, neural, and cognitive mechanisms, which all "appear to have coevolved."[3] Central to these developments is one gene in particular, the manic depression gene, which also "provides a means to date the evolution of the human brain and the emergence of fully human speech capabilities."[4] It is important to note that the speech under discussion here is neither primitive nor rudimentary, but rather fully modern, which together with simultaneous development of language and cognition enables Lieberman to state that these humans "were capable of talking and acting as we do."[5] The date suggested by Lieberman for these developments lies sometime in the period between 90,000 and 50,000 years BP (before present). This gives good agreement with Holden who can say that the final mutation of the FOXP2 gene may have taken place "fewer than 100,000 years ago . . . . perhaps laying the groundwork for a new level of linguistic fluency."[6] So, collecting these findings together we may conclude that humans—or to use

---

2. In his discussion of the dispersal of the first colonists from Africa Mellars talks of the "coastal" route taken eastwards beginning with a crossing at the mouth of the Red Sea. (Mellars, "Why did Modern Human Populations," 9385).
3. Lieberman, "Evolution of Human Speech," 52–53.
4. Lieberman, "Evolution of Human Speech," 52–53.
5. Lieberman, "Evolution of Human Speech," 52–53.
6. Holden, "Origin of Speech," 1316.

the jargon of the geneticists—one lineage of humans (L3) were able to communicate fully and fluently with each other approximately 80,000 years ago. Moreover, if, having established the 'when' of this 'event' attention is then directed to where this might have been taking place, we find a small group of humans in the horn of Africa contemplating diaspora:

> ... the initial dispersal was from Ethiopia, across the mouth of the Red Sea, and then either northward through Arabia or eastward along the south Asian coastline to Australasia—the so-called "southern" or "coastal" route.... The strongest evidence at present for the second hypothesis is provided by the mtDNA lineage analysis patterns. These point strongly to the conclusion that there was only a single (successful) dispersal event out of Africa, represented exclusively by members of the L3 lineage and probably carried (out) by a relatively small number of at most a few hundred colonists.[7]

Building then on the picture so far, we find that all non-Africans have descended from this small group of fluently communicating humans originating in Africa some 84,000 years ago.[8] Mellars goes on to suggest that this human diaspora had reached Malaysia and the Andaman Islands by 65,000 years BP, and had colonized Australia by 45,000 years BP.[9] Two further points may be noticed before moving on to a discussion of another group of genes that apparently mutated at the same time as the FOXP2 'speech' gene. Firstly, it should be noted if only in passing, where these fully fluent and recently emigrated humans were now living, that is, in Arabia and perhaps also the Levant—the origin or birth place of the world's largest religions—Judeo-Christianity and Islam.

Secondly, it is pertinent to this argument to note that Australia, has been the home of the indigenous aboriginals for an (until recently) unbroken and completely isolated 50,000 years. These indigenous Australians refer to the time of creation as 'The Dreaming,' although it must be stressed that the word 'dreaming' is used by these people groups as an all-encompassing, spiritual/mystical term best expressed as "everywhen,"[10] and comprising the past, present, and future concurrently. Such an understanding allows any individual aboriginal throughout these long millennia to participate in the Dreaming—an altered state of consciousness (ASC), whilst retaining the idea that it principally refers to the Creation or 'the time before time.' Given that

---

7. Mellars, "Why did Modern Human Populations," 9385.
8. Roberts, *Incredible Human Journey*, 71.
9. Mellars, "Why did Modern Human Populations," 9385.
10. Stanner, *Dreaming and Other Essays*.

the aboriginal way of life (hunter-gathering) has remained largely unchanged since their entry into Australia, there is every reason to suppose that it was continuous with their way of life on the long coastal migration[11] prior to entry. Thus, collecting and integrating these apparently disparate thoughts together we find a small group of fluently communicating humans had arrived in the Arabian peninsula. They were able, not merely to coordinate their activities through speech, but to transmit their lore, stories (and dreams?) to the next generation through this medium. Add to this the suggestion that they are dreamers, then at least two of the basic building blocks of primeval 'religion' are now in place at approximately 80,000 years BP.

Schizophrenia and Bipolar Disorder

Mental illness is a very human and persistent problem, which according to the National Comorbidity Survey (NCS) of mental illness in the United States affected one in four adults (26.2 percent) in the twelve months prior to the survey.[12] Moreover, within these wider bounds of mental illness, schizophrenia in particular "poses an evolutionary-genetic paradox because it exhibits strongly negative fitness effects and high heritability, yet it persists at a prevalence of approximately one percent across all human cultures."[13] Putting it succinctly, the fourteen genes associated with schizophrenia based on HapMap[14] analyses have undergone positive genetic selection.[15] Crespi and his coresearchers are, however, only able to conclude that the forces of 'natural' selection which give rise to the evolutionary preferment of these schizophrenia-associated genes are for the most part unknown. The suggestion offered is that the resistance of these genes to elimination by natural recombination is because they are partly an ongoing and maladaptive by-product of other unspecified, more positive features of human evolution. It does, however, seem odd—to say the least—that genes which impair the quality of life, and indeed threaten life itself, should

11. One group of researchers place the ancestors of the Australian aboriginals in the Arabian peninsula at about the same time (80,000 years BP), eventually splitting from the first Eurasians sometime between 62,000 and 75,000 years BP (Rasmussen et al., "Aboriginal Australian Genome," 97–98).

12. Kessler et al., "U.S. National Comorbidity Survey," 4–16.

13. Crespi et al., "Adaptive Evolution of Genes," 2801.

14. The *HapMap* is a catalogue of common genetic variants that occur in human beings. It describes what these variants are, where they occur in human DNA, and how they are distributed among people within populations and among populations in different parts of the world.

15. Crespi et al., "Adaptive Evolution of Genes," 2803.

continue to be selected over countless millennia, unless some other less obvious benefit is conferred by their selection.

The life-threatening nature of schizophrenia results from dangerous behavior such as self-harming (leading potentially to suicide) or other violent activities, which is interesting given that some of the genes associated with schizophrenia "are also known to affect liability to bipolar disorder."[16] Schizophrenia and bipolar disorder (previously known as manic depression) "in particular exhibit substantial overlap in cognitive symptoms as well as their genetic basis."[17] Those cognitive symptoms include aberrant behavior, and as recently as the year 2000 the Diagnostic and Statistical Manual of Mental Disorders, Fourth Edition (DSM-IV) of the American Psychiatric Association classified such hallucinations, delusions, and auditions as psychosis. In addition, however, DSM IV included other imagery and ideation such as revelations, mysticism, and religious experiences in the same definition of psychosis.

Significantly, four of the fourteen genes associated with schizophrenia (and presumably also the bipolar disorder which substantially overlaps it) were found in the Crespi study to have undergone "extremely recent selection . . . since the time of human demographic expansion out of Africa."[18] Thus, the picture now emerging of the new colonists is becoming much more recognizable as thoroughly modern, even though in terms of lifestyle (nomadic, hunter-gathering) it is completely dissimilar to our own, and that picture includes fully developed fluent speech, and strangely depression with its known effect on sleeping pattern and dreaming in particular.[19] Consequently, all the factors now exist for the oral (and the much, much later written) transmission of dreams from one generation to the next, only requiring the development of formulaic storytelling to ensure the content remains incorruptible.

The Time before Time

Formulaic storytelling is clearly a particular forte of the Australian aboriginals, and in referring to an Australian aboriginal tale[20] the biblical scholar, Susan Niditch, points to certain similarities between it and the Paradise

---

16. Crespi et al., "Adaptive Evolution of Genes," 2806.
17. Crespi et al., "Adaptive Evolution of Genes," 2806.
18. Crespi et al., "Adaptive Evolution of Genes," 2803.
19. The relationship between sleep and depression is dealt with more fully in chapter 3.
20. Parker, *Australian Legendary Tales*, 24–25.

'myth' of Genesis. She does this over and against the more common scholarly comparisons made between the Genesis stories and the creation myths of Mesopotamia:

> This myth from a culture far removed from the ancient Near East opens our eyes to structural and conceptual aspects of the Genesis myths which we might have missed; we are in a sense too used to usual interpretations of them, to seeing their meaning and message solely in an Israelite, Yahwistic, or at least an ancient Near Eastern context.[21]

It would seem Niditch is one of the few scholars to see common ground between the creation myths of Genesis and the tales of ancient, stone-age people groups, and this is the more remarkable given the fact that "attempts to find an ancient Near Eastern myth whose basic plot matches that of the Paradise story in Gen 2,4–3,24 have essentially failed."[22] Indeed, scholars often refer to the dependence of the Genesis stories upon primeval traditions,[23] but few attempts are made to locate and compare them.

Niditch's fundamental thesis concerns what she refers to as two major thematic chains which run throughout Genesis 1–11. These chains:

> ... describe two key transformations in the Israelite concept of the becoming of the universe. One involves the passage from an initial state of chaos to an ideal cosmos in which all of nature is beautifully arranged and ordered. The other involves the passage from this ideal state to reality, for the first movement from chaos to cosmos stops short of creating those social structures, hierarchies, and definitions which mark real time and the human being's everyday status in the world. These two passages emerge most clearly in the myths of Genesis 1—3.[24]

In this first statement of core thesis, Niditch makes a number of propositions, beginning with the belief that an "ideal state," once existed in what is termed pre-reality,[25] or should one say, in Paradise? Secondly, she affirms that this ideal state was translated into "reality," but fails to define that reality, leaving the reader to conclude that by reality she means physical,

---

21. Niditch, *Chaos to Cosmos*, 27.
22. Sparks, "Problem of Myth," 277.
23. "The events take place in the very distant past, *in illo tempore*" (Mettinger, *Eden Narrative*, 14). See also Westermann, *Genesis 1–11*, 195.
24. Niditch, *Chaos to Cosmos*, 6.
25. Niditch, *Chaos to Cosmos*, 29.

sense-reality as it is understood in modern, (scientific?)[26]Western culture. Thirdly, she uses the term "real time," which again is related to the modern, Western view of reality. Finally, there is the implicit statement that the progression of these two major thematic chains in the Creation/Paradise account is intended to lead inexorably to the creation of "social structures, hierarchies, and definitions."

Niditch's first proposition of an "ideal state," which lies between chaos and reality has great merit, if only insofar as she is suggesting that the meaning of the Creation/Paradise accounts are fundamentally about reality. This reality is for Niditch the everyday reality of social differentiation, but importantly she suggests in this a movement from an 'ideal time' (the time before time?) to "real time." In so doing, she is making the case for a transition from an 'ideal reality' to physical, sense-reality as moderns would understand it, but such an explanation fails to take account of the differences between the modern, Western view of reality, and that which prevailed in ancient times. The most significant feature of the Ancient Near Eastern concept of reality concerns the way in which altered states of consciousness (ASCs) were viewed. In particular, the ancients did not consider dreaming to be an integral part of being asleep, but rather a separate state much more akin to waking reality, or to put it succinctly; dreaming was considered to be continuous with waking reality rather than the insensibility of deep sleep. Although the ancients distinguished between experiences when awake and when dreaming, "to them the difference was not, as for us, one of kind, that is, real or unreal, but one of degree."[27] Thus, if it could be shown that the Creation narrative in Genesis 2 contained a dream or dreams, then this would not be inconsistent with the ANE view of reality. It would be for them a true account of real events. Moreover, any adoption of this ANE view of reality has implications for the genre of both the Creation and Paradise stories: It means that for the author, these stories were neither myths, novellas nor any other kind of fictive work.

Notwithstanding the differences between the ANE view of reality and that of modern times, dreams remain dreams, and as such, often contain extremely bizarre content. Indeed, one has only to think of the dreams of Pharaoh in Genesis 41 where 'hungry' (thin) ears of corn ate other (good) ears of corn, or the man-eating fish in Jonah 2[28] to know that this is so. Similarly, viewing the Creation/Paradise narratives as a sequence of dreams

26. A further question is posed here. This concerns the very nature of science itself!

27. Jacobsen, "Graven Image," 19.

28. I have previously shown that the book of Jonah contains very little 'waking reality' and is primarily a sequence of altered states of consciousness, amongst which chapter 2 comprises part of a dream sequence. See Appendix.

permits an understanding of the serpent and the trees of knowledge and life as further examples of dream symbol. Moreover, Niditch's references to a lack of consciousness of sexual differentiation,[29] and differentiation from God[30] is entirely understandable, but stems from the 'equality of status' between all the things, animals, and persons encountered in the immaterial world of dreams. None of this is discounted by the couple's realization of their nakedness and their need of clothing (v. 3:7), which is simply an outcome of the thematic progression of the dream, and actual procreation by the couple only takes place in waking reality after Eden (Gen 4). In mooting this thesis, I do not want to pre-empt a fuller validation of the methodology and exegesis of the text, but would make one further point: if it turns out that up to 60 or 70 percent of the content of Gen 2:4—3:24 takes place in an immaterial realm (dreams), then this has monumental importance for the unity, meaning, and theological derivations of the Creation/Paradise story.

Depression and Psychopathology

So, where does depression fit into this picture? Perhaps the best answer to this question is to be found by looking at the incidence of 'mental illness' in general and depression in particular, where this occurs amongst present-day, pre-modern people groups. Observations of psychopathology have long been a feature of ethnological studies,[31] and Eliade records the incidence of neuropathic, epileptoid or morbid illness[32] as a precondition for election to the vocation of (prophet) shaman.[33] He does this under the

---

29. Niditch, *Chaos to Cosmos*, 30.

30. Niditch, *Chaos to Cosmos*, 31.

31. Depression has often been acknowledged as a component part of certain prophetic narratives in the Hebrew Bible, most notably those about Elijah (Rowley, *Men of God*, 64, and Evans, *Prophets of the Lord*, 44). Longer studies have been somewhat less frequent, but see Wiener, *Elijah*, and also Lacocque and Lacocque, *Jonah*.

32. Eliade, *Shamanism*, 25–32.

33. Following Eliade and Lindblom, 'shaman' is a term that has now gained wide acceptance as a description of "men and women who can be characterised as *homines religiosi* (and) can be called *the prophetic type*" (Lindblom, *Prophecy*, 1). Lindblom, however, would equate the shaman only with practitioners of what he describes as "primitive prophecy" in Ancient Israel (Lindblom, *Prophecy*, 5–6). In similar vein, Kapelrud considers the "*nabi* phenomenon" in Israel to be Canaanite in origin before going on to suggest "that the difference between a shaman and a *nabi* was small" (Kapelrud, "Shamanistic features in the Old Testament," 92). Overholt following Wilson has grouped together various roles and functions (prophet, shaman, medium, and diviner) found in the anthropological data together under the general rubric "religious intermediation" (Overholt, *Cultural Anthropology*, 80). Latterly, Grabbe has adopted an anthropological perspective and likewise draws comparisons between shamans and the early Mesopotamian prophets at Mari (Grabbe, "Ancient Near Eastern Prophecy," 16).

subheading, 'shamanism and psychopathology,' and while discussing the alleged higher incidence of mental instability in Arctic communities, he demonstrates that "psychopathic phenomena are found almost throughout the world."[34] Lewis relates how melancholy, weeping, and unhappiness leading to joy accompanied the calling of an Eskimo shaman,[35] whilst Humphrey, in her discussion on how men or women became shamans amongst the Daur Mongols, notes that usually the "young man (or woman) . . . became inexplicably and incurably mentally ill."[36] Eliade does, however, resist the suggestion that mental instability is a precondition for shamanic activity, explaining that religious practitioners—wherever in the world they arise—are regarded by their communities as perfectly normal.[37] Moreover, both Eliade[38] and Wilson[39] would accept that the prophet-shaman can step over the line into lunacy, but that this is recognized by the community, which then prohibits them from continuing to practice.

Ethnological studies of religious personnel would therefore appear to display a continuum between the normal and the abnormal, the healthy and the diseased, the spiritual and the insane, which, Eliade notes, went largely unnoticed in some early work.[40] This continuum or spectrum may be depicted as follows:[41]

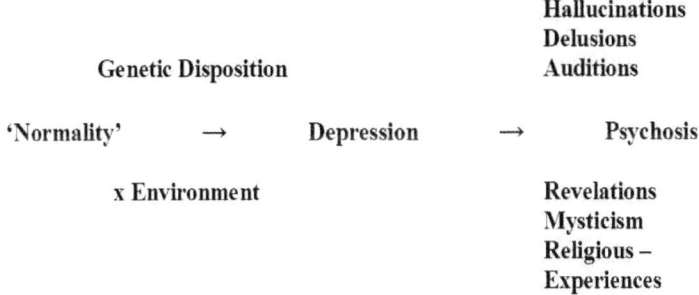

Fig. 1– 'Normality' - Psychosis Continuum

34. Eliade, *Shamanism*, 27.
35. Lewis, *Ecstatic Religion*, 32.
36. Humphrey with Onon, *Shamans and Elders*, 185.
37. Eliade, *Shamanism*, 31.
38. Eliade, *Shamanism*, 26–27.
39. Wilson, *Prophecy and Society*, 46.
40. Eliade, *Shamanism*, 27.
41. The Diagnostic and Statistical Manual of Mental Disorders, Fourth Edition (DSM-IV) of the American Psychiatric Association classifies all of the ideation and imagery in Fig. 1 as Psychosis.

As already noted, the Geneticists are at a loss to explain precisely what, if any, factors are at work in the environment, which might have brought about the positive genetic selection of schizophrenia and bipolar associated genes. Importantly, however, this continuum does exist if only for about one percent of the human population, a number of whom may go on to develop major depressive disorder. Major depressive disorder (MDD), where it involves 'hallucinations' or 'delusions,' has been categorized as a subtype of depression and labeled 'psychotic depression.' Significantly, "the depressive symptoms usually begin before the psychotic ones," within this syndrome,[42] and some recent researchers have suggested that:

> Depression may not only be phenotypically, but also aetiologically intermediate, at least to a degree, between normality and psychosis.[43]

Moreover, "depressive symptoms are typically more severe when they are accompanied by psychotic features," and suicidal ideation as an exemplar of the severity of depression is found in strong association with 'delusions.'[44] It may also be noted with Coryell that the presence of 'psychotic' features tends to predict a re-diagnosis from unipolar depression to bipolar depression where the latter term is the newer name for manic depression. Emotional turmoil and distress concurrent with psychosis/altered states of consciousness appear to be features commonly manifested by the religious personnel (prophetic types) of many pre-modern peoples, especially during the initiatory phase of a shamanic career.[45] Similarly, emotional turmoil and distress seem to figure prominently in the lives of the prophets of the Hebrew bible, where 'suicidal' ideation as an indicator of the severity of that emotional distress can be found, and where arguably, other features of both unipolar and bipolar depression may be seen juxtaposed with psychosis/altered states of consciousness.

Support for the existence of such a continuum also comes from psychology, or more particularly from transpersonal psychology, wherein that continuum has been dubbed psychoticism. It remains disputed "whether

42. Coryell, "Psychotic Depression," 49.
43. Van Os et al., "Self-Reported Psychosis," 463.
44. Coryell, "Psychotic Depression," 27–28.
45. Peters, "Are delusions on a continuum," 201. Winkelman does, however, point out that this kind of observation requires the shaman's condition to be viewed from the Western "perspective of psychopathology," rather than as a transitional stage in an indigenous process ultimately leading to enhanced mental health (Winkelman, *Shamanism: Neural Ecology*, 81). One study has argued that "in some ways, the psychotic person is behaving like a prophet lacking followers" (Price and Stevens, "Evolutionary Approach," 201).

psychoticism is truly a personality trait (or set of traits), or whether it merely signifies a subclinical form of disease."[46] On the former view psychoticism is a set of psychotic traits of personality ('dimensions'), which are just like any other personality characteristics, and "according to (this) fully dimensional view of continuity, psychotic traits, in and of themselves, are not pathological, but merely represent personality variation."[47] The problem that now presents itself is this: How is it possible to demonstrate the incidence of clinical disease (psychopathology) or otherwise in a text that is something like 2,500 years old? There is, however, a 'marker,' which when found in scripture indicates the presence of (what physicians would call) clinical depression, and it is to that we now turn.

Psychosis and Psychopathology

The material so far presented has suggested that a number of factors in the evolutionary development of modern humans came together at or about 80,000 years BP, and these factors included dreaming and the capacity (fully fluent speech) to transmit those dreams to subsequent generations. It follows that formulaic oral traditions begun in the mists of prehistoric antiquity could have reached the earliest stages of the compilation of written texts, as indeed Niditch points out:

> The oral and the written exist on a continuum or a sliding scale (such that) each modality overlaps with the other in the form, orientation, and context of a work, in its composition and transmission.[48]

In chronological terms the two traditions (oral and written) could have coexisted with, and cross-fertilized each other for a period of some 500–1500 years, beyond which the oral tradition may not have remained extant. This means, in effect, that many of the primeval stories of Genesis 1–11, including the creation account (Gen 2–3), were 'frozen' in content and form, if only because the authors were just as culturally bound as the storytellers before them, to transmit the lore in a faithful and therefore formulaic manner.

As already noted, Niditch has suggested that the Genesis accounts bear structural and conceptual similarities to the Aboriginal creation accounts, or the 'Dreaming' as they are more familiarly known. Consequently, if the structure of Genesis 2–3 could be shown to be dreamform, then that

46. Claridge, "Spiritual Experience," 95.
47. Claridge, "Spiritual Experience," 96.
48. Niditch, *Oral World*, 44. Parenthesis added.

would constitute the necessary 'marker' or formula previously alluded to, especially if that dreamform could be shown to be characteristically that of a depressed dreamer. Finding structural evidence of depressive dreaming in this biblical creation account would therefore give good agreement, not only with the Aboriginal 'Dreamtime' tradition, but also with the genetic dating of Schizophrenia and Bipolar Disorder to around the time of the out-of-Africa diaspora. In summary, it may be said that finding evidence of depressive dreaming in the text of Genesis 2–3, together with the genetic dating of speech, psychosis, and psychopathology and the well known and accepted interplay between oral and written traditions, may be indicating that this text could effectively be an authentic written record of creation itself! This, despite begetting the problem of precisely what it was that was created when this small people group left Africa 80,000 years BP?

2

Genesis

THE STORY OF THE Garden of Eden is known throughout the world and is perhaps the best known story about human beginnings to have come down to us from ancient times, but to ask whether it is fact or fiction seems to be an irrelevance in an age that has produced *The God Delusion*.[1] Within biblical scholarship, however, the question continues to be raised from a variety of perspectives, not the least of which is the cultural viewpoint, if only because a quite different answer might be expected from the culture in which the text was first written down. Dating the text produces results that range from the 10th or 9th century BC[2] through to late post-exilic times and "even to the Persian period,"[3] but the date of authorship is, of itself, not of paramount concern to any answer to this question. Indeed, Niditch has pointed out that oral traditions continued to be passed on alongside the written forms to which they gave rise throughout much, if not most, of the first millennium BC.[4] Any classification of this story (Genesis 2:4b—3:24) as fact or fiction must, to a significant extent, depend on the worldview of the culture within which the text had its birth, since the use of categories such as fable, legend or myth in any modern comprehension of these terms could prove misleading.

Going further, one might say that the story's classification will depend on the 'culture' within which the oral tradition(s) had its origin, and in this regard one prominent commentator suggests a very early pre-Hebrew provenance, which he repeatedly designates as 'primeval.'[5] Indeed, the tradition-history approach to understanding the text of Genesis 2–3 is exemplified in

---

1. Dawkins, *God Delusion*.
2. Westermann, *Genesis 1–11* 1.
3. Mettinger, *Eden Narrative*, 11.
4. Niditch argues, "the oral and the literal interact throughout Israel's literary history" (Niditch, *Oral World and Written Word*, 134).
5. Westermann uses the word 'primeval' to describe Genesis 2–3 some dozens of times, notwithstanding his insistence on the whole passage being a confluence of numerous and often, seemingly disparate traditions. Westermann, *Genesis 1–11*, 275.

Westermann who can say: " ... the basic motifs of the narrative did not begin in Israel, but belong to the traditions of the human race which stretch both geographically and chronologically into the far distance and whose origins cannot be determined."[6] Earlier adherents of the tradition-history approach include Gerhard von Rad who, when speaking generally about the Genesis narratives, is able to use the term 'saga' as a descriptive term for narrative traditions that came into existence in preliterary times. He is at pains to point out that the saga in "its simplest and most original purpose . . . narrates an actual event that occurred once for all in the realm of history. It is therefore to be taken quite seriously—it is to be 'believed.'"[7] It is perhaps unfortunate that history in its modern, Western sense tends to be the lens through which we view such ancient and venerable tales, and von Rad acknowledges that the saga "lives and grows at a time when the power of rational and logical historical perception is not yet fully liberated."[8] He is nevertheless clear that the society in receipt of the saga believed it implicitly.

It would seem then that a saga, although recording a real event in (the realm of) history, does so in a manner that is acceptable to the ancient hearer, but not to modern, Western ears. On asking why this should be so, the usual answer given has been to suggest with von Rad that the ancients were at a 'primitive' stage in rational and logical thought, which presumably allowed them to exceed the boundaries of what is currently accepted as history. Perhaps a better approach might be to ask why ancient peoples—and the ancient Hebrews in particular—thought that these stories were a true account of actual (real) events in history. Indeed, von Rad, albeit tangentially, touches upon this when he notes that "in its sagas a people is concerned with itself and the realities in which it finds itself."[9] Reality is indeed at the heart of this issue, in particular, reality as it was experienced by these ancient people groups, and again von Rad comes close to describing that reality when he talks of sagas being understood in a mantic way. Interestingly, and in connection with this point about reality, von Rad is able to say that "the Yahwist, in shaping the individual narrative, probably did not go beyond some trimming of the archaic profiles and making definite fine accents."[10] Consequently, it seems one must understand this as referring to the entry of some oral tradition(s) into the written record in largely unchanged form. Indeed, without taking anything away from the Yahwist's creativity, one may

6. Westermann, *Genesis 1–11*, 275.
7. Von Rad, *Genesis*, 32.
8. Von Rad, *Genesis*, 33.
9. Von Rad, *Genesis*, 33.
10. Von Rad, *Genesis*, 37.

say that ancient oral traditions (sagas) complete with their perception of reality are being preserved in and by the written record. It will be one of the tasks of this present work to use different methodologies to confirm that this is in fact, the case, and to elucidate how reality was comprehended in the Ancient Near East. The remainder of this chapter will, however, concentrate—in a somewhat less than exhaustive way—on previous solutions to the many problems presented by the text as we have it.

Past Approaches to Genesis 2–3.

As already noted, it is not the intention of this chapter to produce an exhaustive study on all previous interpretations of this text, but rather to present in outline form the two main approaches that have been employed in modern exegesis, and to discuss any perceived deficiencies. Significantly, the first of these, the literary approach, could be considered to have incorporated a third perspective—the use of comparative material from surrounding cultures. This is certainly the view of one commentator who traces the development of comparative studies to a terminal date of 1990.[11] Indeed, Hess follows the evolution of comparative studies by firstly noting that up to World War I there was a "common assumption (of the) antiquity and superiority of Babylonian culture (relative) to Israelite culture."[12] Between the wars, the consensus appears to move towards the acceptance that both the Babylonian creation accounts and those in Genesis have a common source. Moreover:

> The option that seems to be preferred is that of a common origin (and) this attitude is characteristic of the comparative approach in biblical studies in the years following World War II.[13]

Hess concludes his essay with a review of the years from 1970–1990, and in his first point confirms "the continuing interest in the comparative application of cuneiform materials to the study and interpretation of Genesis 1–11." It is clear that "modern literary methods and approaches have not cast aside the comparative method," but rather it appears they have in some sense subsumed it, and "the comparative task has now become a part of the interpretation of the biblical texts." That this is so may, in part, be due to the relative paucity of "literary criticism in the interpretation of ancient Near Eastern myths." Secondly, the point is made that "the literary study of the

---

11. Hess, "One Hundred Fifty Years," 3–26.
12. Hess, "One Hundred Fifty Years," 7.
13. Hess, "One Hundred Fifty Years," 11.

Bible is enhanced by the comparative method, not diminished, and if we are to understand the biblical text in terms of its own message, the comparative approach is necessary to show parallels and points of incongruence."[14]

Thus, in summation it would appear that the trajectory of comparative studies, at least until the closing decade of the C20th, has been a move away from the perceived greater worth of Mesopotamian material. The path then proceeded via the suggestion that both sets of material relied upon a common or shared origin, towards a more 'symbiotic' approach in which biblical and cuneiform materials can be used to 'cross-fertilise' each other.

Any literary approach to the creation and paradise story must it seems, necessarily be bound up with the question of genre, and for many, perhaps most interpreters, this story (or stories) is regarded as 'myth.' Mettinger is clear that the genre of the Eden Narrative is myth, and in this regard considers that the function of myth (in comparison with a "true history") may be to "contribute to our understanding of what it means to be a human being."[15] Importantly, for Mettinger:

> The narrative in Genesis 2–3 moves on the level of metaphors and symbols. If we were to find a text of the same type as the Eden Narrative in any other culture, we would certainly designate it a myth. There is no need to avoid this label when we discuss the Eden Narrative. It is a myth.[16]

Moving on the level of metaphors and symbols is, of course, not confined to myth, since they are also prominent features of dreams. An understanding of the Eden Narrative as dream is in agreement with Mettinger's description of "myth as a statement of primeval reality,"[17] but it is precisely what constitutes reality that is the problem. If it is accepted that reality may be culturally defined, then it becomes inaccurate to designate the Eden Narrative as myth, that is, in the harshest, modern sense of having neither factual nor historical authenticity. Writing about the Paradise/Fall story of Genesis 2:4 ff., Sparks, having defined myth as " a story about gods and heroes that explains and sanctions the present natural or cultural order,"[18] goes on to raise a number of questions concerning the story. He raises fundamental issues about the relationship of myths to the ostensibly historiographic matrix in which they are found:

---

14. Hess, "One Hundred Fifty Years," 24.
15. Mettinger, *Eden Narrative*, 67–68.
16. Mettinger, *Eden Narrative*, 67–68.
17. Mettinger, *Eden Narrative*, 70.
18. Sparks, "Problem of Myth," 270.

Did the Yahwist compose the myth or did he borrow it? If he composed it, what elements were borrowed and what contributions were his own? Did the biblical writer recognize the story—whether borrowed or composed—as "fictive", and would his contemporaries have recognized this as well?[19]

Sparks concludes his opening section by coalescing these questions into a unified enquiry concerning "the role of myth within an otherwise historiographic literary context," and more specifically, directs this enquiry to the role played by myth "within the Paradise/Fall story of the Yahwist's history?"[20] Going on to speak about 'historical myths,' Sparks sets out his own position with clarity:

> We tend to believe that the freehanded composition of a literary piece that addresses mythic themes must necessarily imply that the sane author knew it to be fictive and legendary, ... But I have become increasingly convinced that a set of "facts" presumed by an author, combined with the author's unique *Tendenz*, can produce a creative narrative that is for the author anything but fictive.[21]

Thus, it can be seen that in circumstances where a culture believed that altered states of consciousness (ASCs)—for example dream—permitted access to an alternate or extended reality,[22] a reality within which the gods could be encountered, then any "facts" obtained would certainly not be deemed fictive. Moreover, if those facts were obtained from an oral tradition passed on within an accepted, enculturated, revelatory pattern, then they would be self-validating as historically accurate, and may have entered the literary tradition largely intact.[23] Put simply, pre-modern people groups in general, and the ancients in particular, had a much bigger view of 'reality' than the 'sense reality' of the dominant culture of our own times. Turning to the particular case of the Eden Narrative, Sparks looks at the historical methodology of the Yahwist with regard to this story, together with the Flood and Babel stories. He finds that the latter two stories have corresponding myths within the ancient Near Eastern milieu. "But in the case of the Paradise/Fall narrative something very different is going on, for attempts to find an

---

19. Sparks, "Problem of Myth," 270.
20. Sparks, "Problem of Myth," 270.
21. Sparks, "Problem of Myth," 276.
22. I introduce this term to differentiate experiences of the numinous from those taking place within 'normal' everyday sense reality.
23. On this point reference is made to the work of John J. Pilch.

ancient Near Eastern myth whose basic plot matches that of the Paradise story in Gen 2,4—3,24 have essentially failed."[24]

Thus far, Sparks has accepted that the Yahwist did not believe his sources were 'fictive,' so answering one of the questions he originally posed, and this is certainly the view expressed here albeit based on an entirely different methodology. The other big question for Sparks concerns the extent to which the Yahwist drew upon or borrowed from other sources. The lack of an exact Mesopotamian parallel obliges Sparks to suggest that the Yahwist amalgamates a "completely new myth"[25] from what is really a number of disparate Near Eastern motifs. But rather than referring specifically to the motifs he previously listed, Sparks generalizes the Yahwist's sources to "various primeval and creation traditions."[26] In this he joins Westermann in the use of the term 'primeval,' a term which seems to be used on a frequent basis to obfuscate the issue enough to allow any amount of new creative (and theological) work on the part of the Yahwist. If it is accepted that the Eden Narrative does in fact contain fundamental, theological truths, then the methodology offered here suggests new and more appropriate questions need to be posited. Did the Yahwist create a new myth from a number of known motifs and unknown traditions, in order to construct an explanatory prologue to the Deuteronomistic history for "his exilic readers?"[27] Alternatively, is the Eden Narrative a factual account (for the Yahwist) of creation, received into the written tradition in its entirety from a single oral source, and is as such, a foundational rationale for the Yahwist's history?

Simply formulating the latter question causes fundamental problems for the literary approach to the Garden story, since the many interpretations of the narrative can involve 'philosophical superstructures' which depend to a lesser or greater extent upon the craft of an author. Indeed, perceived theological, anthropological, and feminist interpretations often depend upon understanding the text as the work of a single creative mind, because this appears to be the only way of unifying what are seen as disparate motifs. Any suggestion that the text of the Genesis 2–3 narrative derives from a single oral source could undermine the 'philosophical superstructures' of some distinctive, literary interpretations, as well as interpretations based on the tradition-history approach, to which we now turn.

---

24. Sparks, "Problem of Myth," 277.
25. Sparks, "Problem of Myth," 279.
26. Sparks, "Problem of Myth," 279.
27. Sparks, "Problem of Myth," 280.

The Tradition-History Approach and Context

It is perhaps important to make the point at outset that the two approaches—the literary approach and the tradition-history approach—are not necessarily opposed to each other, it being simply the case that adherents of the latter approach tend to posit interpretations based primarily upon the (supposed?) knowledge of a text's prehistory. Consequently, and despite the fact that most studies concentrate on one or the other approach, the net effect still remains a study of final written form. Of course, the teasing suggestion that knowledge of a text's prehistory might be supposition, or worse, conjecture requires a convincing justification. Such a defense will depend upon a demonstration that the context of the story, as commonly supposed, is heavily dependent upon the prevailing presuppositions of the dominant culture of our own times. When the context is changed, through the removal of those presuppositions other liberating interpretations of the story become possible. Context is everything in biblical studies, and notwithstanding the almost insuperable difficulties presented by the text, most interpretations remain pervaded by a tacit acceptance that Genesis 2–3 describes a real-world environment. Moreover, this belief that the story is set within, describes, and progresses at some physical location within the physical world persists even when it is believed to be a fictional account. It is this etic perspective imposed by Western, cultural presuppositions that is the fundamental problem for interpreters, and this problem can only be addressed by applying an emic approach to the subject culture. In the following chapters, a suite of multidisciplinary methodologies will be applied that will enable a perception of this story as a single, unified narrative set within both an other-worldly and a this-worldly environment. Treating the text in this way has the potential to remove most, if not all, of the difficulties (irregularities, flaws, insertions, links, and amalgamations) usually explained by recourse to numerous, incorporated, vestigial traditions and to editorial activity. It is to those difficulties that we must now turn.

Although written some time ago, David Carr's paper[28] provides by way of introduction to his own perspective, a good summation of the current consensus on the tradition-history of Genesis 2–3. Carr points out that there are a number of "long-recognised indicators of tradition history in the first part of the story (2:4b–15)," and begins by citing the apparently pointless, geographical excursus on the location of Eden and the Garden of/in Eden (2:10–14), which appears to have no basis in fact. Certainly, Westermann

---

28. Carr, "Politics," 577–95.

feels able to rule out any geographical basis for the location of the source of the four rivers, and hence of paradise itself. Indeed:

> The intention of the author in inserting 2:10–14 is not to determine where paradise lay, as the majority of interpreters hold, but rather to point out—by way of parenthesis and at the place where a land (Eden) with its garden is first mentioned—that the "life arteries" of all lands of the earth have their source in the river that watered paradise.[29]

For Westermann this passage is a parenthetical insertion, although he notes that some scholars consider it to be part of the original narrative primarily on the basis of the form of speech used—numerative as opposed to narrative.[30] Accepting for the moment that the passage is a part of the original narrative, and perhaps going somewhat beyond Westermann's assertion that paradise has no real geographical location, it becomes possible to suggest a supernatural or other-worldly 'location' for Eden. The task then becomes one of reconciling each verse of this passage (2:4b–15) one to another, within that composite theme, and if compelling reasons can be offered to support it, this theme can stand in opposition to the tradition history approach.

Context, as already observed, is everything and the problem for the majority (tradition history) position as exemplified by Westermann, becomes one of reconciling a seemingly other-worldly environment (the source of the rivers), with a this-worldly environment within which the 'main' plot apparently transpires. The only realistic solution is to sacrifice these verses, that is, consider them to be of independent origin to the bulk of the narrative. The main difficulty with the latter approach is the basic assumption that the bulk of the story, even though considered mythic, has a this-worldly setting. If, however, it can be demonstrated that the majority of the story has an other-worldly 'location,' then it becomes a possibility that these and other 'problem' verses can be reconciled to the so-called main body of the text.

Amongst those other 'problem' verses is v. 6, which in Carr's estimation is linked with the 'rivers' excursus by the use of variants of *shaqah* (water) in vv 2:6 and 2:10, and which likewise is said to be of independent origin.[31] But such a link can serve equally well to suggest an other-worldly environment for v. 6, especially if the ארץ ושמים (earth and heavens) of 2:4b can be shown to be a comprehensive *hendiadys* that comprises the material (and immaterial)

---

29. Westermann, *Genesis 1–11*, 216.
30. Westermann, *Genesis 1–11*, 215.
31. Carr, "Politics," 578.

heavens, the ground, and the (under)world.³² That link would consist in the supernatural waters of the underworld (2:6) and the supernatural waters of the heavens (2:10). Moreover, when 2:4b–6 is understood in this way as a description of all that is—both material and immaterial—it sets up the possibility that long held interpretations of v. 7 may be flawed.

In accepting, for the moment, that 2:4b ends with the single complex idea already referred to, it may be further conjectured (for the moment!) that the author moves the story along sequentially from one component of the *hendiadys* to another, and back again. Thus, the sequence might be as follows:

> Supernatural/transcendent heavens (v. 4b) → surface of the earth/ground (v. 5) → supernatural underworld (v. 6a) → surface of the earth/ground (vv. 6b–7a) → supernatural/transcendent heavens (vv. 7bc–8??).

Suspending disbelief further—for the moment—the sequence can be seen to carry on with its reciprocation albeit excluding the underworld, which has now become redundant in the developing story:

> → surface of the earth/ground (v. 9a) → supernatural/transcendent heavens (vv. 9bc–10) → surface of the earth/ground (vv. 11–14).

The rivers excursus ends at v. 14 and is followed by v. 15, most of which Carr notes duplicates v. 8b, so bringing "us back to the picture of the human in the garden."³³ But rather than this 'doublet' suggesting that most of v. 15 is a redactional addition, it may be seen as part of the same, ongoing, reciprocating sequence. Thus:

> → supernatural/transcendent heavens (vv. 15–18) → surface of the earth/ground (v. 19a) → supernatural/transcendent heavens (vv. 19bc–20).

Of course, the biggest objection to viewing this so-called doublet as taking place in what could be described as the 'extended reality,' returns us to those long held interpretations of v. 7, and the non-geographical 'location' of Eden—hence the question marks placed after vv. 7bc–8 above. With regard to the first point Westermann makes clear his view on the meaning of

---

32. "Occasionally, *'erets* alone (like Akk. *erṣetu*) can mean the Underworld or in any case point to a connection with Sheol" (Ottosson, "אֶרֶץ," 399). Certainly, it seems generally accepted that ארץ in Gen 2:6 is capable of being read as 'underworld' in this "mythological" setting (Holladay, "*Ereṣ* Underworld," 123).

33. Carr, "Politics," 578.

the נפש חיה (*nephesh ḥayyah*—most frequently translated as 'living being') of Gen 2:7c as follows:

> To exist as a human being then is to exist in undivided unity, as expressed in the last sentence of 2:7. And so it is not at all permissible either to read into the sentence that something of the divine was given to humans at creation . . . or to explain רוח from the Greek or contemporary idea of spirit.[34]

This, then is a clear, unequivocal statement of the current, scholarly consensus concerning the so-called, Hebrew totality concept of the *nephesh ḥayyah*. It is opposed by a few voices, most notably Barr,[35] and is based on other readings of *nephesh ḥayyah*—most importantly where the term is used of animals, e.g. Gen 2:19, but as will be shown subsequently, the citing of *nephesh ḥayyah* in 2:19 may be used to oppose the totality concept. This (v. 7) is the first appearance of the term in the Hebrew Bible, and speaking specifically about Gen 2:7, Von Rad elicits a finely nuanced view of the nephesh:

> V. 7 is a *locus classicus* of Old Testament anthropology. It distinguishes not body and "soul" but more realistically body and life. The divine breath of life which unites with the material body makes man a "living soul" both from the physical as well as from the psychical side.[36]

Importantly, "soul" is found here in inverted comas, presumably to divorce the word from any association with its normal (Greek?) usage, that is, immaterial, separable and in some sense able to survive the body. In a similar vein, the use of the word psyche(ical) would seem to imply a Freudian understanding, suggesting that the unity referred to is psychosomatic in nature. But can it really be true that the ancient Hebrews had such a 'developed' view of the nature of man fully three thousand years ago, or is it more likely that Freudian ideas have permeated all twentieth century thought including recent Biblical scholarship? In the event that the methodologies followed in the ensuing chapters do demonstrate the foregoing reciprocation between a transcendent heaven and (the surface of) the earth, it will become apparent—contra Westermann—that "something of the divine was given to humans at creation." The inevitable consequence would be the abandonment of von Rad's *locus classicus*, in favor of viewing the two components of the creation process not as an undivided unity, but rather as an intermingling of

34. Westermann, *Genesis 1–11*, 206–7.
35. Barr, *Garden of Eden*, 36.
36. Von Rad, *Genesis*, 77.

two very different things. To use an analogy from chemistry, one might say that the undivided unity of a compound, should more properly be regarded as a mixture—separable under certain circumstances.

If we may be permitted to dwell on this issue a little longer we find, having reached v. 21, much dissension amongst interpreters concerning the created status of women. The tradition history approach to vv. 21–24 reveals a description of created connectedness between man and woman that does not appertain in Genesis 3. Indeed, Carr lays stress on the nature of this connectedness, remarking that *"the man is bound to her* because she was built from part of him."[37] Commentators with other approaches, however, find themselves opposed to this position. The anthropologist, Bowie, sees the taking of "Eve . . . from Adam's side" in v. 21 as clear evidence of the building of a subservient woman at this point in the 'creation and fall' story,[38] rather than any later descent to that status in chapter 3. In contradistinction, Trible finds from her exegesis of Gen 2–3 that the woman is not only created as a fully differentiated being, but may in fact be uniquely superior to the man on the grounds that she alone in creation was not taken from the earth![39] This last point is an interesting observation, insofar as it proposes a kind of reverse to Trible's obverse—the essential idea that the woman has been 'built' in a single step, rather than being 'formed' and 'breathed into' as with the two component creation of the man in v. 7. Moreover, the idea of an 'earthless' or aphysical creation lends itself to the Islamic creation tradition that speaks of the woman being created "a soul from a soul."[40] It should be apparent to the reader by now that I will be applying multidisciplinary methodologies to the Hebrew understanding of the 'soul' when returning to this issue in what follows. In doing so, I expect to confirm by an entirely different route both the connectedness of the man and the woman within the tradition-history approach, and also the symbiotic equality of the woman at this point in the creation story.

Context is once again of paramount importance to any interpretation of the 'connectedness' of the man and the woman, and should that context prove to be a transcendent environment involving theophanic encounter, then a number of important questions about gender and sexuality come to the fore. Firstly, one might ask: Was the man created sexually undifferentiated

---

37. Carr, "Politics," 580. Author's emphasis.
38. Bowie, *Anthropology*, 277–79.
39. Trible, *God and the Rhetoric*, 101–2.
40. "O humankind, be careful of your duty to your Lord, who created you from a single soul and from it created its mate" (Qu'ran 4:1a).

as some feminist scholars would suggest?[41] Any answer to this question has implications for the relationship of the genders to each other immediately after the creation of the woman, and most importantly, how, and in what way, this changed following the acquisition of the knowledge of good and bad. Indeed, in the context of an extended reality environment one must ask much more fundamental questions. Is it, for example, appropriate to consider the story to be saying anything at all about sex or sexuality in such an other-worldly environment? Moreover, one must ask what precisely is the nature of said 'connectedness' if sex/sexuality is ruled out?

Positing an other-worldly or numinous environment for the garden of/in Eden poses even more fundamental questions than those raised concerning the created status of woman, for we are obliged to consider the implications of the prohibition in v. 17. If the threatened consequence of eating fruit from the tree of the knowledge of good and bad was death, what should we understand death to mean in this environment, and how, if at all, does such a death relate to normal physical existence? Indeed, the conundrum of death failing to materialize—at least in the conventional sense—brings us right back to the nature of this strange 'land' of Eden about which so little is known, and that immortality, in the sense of the avoidance of death, is to be found there. On the issue of immortality, James Barr reaches the conclusion of the presentation of his thesis by arguing with conviction that the Hebrew understanding of immortality in the Eden story has been colored by later theological ideas. He writes:

> In particular, our story does not speak of 'life after death', nor about the 'immortality of the soul'. The 'living for ever' which Adam and Eve would have acquired had they stayed in the garden of Eden is a permanent continuance of human life.[42]

Acceptance of this understanding of immortality, which as Barr points out is entirely in accordance with Hebrew thinking, once again affirms that the very nature of Eden is central to the story. Crucially, if the nature of Eden turns out to be immaterial, that is, numinous or other-worldly we are again forced to contemplate what death might mean in such an environment, and perhaps more importantly what a permanent continuance of human life there might mean. Returning, however, to Carr's summation of the tradition history approach to these chapters produces a somewhat butchered story, and he is able to state the broad consensus on Genesis 2–3 as follows:

41. Trible, *God and the Rhetoric*, 80.
42. Barr, *Garden of Eden*, 19.

In sum, the arguments ... have distinguished an early creation story (2:4b-5, 7-8, 15bβ, 18-24) from a redactional extension of it into a creation *and* fall story (new verses include 2:6, 9-15abα, 16-17, 25 and most of chap. 3).[43]

Fundamentally, so the argument runs, these two blocks of material are contextually incompatible due to "contrasts in conceptuality and form,"[44] and as a consequence most of chapter 3 together with the insertions in chapter 2 are a "conscious" redactional extension to an earlier creation account. The reference to most of chapter 3 is here excluding the "'tree of life' texts in ... 3:22, 24 (and possibly 3:20)," which "may be remnants of a separate source or later redactional additions,"[45] and which Carr groups with 2:9b. Indeed, Westermann considers that 3:23 was the original conclusion of the narrative, and that vv. 22, 24—the 'tree of life motif'[46]—were added to the narrative, and this would appear to be a reasonable supposition using the tradition-history approach. Most interpreters would agree that these verses are either a second vestigial tradition amalgamated with the larger whole or else later redactional additions, and the fact that the plot is seemingly concerned with just one tree—the tree of the knowledge of good and bad—has suggested to some that there was in fact only one tree.[47] But if much of the action of the entire narrative is considered to take place largely in an altered state experience (dream) in the extended reality, as proposed above, then the 'tree of life motif' may take on significantly more importance than has hitherto been allocated to it, even to the point of becoming the dominant theme. Moreover, any demonstration that the (inter)actions of the characters within the story takes place in dream will create a continuity in the narrative that has so far eluded interpreters, and required the elaborate (de)constructions of the tradition history approach. In a context where the scene constantly shifts from a 'this-worldly' environment to an 'other-worldly' environment, but which is unified by a continuum consisting largely of dream, the 'tree of life' takes on primary significance insofar as it becomes the central, (sic) anthropological/theological theme of the story. This centrality derives from 2:7-9, since if 2:8 is deemed continuous with 2:7,[48] and thus with the first doublet (2:8/9),[49] it may be concluded that the tree of life appears in the text more or less

43. Carr, "Politics," 581.
44. Carr, "Politics," 582.
45. Carr, "Politics," 583.
46. Westermann, *Genesis 1-11*, 274.
47. Von Rad, *Genesis*, 78.
48. Westermann, *Genesis 1-11*, 208.
49. Westermann, *Genesis 1-11*, 211.

simultaneously (that is, at the beginning!) with the appearance of the man. Present at the beginning, the words 'tree of life' being the very last words of the text conclude the narrative, with both the tree and the man disappearing together. Effectively, the whole story is enclosed by this motif.

Dream

The reciprocation/oscillation suggested above between a this-worldly and an other-worldly environment has been said to take place largely within dream, and aspects of the text have previously been recognized as having dreamlike qualities by one interpreter in particular. Dan Burns is quite clear that Gen 2:4b—3:24 is a literary construct, the inconsistencies of which "are problematic only if we expect the narrative to conform to logical standards rather than literary ones." Continuing, he suggests that the central part of the narrative:

> . . . is numinous, and has the characteristics of dream, including transformation, sudden juxtaposition, paradox, riddle, and masking.[50]

It would be inappropriate at this point to take issue with Burns over his apparent belief in an absence of "logical standards" in the narrative, (presumably these are the province of later Greeks), and simply be content to discuss the "triptych" structure he proposes for the story. In Burn's view an opening section (2:4b–20) sets the scene, following which "Adam is put to sleep (2:21)," and this in turn is followed by "events in the centre of the narrative (2:22—3:6), which may be read as if it were Adam's dream," before finally 3:7–24 concludes the three-part format.[51] Clearly, then for Burns the deep sleep of the man in 2:21 signifies the beginning of the dream, which he then convincingly expands upon by recourse to Jungian theory.

Notwithstanding my own contention that dream occupies a significant proportion of the text of Gen 2–3, I must take issue with Burns, or at least reach a synthesis with him, on a number of points. Whilst agreeing with Burns that Phyllis Trible is a formidable exegete (whose work I will likewise later utilize) I feel that he makes a quantum leap from Trible's work when he posits that the "dream" woman is a construct of Adam's dream. Although the formation of the woman from the man (as quite distinct from his own creation process) is a singular feature of the story, it would be inappropriate to explain this entirely on the grounds of analytical psychology. Trible and Burns are absolutely

50. Burns, "Dream Form," 4.
51. Burns, "Dream Form," 5.

correct to highlight the formation of the woman from the man's rib/side, but is Burn's suggesting this 'illogical' author has a comprehensive grounding in modern Jungian theory? The fundamental premise of this theory is said to involve individuation, a process in which through dreams the man projects an "inner figure as a female personification of his unconscious."[52] In the paradise story individuation or the birth of self-consciousness takes place in 3:7 when "the eyes of both were opened." Thus for Burns:

> Trible's analysis provides evidence which suggests that Eve appears in Adam's dream as a projection of his unconscious, that she acts out his prohibitions, and that she is externalized when his eyes are opened, at which point procreation can begin.[53]

Significantly then, it would appear that the dream has now ended (3:7), and a return to normal waking reality takes place within which procreation can occur, but which does not in fact do so until Gen 4:1, that is, after expulsion from Eden! In the interim, however, the man—who arguably is never sufficiently individuated to be called by the personal name, Adam[54]—continues to engage with the woman (hiding with her, naming her), and continues to engage with YHWH. Indeed, he has engaged with YHWH before the dream as well as after it, since he took instructions (2:15), received warning/direction (2:16–17) and accepted devolved authority (2:18–19) from YHWH. Consequently, it becomes legitimate to ask why these interactions seem to be taking place outside the dream (presumably in normal waking reality), when it would be more in keeping with other theophanic encounters (e.g. Gen 15:1 ff) for them to be within dream/vision?

Burns has used an innovative approach to Gen 2:4b—3:24, which he describes as "an ancient prototype of literature whose structure is invested in the fairy tale," and to which he then applies the insights of modern, Jungian, analytical psychology. The problem that arises when psychological insights are applied to Ancient Near Eastern texts stems from the incompatibility of those cultures with the dominant culture of our own times. As with insights from psychiatry, it is unwise to expect to find psychological or behavioral characteristics recorded with any certainty in ancient texts except where the behavior in question is universal in nature. Put simply, only behaviors that

---

52. Burns makes note of the fact that the Jungian term for this dream woman within is the latin 'anima' a term which the author of the story could only have understood as *nephesh* or soul (Burns, "Dream Form," 6).

53. Burns, "Dream Form," 5.

54. There are only four appearances of the word ʾādām without the definite article in Gen 2–3, and one major translation (NRSV) does not use this word as a proper noun at all until Gen 4:25.

take place in all cultures and at all times can be relied upon to contribute valid information to the interpretative quest. Now it may be argued that Burns has identified one such universal behavior, that is, dreaming, but dreams occur within sleep and it is the overall pattern of sleeping that needs to be identified, before supplementary analysis of dreaming can take place. At that point the insights of analytical psychology may be applied to good effect. Unfortunately, the (premature) application of Freudian or Jungian psychology to the texts of ancient cultures effectively constitutes the imposition of an etic view on the culture concerned, and must be avoided at all costs. A better approach might be to use the techniques of cross-cultural psychology to obtain a derived etic view of the ancient text, one in which only those features that are universal are taken into account. We will return to this subject when developing appropriate methodologies in the next chapter.

Interestingly, unless the overall sleep pattern is identified by the techniques of cross-cultural psychology it becomes difficult, if not impossible, to determine where any particular dream begins and ends. In demarcating a single dream running from Gen 2:22 to 3:6, Burns appears to have relied upon a literary delineation of the middle portion of his suggested triptych structure commencing after the man's sleep in 2:21. The terminus of the dream is then confirmed, as already noted, on the basis of psychological analysis at 3:6. Significantly, however, the dream is said to include 2:24—3:1a—verses that are arguably regarded as narrated/editorial insertions in the text. Certainly, for Westermann v. 25 is considered to be a narrated link verse,[55] indeed he considers "the narrative would be quite complete,"[56] if it ended at v. 23. The important point here is that narrated insertions whether redaction or separate traditions are precisely that—narrations, and more properly contribute commentary on social norms rather than being dream (or indeed plot) content.

Having suggested that these 'link' verses (vv. 24–25) are outwith Burn's dream section, one might be tempted to dismiss his entire premise, but that would be a mistake, and although a synthesis of the dream (middle) portion of the triptych with Westermann's link verses destroys viewing the passage as a single dream, it does create other options. It remains the case that despite their separation the two 'pieces' of dream (2:22–23, 3:1–6) continue to retain the dream qualities enumerated by Burns, that is, transformation, sudden juxtaposition, paradox, riddle, and masking. Moreover, the first of the two dreams would terminate at the end of v. 23 in agreement with Westermann's

55. Westermann, *Genesis 1–11*, 234. In a similar vein Trible argues that v. 25 is "third person narration" (Phyllis Trible, *God and the Rhetoric*, 105).

56. V. 24 is considered by Westermann to be an "etiological addition" (Westermann, *Genesis 1–11*, 232).

suggested termination of the first (creation) narrative. At this point it becomes apparent that the so-called link verses can equally well be linking two dreams as quite distinct from two (creation and fall) narratives, and to suggest that two dreams are linked together here raises the further possibility that there may be more dreams, and that a sequence of dreams is in prospect here.

Viewing 2:15–20 as a further period of dream would, as previously noted, be very much in keeping with other theophanic encounters within dream/vision, and this would leave the man's induced deep sleep תרדמה (*tardēmā*) separating this dream from the one following it. Clearly, for this to be the case, it would be necessary for *tardēmā* to be understood as deep dreamless sleep, such as that which separates dreams during a normal night's sleep,[57] and a number of interpreters have been drawn to this conclusion. Indeed, although Lindblom had early associated *tardēmā* with dreaming,[58] it was left to Lipton to suggest that "the term may refer to a certain quality of sleep that was achieved, without waking, during the night."[59] Moreover, Lipton whilst acknowledging with McAlpine the "divinely–given" nature of "this particular form of deep sleep," notes in passing that *Genesis Rabbah* describes it as the torpor of prophecy.[60] Such a description finds agreement with Von Rad for whom "'*Tardēmā*' is a deep sleep in which the natural activities of spirit and mind are extinguished,"[61]—a feature which would appear to rule out any possibility of revelatory dreaming, unless this resumed after a cessation of *tardēmā*, that is, after v. 21.

Acceptance that a sequence of three dreams runs from 2:15 through to 3:6 (and perhaps beyond) brings a partial continuity to the whole story, but is simultaneously at variance with Burn's triptych structure and Westermann's *Geschehensbogen* structure. Westermann applies his idea of a carefully constructed arch, or *Geschehensbogen*, to the (now composite) stories of creation and paradise, which are identified as originally separate stories that have been assembled together by the Yahwist. Accolades such as "great ingenuity," and "impressive theological plan" are applied to the Yahwist within Westermann's perceived arch or bridge structure for his suggested literary construct.[62] But to propose such a sequence of dreams complete

---

57. Leonard, *Fundamentals*, 176.
58. Lindblom, "Theophanies," 94.
59. Lipton, "Revisions," 191. In a similar vein, Robinson argues that Zechariah 4:1 where the prophet describes being awakened 'like a man that is awakened out of his sleep' could refer "to an awakening to a revelation during the sleeping state" (Robinson, "Dreams in the Old Testament," 16).
60. Lipton, "Revisions," 191.
61. Von Rad, *Genesis*, 187.
62. Westermann, *Genesis 1–11*, 194–95.

with their theophanic encounters is entirely consistent with the previously mooted reciprocation between an earthly and a transcendent 'location.' It will be recollected that the reciprocating sequence was left at 2:20 just prior to the man's deep sleep, and an extension of that pattern can now be seen continuing during and beyond this period of sleep. This continuation of the pattern very much depends upon the unconscious nature of the *tardēmā*, a feature which necessarily means that the man will not be capable of interacting with either the earthly or the heavenly environments. As a result, YHWH is free to effectively 'clone' the man, operating upon both of the originally created components (v. 7) at once—a feat that would appear at least capable of being accomplished on a senseless, earthbound body. Thus, the sequence may be seen to continue as follows:

> supernatural/transcendent heavens (vv. 19bc–20) → surface of the earth/ground (v. 21) → supernatural/transcendent heavens (vv. 22–23).

Crucially, therefore, there seems to have been an unbroken and symmetrical reciprocation between the earth and the heavens throughout the entire story from v. 2:4b to v. 23, the point at which the narrated verses begin, and which create the link between Genesis 2 and 3. This supposed pattern of reciprocation has taken us a long way—some might say out on a limb—but before assembling and applying appropriate methodologies by way of support, it might be useful to recap on all the points raised.

A Third Approach

As we have seen, past approaches to the text of Genesis 2:4b—3:24 have recognized a unified story only on a literary level, and irrespective of the mooted tradition history of the received text it is only with considerable difficulty that the 'irregularities' within the narrative can be reconciled to each other. In the following chapters, however, we will collect together and précis the arguments that suggest the story has a fundamental unity, which derives directly from a single, primeval, oral counterpart that coexisted for a time with its written heir. Indeed, a third approach will be offered, which posits that this single, oral counterpart has undergone very little (editorial) supplementation when transposed into the written form, save where this has been required to preserve a basic preliterary form.

At this stage, it must again be freely admitted that the argument presented of a this/other-worldly reciprocation from Gen 2:4b onwards has been made without the benefit of a detailed, methodological presentation. But the argument is only intended to infer that the Hebrew might be capable of supporting such a context of continually shifting 'location' between the 'real' world and the world of the numinous. Continuing on the basis that such a context does in fact appertain, the discussion moved on to threaten, or at the very least question, certain long held tenets concerning ancient Hebrew thinking. Amongst these is the so-called, Hebrew totality concept of the created status of mankind, wherein the *nephesh ḥayyah* is, in effect, thought to be that thoroughly modern concept—a psychosomatic unity. Similarly, one is obliged to question the created status of woman, since the proposed numinous/transcendent environment would appear to completely preclude viewing that status as in any way concerned with sex or sexuality. More importantly, in positing a transcendent environment, or at least reciprocation between the earth and the heavens (accessed through dream), we are compelled to view the threatened death following the eating of the fruit (2:17) in a completely new light. Then there is the puzzle of the 'tree of life' motif, which appears and disappears simultaneously with the appearance and disappearance of the man, yet is considered to be an incorporated, vestigial aside by most commentators even though it almost completely encloses the entire Gen 2–3 narrative. Intriguingly, this tree is arguably present to both this world and the world of the numinous at the same 'time'.

Having enumerated and briefly discussed these issues as consequences of the proposed numinous environment, the discussion moved on to suggest that such a context was consistent with dreamform. Reference was made to a previous attempt (Burns) to relate at least a portion of the Gen 2–3 story to dream, on the basis of a literary approach involving a tripartite division of the story. Whilst highlighting the features of the story that point to dream, Burns' approach partially fails insofar as it relies overmuch on a literary perspective inauthentically supported by modern analytical psychology. It was noted that the use of modern disciplines in this way, although invalid, is quite acceptable when used in secondary support of more appropriate cross-cultural methodologies. Moreover, it was mooted that the essential problem with viewing any or all of Gen 2–3 as dream stems from a failure to address the relationship between sleep and dream, both within the modern West and the Ancient Near East. Nevertheless, beginning with Burns' important identification of dream categories, an initial argument was presented—pending methodological support—for viewing most of the direct and reported speech/action in Gen 2–3 as dream, and that this is entirely consistent with other theophanic encounters found in dream/vision elsewhere in the Hebrew Bible.

3

"To Sleep, Perchance to Dream . . ."

FOLLOWING ON FROM THE preceding chapter, and collecting together the ideas presented there, allows the development of a 'third' approach and its application to Gen 2–3—a third approach that is dependent on a clear demonstration that the structure of the narrative is dreamform, set within an overall context of sleep. This previous discussion was concerned with the plausibility that real, nocturnal behavior is an incorporated feature of the text, on the basis that 'reality' for this pre-modern culture comprises both a variety of altered states of consciousness (ASC's) and sense experience. In support of this contention it may firstly be noted that in the Western cultural purview dreaming is considered to be merely one mode or form of sleep, which is considered to be integral with engaging in the act of sleeping as a whole. But this is an entirely different concept from that found amongst premodern people groups—including those of the Ancient Near East. Indeed and as previously noted, although the ancients distinguished between experiences when awake and when dreaming, "to them the difference was not, as for us, one of kind, that is, real or unreal, but one of degree."[1]

The close conceptual relationship between waking and dreaming experiences would also be consistent with what Oppenheim reports is the "Egyptian (and Coptic)" understanding of the dream experience, one in which, "the term for dream *rswt* . . . conceives of the dream as a specific state of consciousness between wakefulness and sleep,"[2] as quite distinct from a state of consciousness within sleep. Moreover, it may be observed that a dream (*šuttum*) at Mari in Mesopotamia involved receipt of revelation through vision, and hearing could also be involved.[3] Similarly, the Egyptian word for dream (*rśw.t*) indicates a visionary experience that has "an open eye as its determinative, apparently representing dreaming as a special state

---

1. Jacobsen, "Graven Image," 19.
2. Oppenheim, "Interpretation," 226.
3. Botterweck, "חֲלוֹם," 426.

of consciousness, something like 'watching during sleep.'"[4] An awareness (by Westerners) of the close relationship between wakefulness and dreaming in the ancient mindset, and therefore the ease with which it would have been deemed possible to switch between these two 'realities,' allows a passage (any passage incorporating sleep) to be viewed more easily as involving a real sequence of separate dreams. Importantly, when sleep is mentioned in a passage it almost invariably refers to deep, slow wave, insensible sleep, which separates the periods of speech/action (dreams) from each other enabling the discernment of a clear nocturnal structure and progression. Consequently, it will be necessary to engage with the findings of modern sleep research in order to demonstrate this structural relationship between sleep and dreaming. Moreover, should that investigation also reveal a connection with clinical depression then this would be resonant with the genetic evidence reported in chapter 1. Indeed, it bears repeating that the essential problem with viewing any or all of Gen 2–3 as dream stems from a failure to address the relationship between sleep and dream, both within modern Western biblical scholarship and the traditions of Judeo-Christianity as they developed after the collapse of the Roman Empire.

In pharmacological terminology, depression has been linked with a deficiency of serotonin in the brain (hypothalamus),[5] which is produced in the body from the amino acid precursor, L-tryptophan.[6] Although it

4. Bergman et al., "חֲלוֹם," 422.
5. Gaskell, "Weighing in," 44.
6. The efficacy of many antidepressants depends on their ability to increase the concentration of the naturally occurring neurotransmitter, serotonin (5-hydroxytryptamine, {5HT}) in the brain. "One of the most abundant neurotransmitters in the central nervous system, serotonin controls a variety of functions, including the level of arousal, the sleep-wake cycle and mood" (Pufulete, "The Voices Within," 32). Ingestion and catabolism of the serotonin precursor tryptophan proceeds in accordance with the following sequence:

Consequently, the production of a specific known amount of serotonin via this route, followed by its delivery to the appropriate brain receptors, is dependent firstly on the efficient, non-destructive, absorption of tryptophan by the stomach, and secondly on the efficiency of the first two enzyme reactions. It is interesting to note that the third enzyme reaction shown in the above-noted sequence destroys serotonin, and suppression or inhibition of one of the active enzymes, monoamine oxidase, through a class of drugs known as monoamine oxidase inhibitors (M.A.O.I.), can help maintain the

is not doubted that the serotonergic system is intimately involved in sleep, opinions differ as to the precise mechanisms of action, and discrepancies exist between the findings of human and animal studies,[7] with the latter indicating that serotonin (5HT) plays a crucial role in the overall sleep pattern. The two main types of sleep are firstly "non-rapid eye movement sleep (non-REM or slow-wave sleep)" and secondly "rapid eye movement sleep (REM sleep),"[8] and they may be monitored during sleep by using a variety of electrode and other physiological measurement techniques. The whole REM/Non-REM sequence has been represented graphically in figure 2[9], where Non-REM sleep is shown further subdivided into 'light sleep' (stages 1 and 2), and a deeper sleep (stages 3 & 4).

All the stages of sleep are characterized by the respective waveforms they generate on the screens and printouts of the monitoring equipment. REM sleep accounts for perhaps 20 percent of total sleep time for a normal young adult, but this total is typically divided into four periods spread throughout the night and separated by (longer) periods of non-REM sleep. The first period of REM sleep begins at about 90 minutes into sleep and each of the three subsequent periods are of increasing duration, with the last period (just before waking) being the longest and most vivid. Although the precise physiological function of REM sleep is unknown, pharmacological interventions using antidepressants or serotonin precursors are known to affect both its latency and duration. Measurements of the concentration of 5HT during REM sleep reveal that serotonergic activity is totally suppressed.[10] Interestingly, sleep features serotonin deficit in common with a number of other inducing physiological states (illness, fasting, surgical trauma, and intoxication), and significantly this 5HT deficit occurs during the REM phase of sleep—long associated with dreaming sleep.[11]

---

body's own supply of serotonin.

7. Animal studies, unlike those involving human patients, have pointed to a role for serotonin in all stages or patterns of sleep (Mendelson, *Human Sleep*, 71).

8. Leonard, *Fundamentals*, 175.

9. Reproduced from Leonard, *Fundamentals*, 176.

10. Leonard, *Fundamentals*, 96. Hobson, *Sleep*, 132.

11. Leonard, *Fundamentals*, 175.

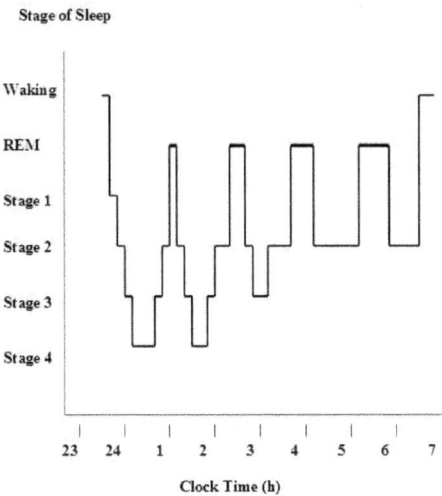

Fig. 2   Typical Hypnogram of a Normal Young Adult

Depression

According to the predominant *Selective Mood Regulatory Theory of Dreaming*,[12] under normal circumstances dreaming as manifested by REM sleep serves to regulate mood across the night. In fact, for normal adults without any history of depression, "a successful night's dreaming has as a consequence an increase in happiness."[13] To use Kramer's expression, the physiological and psychological functions of sleep act as a "thermostat," which adjusts the mood towards a more central level that is neither too high nor too low. It has been found, however, that this regulatory function only occurs within a relatively narrow range of pre-sleep mood levels, that is, there is a "floor and a ceiling effect."[14]

12. Kramer, "Selective Mood," 139.
13. Kramer, "Selective Mood," 187.
14. Cartwright et al., "Role of REM Sleep," 3.

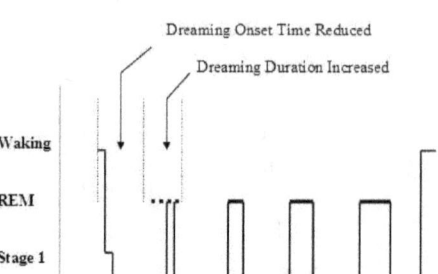

Fig. 3   Typical Hypnogram of a Depressive

In depressives it seems that the pre-sleep negative mood may be too great to be modified by this regulatory mechanism and both the onset and level of eye movement activity of the REM sleep are affected. In depression the early stages of the sleep pattern become measurably distorted with the earlier onset of an extended first REM sleep period, and the typical, characteristic hypnogram produced is shown in figure 3. The content of the dreams as manifested by the level and intensity of the rapid eye movements is greatly increased, with both the number and types of character appearing in the dreams exceeding those recorded for non-depressives.[15] Later research does, however, indicate that REM sleep and dreaming are not isomorphous, and that there is no relationship between eye movements and the visual imagery in dreaming.[16] Depression induced by semi-starvation (fasting) has also been shown to result in an accelerated onset of REM sleep in patients undergoing reduced calorie intake.[17] In summary, it may be said that depression induces the quicker onset of a longer first REM sleep period,

---

15. Kramer, "Selective Mood," 187.
16. Palagini and Rosenlicht, "Sleep, Dreaming," 182.
17. Fichter and Pirke, "Starvation Models," 100.

and this remains characteristic of sleep in depression[18] producing the sleep architecture shown in fig. 3.

The universality of dreaming ensures that it does not become 'medicalised,' but if the 'dreaming state' were to intrude into normal wakefulness,[19] a dilemma is presented to doctors and a choice must then be made between describing the resultant state as visionary on the one hand, or hallucinatory/delusional on the other. In modern Western society choosing between these states can have profound consequences for the individual concerned and is effectively a subjective decision taken by the medical professional. Medical practitioners are forced on a daily basis to decide between mystic and psychotic states. Indeed:

> Religious delusions are a feature of . . . psychotic illnesses. Distinguishing culturally accepted religious-mystical beliefs from bizarre psychotic delusions poses both a practical challenge to clinicians and an epistemologic-theorectical challenge to the foundations of psychiatric nosology. . . . Ultimately, no diagnostic system can irrefutably characterize certain beliefs as delusional, as having no correspondence to objective reality.[20]

Saver and Rabin aver that mystical and psychotic states are both characterized by "apparent delusions, hallucinations, strange behavior and social withdrawal,"[21] and therefore, the medicalisation (alienation?) of any particular altered state of consciousness must ultimately be a cultural decision.[22] In the modern West that cultural decision is normally taken by the clinician (psychiatrist) with reference to his/her personal knowledge of what has now become the sub-culture of religion. Even should an actual reference be made to the religious sub-culture concerned, visionary or auditory contact with the deity may be so proscribed within that group as to deny any validity to the experience. Moreover, 'hallucinations' are characterized for diagnostic purposes within the mystical state as chiefly of a visionary nature, whilst auditions are seen as typifying psychotic conditions.[23] This is, however, an arbitrary dichotomy that is incompatible with the interchange-

---

18. Palagini and Rosenlicht, "Sleep, Dreaming," 182.

19. It should be noted here that dreaming sleep is the shallowest kind of sleep, i.e. the one nearest to the waking state of the five levels of sleep (Leonard, *Fundamentals*, 176).

20. Saver and Rabin, "Neural Substrates," 505.

21. Saver and Rabin, "Neural Substrates," 505.

22. Prince draws the same conclusion regarding the interpretation of "highly similar mental and behavioural states" (Prince, "Religious Experience," 289).

23. Saver and Rabin, "Neural Substrates," 506.

ability between visionary and auditory states found in biblical sources (e.g. 2 Sam 7), and in addition, fails to acknowledge the modern accounts of synesthesia within mystical states.[24]

Cross-Cultural Psychology

The introduction of modern sleep research and psychopharmacology complete with hypnograms (the graphical representation of the progress of a night's sleep) into a discussion about Hebrew scripture begs the question: How/why is it valid to compare the structure of an ancient passage in scripture with the structure of a modern hypnogram? The answer at its simplest relates to anthropological, cultural, and social patterns found in the written passages. Dreamers, visionaries, and all the subsequent contributors to the tradition (both oral and written) shared the same culture-specific wording patterns, and this works to create and transmit a stylized description of nocturnal ASC experiences (dreams) in the time-related matrix (sleeping, dreaming, waking) in which they occurred. Indeed culture offers ways of coping or dealing with different states of consciousness, and "since the social system also specifies the behavioral pattern by which altered states are experienced and interpreted, it is quite plausible that visionaries did behave in just the way the literary pattern reports."[25] Essentially, it would appear that there is an irreducible core preserved at the heart of the final text that relates to, and reflects, real ASC/dream experiences in behavioral terms, that is, in the proportion that each dream bears to the others, and to the other states of consciousness. Indeed, it would be a mistake to consider the stylized descriptions found in the text as entirely the result of literary activity on the part of the author, and "it may well be these cultural patterns that have been too narrowly, exclusively, and conveniently defined as literary forms by biblical scholars."[26] In short, it seems likely that original speech motifs recollecting and describing a real matrix of characteristic, nocturnal (and prophetic) behavior are being featured in these accounts, and that they have not been significantly compromised in the transmission process, on the contrary they have been actively endorsed in that process.

On the basis that real nocturnal behavior is being featured in selected final texts a comparison may now be drawn between the latter, and

---

24. "Synesthesia is the transmutation of sensory modalities, where sound may be seen or color experienced by the sense of smell and so on" (Goodman, "Serotonergic System," 265).

25. Pilch, *Visions and Healing*, 76.

26. Pilch, "Visions in Revelation," 237.

the modern laboratory record of nocturnal activity, that is, the hypnogram. As already noted, however, some discussion needs to take place on the appropriateness of conducting such a comparison, and psychology—based as it is on the behavior of individuals—suggests itself as the most suitable discipline to employ in this regard. Unfortunately, as "Segall and other specialists in cross-cultural psychology point out . . . modern Western psychology is a mono-cultural science, so integrally bound to Western culture and values as to be nearly useless for application to other cultures."[27] Indeed, Segall and his coworkers suggest a different approach is employed, and this process of comparison wherein the researcher seeks to apply an observed behavior found in modern, Western culture to behavior recorded in other, alien (pre-modern) cultures has been depicted in the Venn diagram form shown in figure 4.[28]

The essence of the Segall et al. methodology lies in the avoidance of pressing a Western emic analysis onto the culture in question as an imposed etic view. Indeed, the imposition of a Western, etic view onto ancient, alien cultures should be avoided at all costs by what amounts to the 'enculturation' of the researcher, that is, the investigator seeks to "discover the other culture," or develop an understanding of that culture from its own internal (emic) viewpoint. This is step 3 in the Segall et al. Venn diagram (fig. 4), and follows the abandonment of an imposed etic view (step 2). At this point, comparison can begin between the internal, collective mindsets of the two cultures, that is, between the emic perspectives of Western culture (emic A) and those of (in this case) the Ancient Near East (emic B). "In this stage (step 4), the researcher focuses on culture-specific phenomena like the behaviors, norms, values, customs and traditions of the particular society under study."[29]

---

27. Pilch, "Altered States," 138.
28. Segall et al., *Human Behaviour*, 55.
29. Pilch, "Altered States," 136.

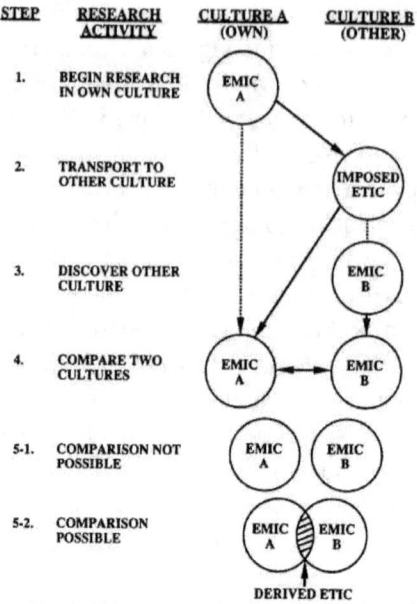

Fig. 4 – Steps in Operationalizing Emics and Etics

The final step (5) in the process involves the bringing together of the two internal perspectives (emic A and emic B) to produce one of two possible outcomes: Either the cultures are not comparable in respect of the behavior under consideration, or comparison is possible "and the Venn diagrams representing an emic A and emic B behavior overlap"[30]—an overlap that Segall *et al.* represent as a derived etic,[31] and which consists in "that aspect of a human behavior that can be considered universal."[32] Given that the behavior under consideration in the present study is ASC behavior (with a particular emphasis on dreaming behavior) an attempt may be made to produce a derived etic from a passage concerned with dreaming. As already observed, the social system specifies the behavioral pattern in which ASCs are experienced and interpreted,[33] and as a consequence the behavioral patterns found in final texts may not simply be the result of literary activity. On the basis that visionaries did behave in the way the literary pattern reports, it is quite plausible that dreaming behavior is likely to have been experi-

---

30. Pilch, "Altered States," 136.
31. Segall et al., *Human Behaviour*, 55.
32. Pilch, "Altered States," 136.
33. Pilch, *Visions and Healing*, 76.

enced and interpreted as part of a nocturnal matrix of sleeping, dreaming, and perhaps also wakefulness in sequence, that is, as a continuous stream of experience. In the view advanced here it is contended that this whole experience of nocturnal behavior, as recorded in the text, may be compared with a modern, electronic record of nocturnal activity (a hypnogram) in a meaningful way supported by the Segall *et al.* methodology depicted in figure 4. In the event that an overlap is achieved between the textual record of speech-action/sleep sequences and such a hypnogram a derived etic is produced, which may then be represented graphically as a 'derived etic' hypnogram of that passage. Moreover, if overlap should occur between the hypnogram of a depressive, as quite distinct from that of a 'normal' person, then this has implications for the way in which the prophetic character or personality is understood.[34] Indeed, a hypnogram derived from the overlap of these two 'accounts' (ancient and modern) of nocturnal activity serves to identify the prophet (to the modern reader) as a depressive, and establishes an equivalence wherein to be depressed is to be a prophet and *vice versa*. The common factor of characteristic, depressive dreaming within a 'derived etic' hypnogram suggests that the two nocturnal behaviors—prophetic and depressive—are equivalent, especially in those instances where the text makes explicit mention of the terms for dream or vision.

It may be objected that characteristic, depressive dreaming is not sufficient evidence in and of itself to allow the prophet to be labeled as a depressive, unless it is supported by other depressive parameters, such as those found in the DSM IV criteria.[35] On the contrary, it may be the only evidence for such depressive labeling, since it depends on a relevant behavioral comparison rather than categories derived from modern Western psychology, which as already noted have little value when applied to other cultures. Moreover, any demonstration that certain 'dream theophany' texts do overlap with modern, depressive hypnograms—thereby suggesting that the dreamer is depressed—may appear to some readers to add nothing to an understanding of the text in question. But the importance of the procedure lies in its transferability to other texts not normally described as dream theophanies, such as 1 Kings 19:2–21, and sections of the book of Jonah, where it has been accepted that other DSM IV criteria for depression are present, criteria which in themselves (unsupported) merely reflect an imposed, Western etic perspective. If a 'derived etic' hypnogram can be

---

34. See figures 2 and 3, which display the differences between normal and depressive hypnograms.

35. For example, recurrent thoughts of death, or poor self-regard (American Psychiatric Association, *DSM IV*, 356).

produced from each of the latter texts, it might better explain (in terms of ASC/dream imagery) many of the more bizarre features found there.

Such features as the earthquake, wind, and fire of 1 Kings 19:11–12, the man-eating fish of Jonah 2:1, or the telescoped life of the plant in Jonah 4:6–7, may be readily understood as typical of the abruptness of dream patterns, despite having often been seen as a function of the poetic license of the storyteller. 'Derived etic' hypnograms can therefore explain features of these stories that are otherwise difficult to interpret without, that is, resort to literary categories such as fable, legend or deliberate fiction-writing (novella). What is important, however, is that these otherwise bizarre features are seen as integral to the behavioral (dream/hypnogram) pattern of the experiences as specified by the social system, irrespective of whether that particular story is deemed factual, fact with interpretation or simply fictional. Put simply, reference is being made at the level of the text to an example of real behavior that would in all probability have been readily recognizable by an ancient author and his 'audience.' It is important to realize that:

> All language derives its meaning from the social world. . . . Since these authors and their original readers (or listeners) shared this social world and were intimately familiar with it, there was no need for an author to spell out the obvious. . . . It is important to realize that . . . far more was left unsaid than in a modern Western context.[36]

With these points on the possible relationship between culture-based experience (of ASCs) and ultimate literary form in mind, it would seem appropriate at this point to attempt a fuller investigation of particular 'dream-theophany' passages, that is, passages containing the Hebrew terms for dream and vision.

Derived Etic Hypnogram—Abraham

When I began research into the significance of psychophysiological factors in prophecy, it was suggested to me that I demonstrate this comparative methodology on a passage containing the Hebrew word(s) for dream or vision, before applying it to other passages that did not include those words. This was a difficult task as most prophetic passages do not use these words (despite many including verses showing the prophet sleeping),[37] for indeed,

---

36. Pilch, "Transfiguration," 50.

37. It is essential for the narrator to point this out, since 'sleeping' in this cultural context is not the same as 'dreaming.'

as previously noted with Pilch, there was simply no need for an ancient author to spell out the obvious. Undaunted, I settled on one especially formative passage in Genesis—the Abrahamic covenant. Indeed, Genesis 15 opens with the words:

> "After these things the word of the LORD came to Abram in a vision, ..."[38]

Now clearly, it might seem obvious (to a Western reader) at first sight of this verse that the word of the LORD came to Abram within a vision/dream. But that would be a Western etic reading of the text, for in its ancient context, it would have been obvious to the listener that Abram received the words through his eyes, that is, Abram heard the words through his eyes. Of course the nature of that visionary experience is not conveyed by the text (and probably its oral antecedents also) because it is likely to have been a synesthetic event that is nearly incapable of description. Indeed, this "mixture of sensory systems ... is common to dream experiences and experiences of the numinous."[39] Certainly, synesthetes have, in what for them is 'normal waking reality,' described the "feeling of a presence or the 'visitor experience'"[40]—a feature known to clinical neurology that correlates with lesions in mesiobasal portions of the temporal lobes:

> These areas of the brain are associated inter alia with the experience of meaningfulness, the sense of self and its relationship to space-time (with its religious and cosmic associations), dreamy states, feelings of movement, and smell.[41]

Consequently, the difficulty presented to the narrator/editor and probably also the source visionary/prophet/dreamer is how to relate an experience which is of its essence strange, yet seemingly not beyond explicit, matter-of-fact acknowledgement,[42] for "the indescribable must somehow be put into human words."[43] Thus, the reason for the presence in the text of the word

---

38. NRSV.
39. Hasan-Rokem, "Communication," 219.
40. Cytowic, *Synesthesia*, 305.
41. Cytowic, *Synesthesia*, 305.
42. See Exodus 20:18 "וכל־העם ראים את־הקולת" (and all the people saw the voices). Taken at face value this expression can refer either to the perceptions of a group of synesthetes in what for them is 'normal waking reality,' or to the synesthetic experiences of a more 'normal' group of individuals during an altered state of consciousness—a visionary or dreamy state. The latter situation is the more likely, since a group of people that by any reckoning was quite large, cannot all have been synesthetes.
43. Gnuse, "Dreams in the Night," 52.

for 'vision,' is not to establish that the passage relates a dream/vision, but rather to state baldly that Abram heard the 'word of the LORD' through his eyes! Fundamentally, the statement in the first verse of this passage (Gen 15: 1–21) that Abram received the 'word of the LORD' in a vision is quite irrelevant to this discussion, and the confirmation (for the modern Western reader) that the passage consists of a sequence of dreams can only be satisfactorily demonstrated by the derivation of an etic hypnogram, using the methodology outlined above.

After the opening verse, continuous speech/action between Abram and YHWH now ensues until the end of the passage broken only by two, possibly three, narrated interjections. These interjections (vv. 6, 12, and perhaps 17a) roughly correspond with commonly accepted junctures in the text—"joints"[44] within the text that have led previous generations of scholars to regard Genesis 15 as being "made up of heterogeneous elements."[45] Thus, a traditional breakdown of the passage might envisage two "units" (vv. 1–6 and 7–11+17–18) into which a third (vv. 13–16) has been inserted allowing Westermann to treat the passage as comprised of "two promise narratives"[46]—Gen 15:1–6 and 15:7–21. Westermann's treatment, however, does not appear to address the nature of this passage, since nowhere do the terms, vision, dream or theophany seem to be discussed. The nature of the passage is important insofar as it may overcome the apparent contradictions—Lindblom's so-called "heterogeneous elements"—that prevent it from being read (in von Rad's view), as "an organic narrative unit."[47]

Classification of v. 6 as narrated interjection is perhaps something of an over simplification, for in von Rad's view the verse is describing (concealing!) further speech/action which is undisclosed. Indeed, the narrator does not describe the actual occurrence upon which the theological assertions of v. 6 about faith are based, but:

> It appears to concern something that cannot be described. This belief is not described but only asserted. Approached from without, this concealed event of believing is rather negative; it is muteness—silent listening and looking.[48]

Von Rad's words touch the heart of this experience and recall once again Cytowic's association of "dreamy states" with the synesthetic transfer of

---

44. Von Rad, *Genesis*, 182.
45. Lindblom, "Theophanies," 94.
46. Westermann, *Genesis 12–36*, 230.
47. Von Rad, *Genesis*, 182.
48. Von Rad, *Genesis*, 184.

information through the eyes. When v. 6 is understood in this way the whole passage (vv. 1b–11) may more readily be seen as a single visionary interlude, albeit that it may now be seen to consist of three discrete—yet continuous—sets of visionary events (vv. 1b–5, 6 and 7–11) rather than two disparate ones as commonly supposed. It might be argued that the apparent disparity between the content of each (of three) speech/action sequences makes an even stronger case for viewing the passage as heterogeneous, but this argument may be countered by noting the fluidity of dream states in common experience. Dreams are of their essence capable of enabling a rapid translation from one visual event to another, in a way not possible during 'normal' waking consciousness. Clearly, for many scholars new narrative content begins at v. 7,[49] but von Rad equivocates insofar as he raises doubts concerning the 'normal' scriptural usage of the divine self-introduction, אני יהוה. On v. 7 he argues:

> It is obvious that the redactor is attempting to unite the event about to be described closely to the one that has proceeded; for a narrative cannot have begun with v. 7 only.[50]

Von Rad supplements this point by adding that it was necessary for God to step out of "his incognito," in order to differentiate himself from other denizens of the "world of the numinous" who could so affect the lives of mortals.[51] Viewing vv. 1a–11 as a continuous vision-dream interlude finds support from Lichtenstein who considers that Genesis 15 reports two tracts of visionary experience:

> Thus, in Genesis 15 two distinct divine oracles are preserved, one is delivered במחזה "in a vision" (vv. 1–11), while the other is introduced by the notice נפלה על אברם ותרדמה "And sleep overcame Abram..." (vv. 12 ff.).... The usage of תרדמה "sleep" in v. 12, ... serves to introduce an oracle delivered in a dream.[52]

---

49. So, for example, Von Rad, *Genesis*, 223. Turner, *Genesis*, 74. Waltke, *Genesis*, 242.

50. Von Rad, *Genesis*, 1186. See also Van Seters who considers that this "new theme (v. 7) cannot be regarded on the literary level as an entirely new beginning, because both the subject and the indirect object of the opening verb have their antecedents in the previous unit" (Van Seters, *Abraham in History*, 257).

51. Von Rad, *Genesis*, 1186.

52. Lichtenstein, "Dream Theophany," 46. Gnuse is uncertain "whether there are two revelations in vv. 1–11 and vv. 12–21, or whether the text portrays this as one theophany" (Gnuse, "Dreams in the Night," 35).

It is clear, however, that in the view of Lichtenstein תרדמה (*tardēmā*) is a deep sleep during which the dream oracle of vv. 13–21 is delivered,[53] and in this respect he agrees with Lindblom who also associates *tardēmā* with dreaming.[54] What is certain is that v. 12 in general, and *tardēmā* in particular, are pivotal to the achievement of any understanding of this passage. Gnuse considers whether Abram's "deep sleep" should be classified as further dream revelation but remains undecided[55] whilst, significantly, Lipton suggests, "the term (תרדמה) may refer to a certain quality of sleep that was achieved, without waking, during the night."[56] Moreover, Lipton whilst acknowledging with McAlpine the "divinely-given" nature of "this particular form of deep sleep," notes in passing that *Genesis Rabbah* describes it as the torpor of prophecy.[57] Such a description finds agreement with von Rad for whom "'*Tardēmā*' is a deep sleep in which the natural activities of spirit and mind are extinguished,"[58]—a feature which would appear to rule out any possibility of revelatory dreaming, unless this resumed after a cessation of *tardēmā*, that is, after v. 12.

Collecting these ideas together suggests that the narrator introduces in v. 12 three staccato-like points in quick succession: 1) the temporal reference to sunset, 2) the depth and insensibility of Abram's sleep and 3) the termination of the *tardēmā*. On this last point Lipton makes an interesting comment when she suggests that the אימה חשכה גדלה ("great dark dread") "which descended upon Abraham may have been a standard dream-manifestation of the divine presence."[59] Indeed:

> Additional support for this reading may be derived from the juxtaposition of vv. 12 and 13 . . . Since none of the four preceding verses has mentioned God's name, one might have expected v. 13 to specify that God was speaking to Abraham. The absence of an explicit reference here may indicate that the narrator regarded the great darkness in v. 12 as a divine manifestation.[60]

---

53. Lichtenstein, "Dream Theophany," 46.
54. Lindblom, "Theophanies," 94.
55. Gnuse, "Dreams in the Night," 35.
56. Lipton, *Revisions*, 191. In a similar vein, Robinson argues that Zechariah 4:1 where the prophet describes being awakened 'like a man that is awakened out of his sleep' could refer "to an awakening to a revelation during the sleeping state" (Robinson, "Dreams in the Old Testament," 16).
57. Lipton, *Revisions*, 191.
58. Von Rad, *Genesis*, 187.
59. Lipton, *Revisions*, 196.
60. Lipton, *Revisions*, 196.

To put it slightly differently and in terms of the controlling paradigm of this discussion, Abram appears to have begun a new ASC/Spiritual encounter at this point in the story, and the *tardēmā* of v. 12b is effectively a watershed—bounded on either side by the visionary/theophanic activity of vv. 1–11 and vv. 13–21. Indeed, in expansion of Lipton's insight already noted,[61] *tardēmā* appears to represent a boundary between dreams, yet a boundary that is of little consequence to the modern, Western mindset, which regards dreaming as merely another kind of sleep quite devoid of significance. Here *tardēmā* would seem to herald a crossing of the boundary between sleeping and dreaming—a transition which occurs, as Lipton has pointed out—without waking, thereby giving good agreement with Egyptian, Sumero-Akkadian and Graeco-Roman perceptions of dreaming as an intermediate state of consciousness lying between sleep and wakefulness.[62] With regard to v. 12a Lipton is undecided on whether the sun is setting in reality or in the dream-vision, but favors treating the sunset of v. 12 as another construct of Abram's dream on the basis that the sun had fully set in v. 17. But it is suggested here that Abram's *tardēmā* is being reported as an integral part of a continuous stream of nocturnal behavior that includes real ASC/dream experiences; behavior which has undergone elaboration during the retelling of the story, in order to bring the story into closer conformity with traditional culture-based experience of prophetic nocturnal behavior. Since *tardēmā* follows closely upon the temporal reference "as the sun was going down," this suggests that v. 12a may also have been a feature external to either dream. It is perhaps important to recognize with Lipton the importance of 'darkness' to the development of the narrative at this point (v. 17), for "in terms of the dream-vision . . . the darkness is an all important backdrop to the appearance of the oven and the torch, whose images would have been infinitely less potent in daylight."[63]

61. Lipton, *Revisions,* 191.

62. Oppenheim cites passages in Pindar which indicate that the dream "is a *sui generis* state of consciousness, a hovering between the eclipse of sleep and the stark but dull reality of the day," before going on "to draw attention to the fact that the Egyptian word for dream (*rswt*) is not only etymologically connected with a root meaning 'to be awake' but is also written with the determinative representing an opened eye." Working with an unpublished Sumero-Akkadian vocabulary fragment, Oppenheim suggests that *munattu*—one of a number of synonymous expressions for 'dream'—refers to "an intermediary stage between wakefulness and slumber in which dream experiences of a special nature are said—in classical sources—to occur. Macrobius, in his Commentary to the Dream of Scipio . . . knows of such phenomena and calls them in Greek *phantasma,* in Latin *visum*" (Oppenheim, "Interpretation," 190, 225).

63. Lipton, *Revisions,* 194. Likewise the earlier 'picture' of a star-filled sky (v. 5) could be seen to suggest the relative eminence or status of Abram's descendents by the varying brightness of individual stars, in a way not possible with (daylight) images of

Acceptance that a real, temporal reference point is in view here fixes the whole passage (vv. 1–21), suggesting a dream/sleep/dream sequence running from the mid to late evening (the last of the light) into the night proper, and two dreams of unequal length are in prospect here separated by a discrete period of deep sleep. If a comparison is now conducted between the record of Abram's nocturnal activities (the dream/sleep/dream sequence) and a modern, Western (depressive) hypnogram, it becomes apparent that an area of overlap exists in terms of the Segall *et al.* Venn diagram (fig. 4), and the resultant 'derived etic' hypnogram may be represented as follows in figure 5:

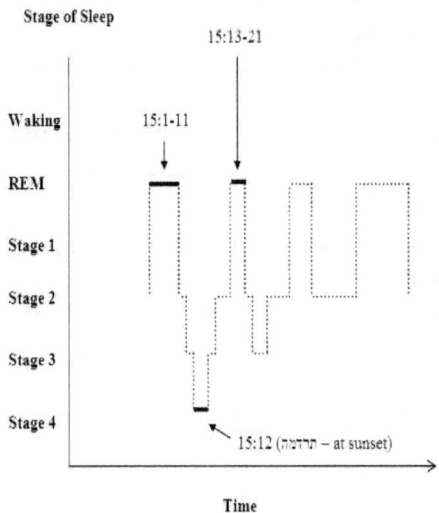

Fig. 5   'Derived Etic' Hypnogram of Genesis 15

This comparison between the dream/sleep/dream sequence of Genesis 15:1–21 and the typical, modern, Western hypnogram of a depressive produces an overlap or match inasmuch as the duration of the first dream—as reflected in the relative length of text allocated to speech/action—is found to be extended/lengthened relative to the following dream. This feature of the passage indicates firstly that the dreams are likely to be the first two in a sequence of four, and secondly it suggests that Abram is being portrayed as a depressive (Western, emic view), because of the characteristic relative

---

'sand' or 'dust,' which Lipton suggests "would have been more appropriate for a daytime setting" (Lipton, *Revisions*, 186).

length of the first dream, despite there being no other (DSM IV) indicators[64] to this effect. With regard to the first point another aspect of the passage supports the contention that a continuation of the dream/sleep/dream sequence might be expected across the remainder of the night. This concerns the apparent 'failure' of the narrator to 'close' the passage, for although in the second dream the content has reached a finite and complete conclusion,[65] YHWH's words are not formally closed[66] either by a further sleep period or Abram waking up. Thus, the narrator leaves his hearer/reader with the impression that although YHWH has finished speaking on that particular topic (the covenant) Abram's 'nocturnal activities' are not yet over. This, when combined with the fixed temporal point of sunset (v. 12), indicates that the two dreams are likely to be the first two of a normal night's sequence of four—a recognizable and culturally-significant (hypnogram) pattern. In this respect, editorial activity[67] may have been responsible for bringing the dream-vision into closer conformity with the traditional culture-pattern.[68]

Thus, the fundamental feature of the Abrahamic covenant of Genesis 15 does not lie in the fact that it is presented by the writer as a vision, מחזה, machazeh (although, as discussed, this in itself is instructive), rather its value lies in the display of a dream/sleep/dream sequence, which directly correlates to a modern hypnogram. Moreover, that dream/sleep/dream sequence is characteristically that of a depressed dreamer, as displayed by the relative proportions that the first dream bears to the second. Consequently, it is the culture-based validity of the methodology that is the most important factor, and this allows it to be extended to include other texts that relate theophanic encounters, but which do not overtly mention dreaming or vision, before finally being applied to Genesis 2–3.

---

64. For example, recurrent thoughts of death, or poor self-regard (American Psychiatric Association, *DSM IV*, 356).

65. The 'completeness' of the list of nations (10) given in vv. 19–21 relative to that given in Deut 7:1 (7) has been noted by a number of scholars. See for example; (Westermann, *Genesis 12–36*, 230 and Waltke, *Genesis*, 246).

66. There is a certain resemblance here between the ending of Genesis 15 and that of the book of Jonah, although in the latter case (Jonah 4:11) the hearer/reader is led to anticipate an immediate response/retort from the prophet.

67. "The majority of exegetes . . . judge vv. 19–21 to be an appendage" (Westermann, *Genesis 12–36*, 229).

68. Pilch, "Transfiguration," 56.

4

Elijah—A Dreamer of Dreams!

IN EXTENDING THE METHODOLOGY derived from cross-cultural psychology to passages with no overt reference to dreams or visions, we would do well to consider the exhortations found in Deuteronomy 13:1–5. Although essentially addressing the pronouncements of false prophets, this passage is clearly indicating that all prophets possess "the standard means (dreams)" through which they may tap "into divine power."[1] Is it, therefore, reasonable to expect any number of texts, which relate prophets' exploits, to exhibit solid evidence of dreaming even though they include no explicit references to visions or dreams? In this regard, it has previously been noted that in ancient texts "far more was left unsaid than in a modern Western context,"[2] and consequently it might reasonably be expected that a behavioral comparison applied to such texts will yield results.

In chapter 3 it was suggested that Genesis 15 is a single, unified story that faithfully records the first two of the four dreams that constitute the normal night's sleep of a depressive. Abram's nocturnal encounters with YHWH follow a prescribed, enculturated, revelatory pattern, and it is this pattern that defines him as an archetypal prophet, rather than the giving of oracles—an activity in which he does not appear to have ever engaged. It follows, therefore, that the identification of this same prescribed, enculturated, revelatory pattern in other 'prophetic' passages is, in itself, sufficient reason to consider such passages as sequences of dreams, even when not so described. It is the overall, behavioral pattern that is important, rather than any initial labeling with the terms for dreams or visions, which may in any case have been applied for different reasons.[3]

The selection of such passages will, however, require the application of certain criteria, chief among which will be that ideally the character concerned should be a known prophet. Secondly, the passage should contain

---

1. Wright, *Deuteronomy*, 173.
2. Pilch, "Transfiguration," 50.
3. On this, see section on synesthesia in chapter 3.

Hebrew terms for sleep (תרדמה,[4] רדם, יָשֵׁן) or words (שָׁכַב, לִין) that are capable of conveying the same sense, and the presence of any of these terms will be an essential prerequisite in demonstrating that a more comprehensive, behavioral pattern exists. Moreover, on the basis that the 'derived etic' hypnogram of Gen 15:1–21 is suggesting that Abram is depressed, it would seem appropriate to limit the search to those texts which contain 'personality traits' (DSM IV criteria) such as 'suicidality' or anger. These affective motifs have previously been taken to indicate depression by some readers, despite such an approach requiring the imposition of psychological categories specific to an alien, Western, cultural purview. Indeed, it may be possible to go beyond this by selecting those passages, which also allude to a known inducing physiological state—for example fasting, famine or starvation.[5] Applying all of these criteria to the available material suggests two potential candidates (Elijah and Jonah), and therefore a discussion of Elijah in 1 Kings 19 follows. Finally, it may be noted that the selection of potential dream-form texts often involves those texts that contain the most bizarre features, as indeed is the case with those of Elijah and Jonah.

1 Kings 18–19

Clearly, if the narrator of 1 Kgs 18–19 had wished to describe Elijah in a state of depression he would not have had a body of clinical nomenclature at his disposal with which to do so. But clinical nomenclature—then as now—fails to convey the subjective reality of depression, and the only means available to do so—then as now—was by the use of metaphor, indeed, the experience of depression "can be described only in metaphor and allegory."[6] Thus it becomes necessary to search the narrative for 'depression motifs,' that is, words and phrases, which although serving as features of the story, fulfill a secondary role as 'markers' of depression. It is the close juxtaposition of two or more of these motifs that 'gives away the subplot,' and in this regard the hyperactivity presented in 18:46—perhaps the most significant marker— is preceded by and grounded in the 'darkness motif' of v. 45. The 'black cloud(s)' of v. 45 parallel a well-known pictorial description often given by modern sufferers from depression. Indeed, "depression operates on a wide

---

4. This term when transliterated reads *Tardēmā*, and is most frequently translated into English as 'deep sleep.'

5. Early studies such as the "Minnesota Experiment" indicated that depression, although a noted result of fasting, was not present in every case (Fichter and Pirke, "Starvation Models," 83).

6. Solomon, *Noonday Demon*, 16.

scale . . . at the bottom is . . . the *black cloud of despair* that seems never ending."[7] Moreover, the black clouds over Carmel were generated from the waters of the western sea late in the day (v. 44)—the direction into which the light regularly disappears bringing with it the gloom of night.

If, indeed there is a subplot describing the development of Elijah's depression then it should be evident both in the juxtaposition of 'depression motifs' and in the progression of the severity of those motifs. Clearly, there appears to be progression from the "little cloud no bigger than a person's hand" in 18:44 through the black clouds of v. 45 to the hyperactive descent of v. 46, and this reaches its nadir in the suicidal ideation of 19:4. The intervening verses (19:1–3) present an apparent discontinuity in this sequence that will be dealt with in the next subsections. From that lowest point (19:4) a succession of divine interventions have the effect of ameliorating Elijah's depression,[8] even though it does not entirely disappear. The first two interventions are recorded in vv. 5 and 7 respectively where Elijah is exhorted to eat (twice) by a messenger, and significantly, Elijah eats a high-carbohydrate meal (bread) on the first of these occasions.[9] The third and final divine intervention is the command by YHWH himself to Elijah to "Go out and stand on the mountain before the LORD, for the LORD is about to pass by" (19:11a). Elijah complies by moving from the depths of the cave to its entrance (v. 13), but significantly he is shown not venturing beyond the entrance. The metaphorical import of 'the cave' is that it is an example of another 'depression motif'—the 'place of confinement,' a dark, inhospitable place involving isolation from the world and from which escape is difficult, if not impossible. Indeed:

> Severe depression is often likened to a prison, . . . a tunnel which admits no light (or) a nightmare from which there is no awakening. . . . Pits, tunnels, and prisons are difficult to get out of. So, too, is severe depression.[10]

---

7. Winter, *Depression*, 11.

8. Hauser remarks on Elijah's second obedience to the angel's command (v. 7) as indicative of his "moving away from the negative attitude expressed in v. 4" (Hauser, "Yahweh Versus Death," 66).

9. Miller notes that "a high carbohydrate, protein-poor meal elevates brain tryptophan thus accelerating serotonin synthesis." Increased production of serotonin would have the effect of lifting Elijah's mood and pertinently Miller makes reference to the hypothesis "that carbohydrate foods will cause more sleepiness post-prandially than protein meals" (Miller, "Psychoneurological Aspects," 188).

10. Barnes, *Dealing with Depression*, 31.

If the metaphor is a true one YHWH has succeeded in bringing Elijah back from the deepest reaches of his depression,[11] but the repetition of Elijah's 'complaint' in 19:14 indicates that the negativity and irrationality that epitomize his condition remain still. It has been argued that the "narrative aim of the theophany . . . seems to be not so much to present a coherent story as to create an overwhelming impression of a Moses redivivus,"[12] and in this regard the 'cave' of 1 Kgs 19:9–13 is considered to be analogous to Moses' refuge in Exodus 33:21–22. Wiseman[13] has drawn the same inference from these passages and this argument would be strengthened if the 'cave' in question turned out to be figurative (internal to the prophet) rather than any 'real' physical feature of Horeb. It is easier for people to share internal experiences than remote mountain summits.

The topography of Elijah's journey from the top of Mt. Carmel to Horeb may itself be symbolic of the progress of his depression. The journey starts on Carmel at a height of some 2,000 feet above sea level, and reaches Jezreel—or at least the 'entering into Jezreel'[14]—by means of a rapid descent down the mountainside. The journey continues southwards—if normal trade routes are followed[15]—along the plains of Sharon and Philistia before heading inland through the southern foothills of the Shephelah to Beersheba. Thus far the height above sea level has been maintained in the 500 to 1,000 feet range, and although this does not significantly alter, Beersheba represents the symbolic low point because it sits in a great natural dish[16] or depression flanked by the Shephelah, the Judean Hills and the Northern Negeb. It is at this point somewhere in the environs of Beersheba that the nadir of Elijah's depression is positioned, that is, the desire to end his life. Beyond Beersheba the route south to Horeb[17] begins to rise inexorably before finally reaching heights approaching 10,000 feet. The whole journey may be seen to represent a parabolic fall in mood from Carmel into the black despair of Beersheba followed by the divinely assisted recovery on the ascent to Horeb—a recovery that doesn't quite restore Elijah.

The 'psychologising' interpretation of these verses (18:44—19:14) offered here has gone much further than previous attempts in the same vein,

11. Kaplan notes that the "Hebrew bible contains a number of suicide-prevention narratives" (Kaplan, "Jonah versus Narcissus," 143).

12. White, *Elijah Legends*, 7.

13. Wiseman, *1 & 2 Kings*, 172.

14. Wiseman, *1 & 2 Kings*, 171.

15. May, *Oxford Bible Atlas*, 49.

16. May, *Oxford Bible Atlas*, 49.

17. The precise location of Horeb within the massif of the southern Sinai peninsular is not known.

if only because it is grounded in the physiology recorded in the text, yet it must still be viewed as a feature of mono-cultural, Western psychology. The physiology tells us that Elijah's rapid descent from Carmel (18:46) has nothing to do with triumph[18] and everything to do with his half-starved condition. Indeed, experiments with animals (rodents) have indicated that food restriction (semi-starvation) induces hyperactivity, which in the case of rats is observed as "a rapid increase in running activity."[19] The realities of the recorded psychophysiology (18:44–46) help explain why Elijah is shown becoming progressively more and more depressed,[20] and also show that there is no lack of psychological coherence between the Elijah of 19:3 who apparently "fear(s) for his life," and the Elijah of the very next verse (19:4) where he "asks Yahweh to take it away!"[21] It is this apparent incongruence that will now be addressed utilizing the more appropriate and valid cross-cultural behavioral comparison introduced earlier.

Elijah's Hypnogram—1 Kings 19:2–21

There has always been a central enigma within the Elijah narrative(s) of 1 Kings 18–19 that has caused several generations of scholars to propose solutions of broadly two different types. Brevard Childs puts this enigma succinctly when he notes the shift in tone from the "victorious and bold prophet" of chapter 18 who "now flees in terror before Jezebel" in chapter 19.[22] The first of these solutions is the historico-literary approach, which insists that two independent stories have been "artificially joined within the Book of Kings." Nevertheless Childs is sure that:

---

18. "Psychologizing interpretations of this narrative have been hard put to explain how the triumphant, high-flying Elijah of 18.46 could suddenly become so frightened (19.3) and despondent (vv. 4–9), but of course this question does not arise for those who recognise the original independence of these passages" (DeVries, *I Kings*, 235).

19. Fichter, and Pirke, "Starvation Models," 85.

20. It is not without significance that king Ahab is seen to eat (1 Kgs 18:42), in contrast to Elijah whom we must presume continues to participate in the Samarian famine (1 Kgs 18:2).

21. Kissling appears to relate Elijah's 'triumph' to his courage—a courage that only holds up when he contends with 'weak' characters such as Ahab, but which fails him when in contention with 'strong' characters such as Jezebel or YHWH. On these latter grounds Kissling rejects psychologising as unnecessary, but fails (as also DeVries) to address the problem of an Elijah who within the space of one verse can both fear and desire death (Kissling, *Reliable Characters*, 101).

22. Childs, "On Reading," 134.

> One cannot use the prehistory of the early levels of the story to destroy the integrity of the final form of the narrative.... The two stories—whatever their origin—have been joined. Therefore they demand an interpretation of the whole.[23]

The second solution to this enigmatic shift in tone is to explain it psychologically, in so far as it was Elijah's reported reaction to the stress of the contest. Elijah's initial response to the success of the Mount Carmel encounter with the prophets of Baal is to run down to Jezreel (1 Kings 18:46) ahead of King Ahab's chariot. The psychologist, Hart, considers this to be the essence of the 'Elijah Syndrome,' a depression brought on, in his view, by "adrenalin-exhaustion."[24] Such 'post adrenalin depression,' is regarded by Hart as the aftermath of a "period of high adrenalin demand" in which "the adrenal system becomes exhausted and switches off when the demand is over, ... it is the body's way of demanding rest."[25] Although it is clear to most commentators that psychological factors are in play in the transition between the two chapters and beyond, they are considered to be isolated observations within the text that are generally remarked upon only in passing. Indeed, for Childs:

> Some of these psychological observations may be true, but is this the message to which the narrative now bears witness within its context as scripture? I hardly think so because there is no hint that such implications were ever drawn within the biblical text.[26]

If the text is at best relating a few isolated psychological observations one is compelled to agree with Childs. But when the juxtaposition and especially the progression of the depression motifs noted above are added to a psychophysiological, structural integrity found running throughout chapter 19, the overall structural integrity of the transitional passage (18:44—19:4) becomes apparent. To answer Childs' question comprehensively it is necessary to consider this transitional passage and the ensuing verses of chapter 19 more fully from a number of other disciplinary perspectives.

Reference has already been made to the hypnogram of a normal, healthy adult[27] and also to the way in which this sleep pattern deforms

---

23. Childs, "On Reading," 134.
24. Hart, *Counselling the Depressed*, 96.
25. Hart, *Counselling the Depressed*, 96.
26. Childs, "On Reading," 134–35.
27. Chapter 3, Fig. 2.

during depression.[28] In general it may be said that the duration of the first REM/dreaming period will elongate from about 3 minutes in the normal young adult[29] to perhaps 20 minutes in depressives.[30] Given that the total REM sleep remains unchanged at 20 percent of total sleep time (typically 80–85 minutes per night), this suggests an abnormal temporal distribution of REM sleep in depressives—a feature that is in fact found.[31] Thus, an increase in early REM% (first REM period x 100 , by total sleep of the night) is balanced by a corresponding decrease in late REM% (sum of remaining REM periods x 100 , by total sleep of the night), and although the tendency of successive REM periods to become progressively longer remained, it was not significant, and indeed researchers in the Vogel study recorded some nights when REM periods tended to become shorter.[32] Typically, however, the first REM period accounted for perhaps 25 percent of total REM sleep—except when the first REM period was abnormally long—leaving the remaining periods of REM sleep proportionately reduced in length, yet still maintaining a progressive increase in duration.

If an examination of the text of 1 Kings 19:2–21 is undertaken it will be seen to break down into four discrete periods of speech/action (19:2b–4; 5b–6d; 7–9a & 9c–21) separated from each other by three equally discrete punctuations of sleep (19:5a; 6e; & 9b).[33] The first period of speech/action is the second longest of the four, and the remaining three periods increase progressively in length with the final period being the longest of all. Interestingly, the intervening sleep periods appear to show a gradation in depth of sleep as represented by the terms used, since in v. 5a Elijah both lies down and sleeps whereas in v. 6e he only lies down, and in v. 9b he merely 'lodges' in the cave. But this cannot easily be demonstrated from other scriptural usages of the terms employed (שכב, ישן and לין), and besides it would in reality have been difficult if not impossible to differentiate between the various depths of sleep (stages 1–4), by reference to culture-based experience of prophets' (or indeed any other) sleep patterns. The latter qualification notwithstanding, the spatial relationship

28. Chapter 3, Fig. 3.

29. Leonard, *Fundamentals*, 176.

30. One study also records that the time of onset of REM sleep (REM latency) may be halved from about 90 to about 45 minutes after the commencement of sleep (Vogel et al., "Improvement of Depression," 248).

31. Vogel et al., "Improvement of Depression," 250.

32. Vogel et al., "Improvement of Depression," 249.

33. Verses are here numbered and lettered according to the puntuation shown in the NRSV, i.e. in phrases. The speech/action in vv. 9c–21 envelopes the accepted narrated interjection, vv. 11b–12.

between the sections of speech/action and the intervening sleep periods in 1 Kings 19:2–21 is easier to see if it is represented graphically. Clearly, the text does not provide any numerical information and therefore it is impossible to draw the structure with an 'hourly scale,' as in figures 2 and 3 (chapter 3). Accordingly, in figure 6 below the sleep architecture between the speech/action and sleep sequences have been drawn in broken line to indicate this absence of information. Likewise, a sleep period before the first speech/action sequence and after the last such period cannot be adduced from the text. Figure 6 has been labeled the 'derived etic hypnogram of 1 Kings 19:2–21,' because the overall pattern of the speech/action and intervening sleep periods can be seen to map directly to that of a modern hypnogram, and moreover, the hypnogram of a depressive[34] as quite distinct from that of a normal, young adult. Indeed, applying the methodology from cross-cultural psychology,[35] a behavioral overlap may be observed between this modern pattern of nocturnal activity and the received record of ancient behavior. Thus, the speech/action sequences of chapter 19 should in reality be viewed as the dreams of a depressive, perhaps the logical outcome of the psychophysiological condition that appears to have finally overwhelmed Elijah at the end of chapter 18. This unique pattern (fig. 6) of four REM-sleep/dream sequences of precisely these relative durations interspersed by three periods of sleep is unlikely to have occurred simply by chance.

It may be observed that the bulk of the revelatory content of the four dreams occurs in the fourth dream, that is, when Elijah "came to a cave, and spent the night there" (1 Kgs 19:9 NRSV), and indeed Lindblom has hinted that this divine revelation should be viewed as a more tranquil form of prophetic ecstasy[36]—in other words an altered state of consciousness. That this long final speech/action sequence is in fact a dream resonates with one suggested use of the verb לין (to lodge or spend the night). Indeed, Oikonomou[37] following Westermann[38] has suggested that לין may be interpreted elsewhere (Isa 65:4) as signifying incubation for dreams, and both scholars point to the support provided by the LXX for this interpretation where that text (Isa 65:4)

---

34. See chapter 3, fig. 3.

35. See chapter 3, fig. 4 and related discussion.

36. Lindblom makes the perceptive suggestion that the theophany might represent a tranquil form of prophetic ecstasy in which divine revelation is received in a passive state of mind. Lindblom likewise appears to believe the angelic exchanges of 1 Kgs 19:5–7 take place in an ASC (Lindblom, *Prophecy*, 56).

37. Oikonomou, "לין," 546.

38. Westermann, *Isaiah 40–66*, 401.

adds the words δια ενυπνια, "for dream oracles."³⁹ Although this is not the usual interpretation applied to לין in 1 Kgs 19:9, it nevertheless appears to lie within this verb's semantic range, albeit in a minority, idiomatic sense.

In the view advanced here, what is presented to the reader in 1 Kings 19:2–21 is effectively 'a night's sleep,' which is exactly what might be expected to ensue for Elijah, who, having run down the mountainside (18:46) now finds himself alone and sheltering from the rain at night. It is, furthermore, entirely to be expected that a Yahwistic narrator would spend approximately nineteen verses (19:2–21) recounting Elijah's successful spiritual encounter in the ecstatic state, after describing the failure of the prophets of Baal to do so in four verses (18:26–29)! On this latter point it may be noted that the surgical trauma commensurate with gashing has been found to produce immunological changes associated with depression, and supplementary empirical evidence is available from some recent medical research that further demonstrates the link between surgical trauma, depression, and altered states of consciousness. Significantly, one study found that mood disturbance was the most common reason for referral for psychiatric consultation following surgery, and mood disturbance accounted for 39.3 percent of all such consultations.⁴⁰ The focus of this study was on the incidence of delirium—a psychosis defined as "altered consciousness with cognitive impairment"—and "more than one-fourth of the patients referred with mood disturbances were found to be delirious."⁴¹

---

39. Oikonomou, "לין," 546.
40. Golinger, "Delirium," 105.
41. Golinger, "Delirium," 105.

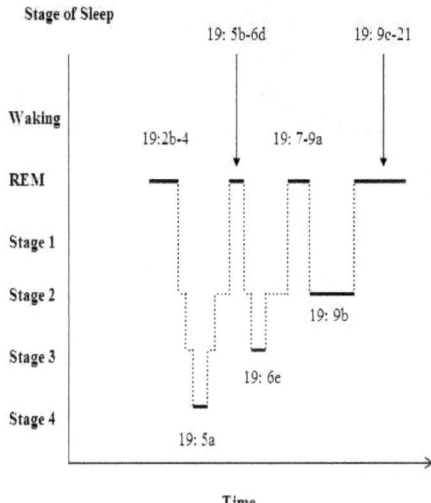

Fig. 6 'Derived Etic' Hypnogram of 1 Kings 19:2-21

Naturally, any consideration of this passage as a succession of dreams must have profound implications for the exegesis of chapter 19 both alone and in relation to the two preceding chapters. Almost without exception previous interpretations have considered Elijah's journey as the portrayal of an actual physical journey beginning with flight from Jezebel (19:3), and this has always required a "repointing" (to use Kissling's term) of 'and he saw' (וַיַּרְא), to 'and he was afraid' (וַיִּרָא).[42] It has to be said that repointing text is a dubious exegetical practice and a more satisfying explanation of וַיַּרְא is likely to lie in the culture-based, direct observation of (prophetic) individuals during dream/vision states. Onlookers observing such states would see rapid eye movements beneath closed eye lids as clear evidence of 'seeing,' but such 'seeing' would be deemed to take place in the extended reality. Auld comments on the difficulties inherent in attempting to separate ordinary sense experience (vision) from instances of altered state seeing or 'second sight' in any given text.[43] This reflects the close conceptual linkage in the ancient mindset between waking reality

---

42. The original text was consonantal and therefore capable of either reading (Kissling, *Reliable Characters*, 103).

43. Auld writes, "the regular Hebrew for 'seeing' (*r'h*) is used not infrequently in the Bible of special, enhanced, second 'sight'. Quite exacting exegesis may often be necessary before deciding that such a sense is appropriate in any given occurrence of the *qal* theme" (Auld, "Prophets," 10).

and dreaming reality already referred to, and a relationship that would probably help to obscure (for the modern reader) certain usages of ראה (to see) within any particular tradition.

The 'seeing' that takes place in this extended first dream period (characteristic of depression) is Elijah's first speech/act[44] in chapter 19 and continues the progression of 'depression motifs' that began in 18:44. This progression concludes with the suicidal ideation of 19:4, and it is noteworthy that the latter (DSM IV) depression motif is found in the text at precisely this point, and not anywhere else. Indeed, two DSM IV parameters (diagnostic criteria) of depression are found in 19:4, that is, poor self-regard as well as recurrent thoughts of death, and it is significant that these criteria were known to feature in the lives of prophets in the ancient world. It was Aristotle who observed that Sibyls, soothsayers, and the divinely inspired (that is, prophetic types generally) were drawn from the ranks of "those who naturally possess an atrabilious (melancholic) temperament."[45] Moreover, it is intriguing to note that the narrator relates both of these features of Elijah's demeanor at a point in the story coincident with the elongated first dream, which is so characteristic of depressive dreaming.

The progressive development of Elijah's depression, which is found to reach its nadir at the end of the first dream (v. 4), refutes the common acceptance of the belief that "it is anachronistic to impose a modern reader's idea of psychological coherence on our (ancient) reader."[46] On the contrary, any failure to evaluate satisfactorily the psychological coherence of this passage is based on an incomplete understanding by the modern, Western reader of the cross-cultural psychology at work here, as quite distinct from the mono-cultural, science usually applied. This (cross-cultural) psychology is inextricably bound up with the underlying physiology of sleep, or rather the culture-based experience of prophetic sleeping patterns that appear to have been so faithfully recorded in the tradition.

The Vogel study on REM sleep deprivation, which remarks on earlier work (Aserinsky, 1969) confirmed an observed tendency for the REM frequency—that is, the number of rapid eye movements per unit time—to increase progressively in successive REM periods.[47] Put simply, this means that the intensity and complexity of the dreaming experience increases in

---

44. Although not conclusive proof this implies a quicker (abrupt!) onset of dreaming, which is again so characteristic of depressives' dreams.

45. Forster, *Works*, 954ª.

46. Kissling, *Reliable Characters*, 101. Kissling's 'readers' are first and second time readers of this text, both of whom are comparatively speaking contemporaneous with the final editor of the text.

47. Vogel et al., "Improvement of Depression," 251.

successive REM/dreaming periods—a feature represented by the increased speech/action found in the fourth dream period of 1 Kgs 19:2–21. The passage also culminates in a dialogue containing increased visual content (1 Kgs 19:11b–12), which can be seen to map directly to the increased REM frequency. From the foregoing discussion and the application of the Segall-derived methodology it may be contended that the overall structure found in 1 Kings 19:2–21 would appear to be one example of a faithful reproduction of the culture-based experience of the nocturnal 'activities' (sleep patterns) of prophets. It is quite plausible that these behavioral patterns rooted as they are in the social system itself have conformed the traditions and ultimately the texts into the final forms found. It may, moreover, be suggested that in the case of 1 Kings 18–19 an altogether different (and validatory) sequence of ASCs has been presented for Elijah, as compared with the prophets of Baal, and it is upon this foundational structure that the triumph over Baal and the superiority of the Yahwistic cult is built in terms of dialogical spiritual encounter.

Spiritual Encounter

The entry of the prophets of Baal into the extended reality by the induction of ASCs (18:26–29) is bracketed by the lack of an answer (18:26, 29) at each end of the pericope, and although the answer they desire is primarily from Baal—within the parameters of the contest—the lack of response is described in much more comprehensive terms. Indeed, the completeness of the sequence "but there was no voice, no answer, and no response,"[48] precludes engagement with any order of spiritual entity. This failure by the prophets of Baal to evoke any spiritual encounter of any kind is to be contrasted with Elijah's later, reported success in this regard. Consequently, before discussing the dreams of 1 Kgs 19 it may prove pertinent to backtrack a little over the events of 18:42–46.

In this pericope Elijah returns to the top of Mount Carmel after the slaughter of the prophets of Baal having left Ahab to his food (18:40–42), and perhaps the whole point of recording Ahab's repast at this point is to emphasize Elijah's fasted condition. Clearly Elijah was in a (enforced) fasted condition (18:2) and Scholem draws attention in his discussion of early Jewish mystics to the "typical bodily posture of these ascetics," remarking that it "is also that of Elijah in his prayer on Mount Carmel."[49] Elijah's posture in

---

48. 1 Kgs 18:29, NRSV. Hebrew: ואין־קול ואין־ענה ואין קשב
49. Scholem, *Major Trends*, 49.

18:42 is that found in the earliest forms of Jewish mysticism[50] and, as Scholem remarks, mystical ascent is always preceded by ascetic practices, indeed the mystic prepares by fasting for "a number of days and lay(ing) his head between his knees."[51] This view has been disputed in recent scholarship; with Himmelfarb in particular maintaining that neither the texts of ancient Judaism nor the earlier apocalyptic (pseudepigraphic) material show any "hint at techniques for ascent." In deriving this conclusion, Himmelfarb lists the activities found in the apocalypses just prior to the ascents noting that: "the most common activity in which the seer is engaged immediately before the ascent is mourning, sometimes expressed through weeping."[52] She goes on to cite the influential *Book of the Watchers* (300–200 BC), which describes Enoch's ascent within a dream and draws parallels between the latter and the "contemplation" found in *The Testament of Levi*. Finally, Himmelfarb reviews the association of mourning with fasting found in *Daniel*, *4 Ezra* and *2 Baruch*, before acknowledging the "clearest example of the relationship of ascetic practice to ascent in the apocalypses"—*The Ascension of Isaiah*.

In her study, Himmelfarb finds a complete absence of "techniques of ascent" in the apocalypses, despite having repeatedly pointed to circumstances that are intimately related to depression. Indeed, an inducing, physiological state (fasting) is found associated with mourning, grieving, and weeping, which together can describe the reactive depression found following bereavement. Moreover, research into parental loss reveals a "statistical association between death amongst first-degree relatives and the occurrence of an eating disorder in the family,"[53] perhaps pointing to a familial, psychological factor at work supplementary to the incidence of fasting within ancient near eastern mourning rites. Such loss would be a common experience for the Jews of Palestine in the period during which the apocalypses were composed, that is, under Seleucid and later, Roman rule.[54] Significantly, the *Book of the Watchers* shows the ascent taking place

---

50. "The earliest Jewish mysticism is throne-mysticism. Its essence is . . . perception of (God's) appearance on the throne, as described by Ezekiel." This perception is achieved via a mystical ascent to the throne room of God that is always preceded by ascetic practices (Scholem, *Major Trends*, 44).

51. It is interesting to note that this position also features in the 'Three Dreams of Gilgamesh' where just prior to Gilgamesh falling asleep and entering into altered consciousness (dreaming) he "planted his chin on his knees" (Scholem, *Major Trends*, 49). Significantly, this episode also takes place on a mountain (Oppenheim, "Interpretation," 248).

52. Texts cited include; *Second Enoch*, *The Testament of Levi*, *3 Baruch*, *Daniel*, *4 Ezra*, and *2 Baruch* (Himmelfarb, "Practice of Ascent," 130).

53. Eisler, "Family Models," 158.

54. It is acknowledged that the provenance of some of these works is not known

within a dream, and *The Ascension of Isaiah* relates the ascent within an ASC[55] directly to the fasting that precedes it. Although deliberate ascetic technique, practice or regimen prior to ascent would appear to be absent from the report of Elijah's Mount Carmel experience, he is clearly engaging in (enforced) fasting, he is depressed and he is found in an ASC (18:46) before finally dreaming in the following chapter (19:2–21). All of these factors, saving the dream, finally cohere simultaneously in 18:46.

Scholem, having noted the parallel between the 'ascent posture' of the Jewish mystics and Elijah's posture[56] on Carmel (18:42), remarks on the significance of this posture as:

> An attitude of deep self-oblivion which, to judge from certain ethnological parallels, is favorable to the induction of pre-hypnotic autosuggestion.[57]

There are several facets of this state of self-oblivion that are worthy of note. Firstly, deep self-oblivion is an ecstatic or meditative state[58] in which the subject temporarily forgets self for the duration of the exercise, and this is to be distinguished from the permanent states of amnesia typical of shamanic, public, ritual trance exhibitions. Secondly, ethnological parallels reveal that Elijah's reported posture ("face between his knees") following fasting has bearing on the practice of conjuring[59] or adjuring[60] spirits. Scholem acknowledges the aetiological nature of the ascetic preparations in facilitating entry into "a state of ecstasy"[61] immediately following his comparison of

---

with certainty.

55. Himmelfarb, "Practice of Ascent," 131.

56. A modern cross-cultural analogue of this posture is to be found in present-day Ethiopia in the "living tradition of Ethiopian eremitic asceticism.... Ethiopia possesses the last remaining large-scale tradition of Christian eremitic asceticism in the world ... which became established in this country beginning at the latest in the fourth century CE." Bushell cites a personal interview with an ascetic, Ethiopian hermit who described the regimen thus: "First, one engages in fasting and prostrations until the knees are wounded, then God sends the spirit [i.e. the Holy Spirit] to encourage" (Bushell, "Psychophysiological and Comparative," 553–56).

57. Scholem, *Major Trends*, 49.

58. "Resort to this meditative position in mystical circles is known in postbiblical and medieval Judaism and in Islamic Sufism" (Cogan, *1 Kings*, 444).

59. Cogan, *1 Kings*, 444. The reference is to a Chinese somnambulist who conjures spirits in the 'head-between-knees' position (Dennys, *Folklore*, 60).

60. Himmelfarb observes that the Hekhalot texts prescribe fasting as a necessary precursor to the adjuration of angels, and that instructions for "adjuring the Prince of the Torah" in Hekhalot Zutarti require fasting followed by a recitation conducted with the head between the knees (Himmelfarb, "Practice of Ascent," 127–28).

61. Scholem, *Major Trends*, 50.

Elijah with the Jewish mystics and the Chinese somnambulist/medium.[62] Moreover, according to Scholem "the adept begins his journey,"[63] that is, begins his ascent in this state of ecstasy, and the implication must be that Scholem considers Elijah to be such an adept about to begin a journey. Certainly, there are clear parallels between these mystical ascents and the vision quests of a prophet-shaman such as Elijah, but more immediately the import of 18:42 lies in Elijah's entry into the extended reality via an ASC (ecstasy) as an outcome of pre-hypnotic autosuggestion. Elijah's posture is a function of his will—the desire to enter the ecstatic state—and although Rouget makes a clear distinction between ecstasy and (public, ritual) trance his comments on the latter apply equally to private, quiescent states of ecstasy:

> It would be a fundamental error to reduce these various forms of trance to no more than various forms of corporeal technique. . . . The technique operates only because it is at the service of a belief, and because trance constitutes a cultural model integrated into a certain general representation of the world. Here we have an essential intellectual datum, which underlies both the psychology and physiology of trance. . . . Entry into trance always seems to depend upon a kind of restrictive clause: however well prepared one may be, physically and psychologically, one must still be prepared intellectually, and have made the decision (more or less unconsciously) to succumb to the trance state.[64]

Thus, the application of all of the foregoing insights to the text (18:42–46) produces quite a different exegesis from that normally offered, and the picture presented is one in which Elijah is seen to be deliberately and purposefully entering into an altered state of consciousness. Elijah's initial purpose—in the confident assurance of his abilities as the master of a spirit—is to conjure or invoke his spirit servant (18:42),[65] and then constrain and compel him to perform the duties recorded in 18:43–44. In this regard, it is interesting to note with Hauser, the repeated (sevenfold) use of the verb

---

62. The results of a study by Alvarado "supports the idea that sleepwalking is related to the frequency of parapsychological experiences. This, in turn provides further evidence of a low-magnitude association between parapsychological experiences and dissociation" (Alvarado, "Sleepwalking," 349).

63. Scholem, *Major Trends*, 50.

64. Rouget, *Music and Trance*, 320–21.

65. Given that Elijah has entered into a (quiescent) ASC at this point, it follows as a consequence that his subsequent 'conversations' will be exclusively with spiritual entities (deities, demons, tutelary spirits, even the spirits of humans) in the extended reality, but quite distinct from normal, verbal discourse with humans.

עלה, 'to go up,'[66] in 18:41–44, and whilst its final use in v. 44 may be idiomatic it is intriguingly difficult to comprehend its use in v. 43. Given that the use of this verb immediately before and after v. 43 conveys the commonplace sense of climbing or ascent it would appear reasonable to assume this same sense in v. 43, and since Elijah is at the top of Mount Carmel and speaking to a spirit, only an ethereal 'going-up' by his spirit-servant seems plausible.[67] Elijah's (master/servant) relationship to the spiritual entities of the extended reality now comes into sharp focus, as only two verses later (v. 46) the master of spirit(s) is seen to become again the servant of YHWH, when the narrator has the "hand of YHWH" come upon him.

Although reference has been made to Elijah's ecstatic condition in 18:46a where the "hand of YHWH was upon him," it seems at first to be entirely inconsistent with the immediately following hyperactive run[68] down to Jezreel. Indeed, this private, quiescent ASC (v. 46a), which would appear to be continuous with entry into the extended reality (v. 42b), seems to have been closely linked, indeed integral with, the running activity of v. 46b. David-Neel in her much reproduced *Magic and Mystery in Tibet* records parallel behavior by the lamas of Tibet who engage in *lung gom pa* running.[69] These runners are able to cover immense distances in a swift, leaping gait whilst alone and in a quiet, ASC that cannot be interrupted.[70] It is interesting that David-Neel's informant avers that to break into their meditation would cause the "god who is in them" to escape, with the result that "he shakes them so hard that they die."[71] Thus, the recorded behavior following Elijah's entry into an altered state of consciousness (v. 42) is to be expected from a cross-cultural perspective, as well as from the biomedical data on semi-starvation reviewed earlier.

With the scene now set in terms of allied ASCs, any continued activity could easily take place within dreamform, and the secure mapping of the speech/action-sleep sequences in 1 Kings 19:2–21 to the hypnogram of a

66. Hauser, "Yahweh Versus Death," 57.

67. Hauser implies that 'the lad' ascended the mountain in like manner to Ahab and Elijah, but nowhere can this be adduced from the text (Hauser, "Yahweh Versus Death," 57).

68. Bushell citing Yates (1991) and Richert and Hummers (1986) observe that "the number of hours that men spend running correlates positively and significantly with the stringency of their diets and with their abnormal attitudes toward food and eating" (Bushell, "Psychophysiological and Comparative," 555).

69. David-Neel, *Magic and Mystery*, 184.

70. This may well be at the root of Obadiah's expressed fears about Elijah in 1 Kings 18:12: "As soon as I have gone from you, the spirit of the LORD will carry you I know not where."

71. David-Neel, *Magic and Mystery*, 186.

depressive will have profound consequences for the exegesis of this passage. As already noted, the opening Hebrew expression (וירא) in v. 3 should be understood as "and he saw," that is, 'seeing' in its special, 'second-sight' sense, rather than the "and he feared" of most English translations. But precisely what does the narrator have Elijah 'see' in his dream? The answer to this question would at first seem obvious with the term appearing to refer to Jezebel's messenger in the preceding verse (v. 2a). Although this may be so, it could also refer synesthetically to the message itself (v. 2b), which immediately precedes it, that is, the message was as much seen as it was heard.[72]

Alternatively, if the narrative force of the sequence "he saw, he arose and he went"[73]—within a larger sequence of waw consecutive imperfects (vv. 1–3)—is entirely forward-looking, then וירא might simply refer to Elijah's entry into the 'seeing mode' of the 'seer' in its 'second-sight' sense (i.e. he began to do what a 'seer' does), thereby indicating the beginning of the first dream. The loss of 19:2b to the total content of the first dream would not significantly affect the overall shape of Elijah's 'derived etic' hypnogram (fig. 6), and each of the four speech/action sequences would continue to bear the same relationship to each other in terms of relative length. This would create an even more abrupt entry into the first dream in v. 3, thus giving the impression of the quicker onset of dreaming so characteristic of depressives' dreams. On this view v. 2b would belong to Elijah's ecstatic state of the previous evening (18:42–46)—a 'waking' altered state of consciousness that appears to have undergone an almost seamless transition into dream/vision quest.

Spiritual Encounter within the Dreamform

The messenger (מלאך) Elijah meets in this first ASC can be equated with the other messengers of the second and third dreams, that is, those recorded in vv. 5 and 7 respectively, and this equivalence would avoid insisting that the narrator is using different meanings for מלאך (messenger *vis-à-vis* angel, NRSV) within the space of a few verses. It is the ecstatic state that is the unifying factor here, making all three of these messengers supernatural envoys rather than human agents. In Hallevy's view:

> Mal'akh, . . . was erroneously translated as "angel." The word is connected with מלאכה, "work, duty," and the Mal'akh carries out the work of those who sent him. Mal'akh ought therefore

---

72. This seems to be the interpretation—as distinct from translation—placed on וירא by the KJV where the expression is rendered "and when he saw that."

73. 1 Kgs 19:3, KJV. Hebrew: וירא ויקם וילך

to be translated as "messenger." This epithet is given in the Bible both to men and to superhuman beings. It is hard to say when the epithet refers to either of the two, so that the meaning of the name should be ascertained in each individual case.[74]

Certainly, if in the later speech/action passages or dreams *mal'akh* is considered to refer to a superhuman being, then so also should this be the case in the first ecstatic state. If each of these speech/action sequences is a visionary or altered state of consciousness, then it follows that any characters appearing therein will not be 'real' human beings. The narrator, it seems, shows Jezebel sending a supernatural apparition of some kind to Elijah, and a fuller consideration of what this could have been is appropriate.

Trible in dealing with the difficulties presented by 1 Kings 19:2 makes reference to both the Septuagint and Old Latin versions of the story where, unlike the Hebrew, Jezebel is quoted with the additional words: "If you are Elijah, then I am Jezebel." Trible goes on:

> This stark juxtaposition of their names bespeaks the theological antithesis of YHWH God versus Baal the Prince. The juxtaposition also encapsulates the human battle.[75]

Theological antithesis is hardly an appropriate description of this battle that takes place in the extended reality, that is, within this first ASC/dream. Theological antithesis there may be in this story, but it is not the central issue, for what is at issue in this juxtaposition of names are the spiritual realities which stand behind the people as described by their names: Elijah is the "Divine Man . . . endowed with superhuman, divine qualities and powers" who stands before YHWH and who possesses "something of the nature of the divinity."[76] Jezebel on the other hand can be considered to be the dwelling place[77] of Baal, and is as a consequence an awesome spiritual opponent. The battle, however, remains exclusively between two great shaman-prophets, and although the human battle—insofar as there ever was one (I Kgs 18:19–40?) is over—the spiritual battle (between the generals) is about to commence.

The story recounts the spiritual battle of 19:2b–3, a battle that takes place in the extended reality and consists of Jezebel's counterattack, an

---

74. Hallevy, "Man of God," 239.
75. Trible, "Exegesis," 8.
76. Hallevy, "Man of God," 237.
77. Bronner notes that 'dwelling place' is one of the three concentric meanings of '*zbl*'—the latter part of Jezebel's name, and that this was true of both the Ugaritic and Hebrew occurrences of the word (Bronner, *Stories*, 10).

attempt to oppress Elijah whilst he is in a vulnerable 'place,' that is, whilst he is in an ASC. Jezebel is effectively bewitching or hexing Elijah at a distance, and this accounts for Ahab's familiarity with a term typically translated as 'trouble' (עכר, 1 Kgs 18:17) in the versions, but which is translated by DeVries as 'hex'.[78] That Jezebel was a known practitioner of witchcraft is made explicit in 2 Kings 9:22 in Jehu's response to Joram, Jezebel's son, and her 'hexing' of Elijah at a distance is supported by the Greek of the LXX which states that Jezebel 'sent out' (απεστειλεν), yet without recording the object of that sending out. In her opening discussion of witchcraft, Bowie describes a "peasant" worldview, which holds the fundamental idea of a "life force, essence or energy" present within people.[79] This life force is then depicted as something that is vulnerable to attack or harm by others who are more powerful or malevolent. Indeed, "this harm is effected at the psychic level, but will be reflected in the biological and material state of the victim."[80] In Lewis's view, the shamanic capacity for witchcraft—interpreted psychiatrically as "projective"—may be compared to possession, which is seen as "introjective." Both of these ideologies may be seen as "different facets of the same role."[81] Bowie illustrates her own definition of witchcraft (as a spiritual onslaught) by referring to Idowu's description of African witchcraft:

> African concepts about witchcraft consist in the belief that the spirits of living human beings can be sent out of the body on errands of doing havoc to other persons in body, mind or estate.[82]

Idowu acknowledges that it is the *ethereal* or extended, spiritual human 'body' that is attacked and although he is primarily discussing the human spirit of the witch as the entity being sent, there is a parallel here with shamanic sendings of spirits over whom the shaman has mastery. This latter may be the more likely interpretation of the Hebrew text of 1 Kings 19:2, with the LXX reading capable of either interpretation, and certainly, this is the case with the so-called "witch of Endor" (1 Sam 28:7) who was in fact "a (female) master of a spirit."[83] In Idowu's view:

---

78. DeVries, *I Kings*, 217.

79. Bowie, *Anthropology*, 219.

80. Bowie, *Anthropology*, 219. Humphrey concurs, confirming the peculiar 'action-at-a-distance' character: "When your soul was oppressed your consciousness was taken over by the spirit, that is, by actions that might be taking place somewhere else or at another time" (Humphrey with Onon, *Shamans, and Elders*, 219).

81. Lewis, *Ecstatic Religion*, 180.

82. Idowu, *African Traditional Religion*, 175.

83. "A woman possessing a familiar spirit" 1 Sam 28:7, YLT. Hebrew: אשת בעלת־אוב.

> The operation is the operation of spirits upon spirits, that is, it is the ethereal bodies of the victims that are attacked, extracted and devoured; . . . Thus, in the case of witches or their victims, spirits meet spirits, spirits operate upon spirits, while the actual human bodies lie 'asleep' in their homes.[84]

Idowu connects such an "exudation of personality"[85] with telepathy, and thereby with the psychological imposition of the will upon others at a distance. Idowu also provides insight into the strange form of words put on the lips of Jezebel in 1 Kings 19:2 when he refers to "the power of the word" backed by the personality of the one who utters it. The inference of such an understanding being that Jezebel's long, convoluted statement (19:2b) effectively amounts to a spell, which only requires the passage of time to accomplish her intent. Moreover, the victim is attacked by a "draining" of their own life force by the aggressor who may use "incantations, spells, ritual objects, and actions in order to . . . harm the life force of the victim."[86] This may go some way towards explaining Jezebel's long drawn-out expression: "So may the gods do to me, and more also, if I do not make your life like the life of one of them by this time tomorrow" (19:2b). It explains this most rambling of death threats, particularly the odd time delay, by suggesting a sequence of firstly psychic and then physical attack. The life force or "vital essence is conceived as liquid and the victim is *drained*"[87]—once again connoting a process that takes time to effect. The importance of the time factor—a full day's delay before Elijah's anticipated demise—also has relevance to the *modus operandi* of the witch, which chiefly involved inflicting sicknesses of various kinds upon the victim, Indeed, the infliction of sicknesses by witches is known to have occurred beyond the Euphrates during the first half of the first millennium BC (900–600 BC), and "harm thought to be caused by witches ranged from insomnia to death, but certain maladies and misfortunes were especially characteristic."[88] Moreover, it was believed that "the personal god of a witchcraft victim deserted him"[89] in the course of such an attack, and this latter feature might have been an important object of the exercise.

---

84. Idowu, *African Traditional Religion*, 176.
85. Idowu, *African Traditional Religion*, 177.
86. Bowie, *Anthropology*, 220.
87. Bowie, *Anthropology*, 220.
88. Rollin refers to two "lists of ills ascribed to witchcraft" the second one of which includes "weakness and paralysis." Rollin, "Women and Witchcraft," 40.
89. Rollin, "Women and Witchcraft," 41.

In the next verse (19:3), the narrator relates Elijah's response. Having encountered Jezebel's spiritual messenger he responds by 'rising' (ויקם) above his static, sleeping body and 'going' (וילך) into (אל)[90] his extended, ethereal 'body' (his *nephesh*),[91] before "entering into Beersheba which belongs to Judah." Hauser uses "this rapid-fire sequence of three verbs (to depict) sudden, animated terrified activity by Elijah,"[92] in order to support his contention that the real struggle in 1 Kings 17–19 is between YHWH and death. Certainly, it can be agreed that there is sudden, animated[93] activity on Elijah's part, but there is no terror to be found here. On the contrary, the dream symbolism of 19:3b can be interpreted as a great victory for Elijah, and together with the foregoing dream/vision-quest explanation of v. 3a, provides an alternate explanation of this pericope that avoids the problem of the apparent "contradiction in moods"[94] between v. 3a and v. 4b. In this regard it is important to note the obvious superfluity on the narrator's part of noting that Beersheba belongs to Judah,[95] since this would be common knowledge for any first reader of the text. Symbolically, however, it serves the purpose of depicting Elijah 'travelling' from the Phoenician (north-western) border of the Northern Kingdom to the southern extremity of Judah—a distance of some one hundred miles—in an instant. The narrative effect is that of reinforcing the rapid-fire verb sequence found at the beginning of v. 3, by

---

90. It is interesting to note that most if not all English versions of the Bible translate the preposition 'אל' in v. 19:3 as 'for,' when in general "the prepostion expresses primarily motion toward someone or something ... the motion sometimes carries "into" that which is approached." Moreover, the term may be used of "mental motion" (Scott, 'אֶל,' 41). It is to be noted, however, that "when used with other particles its force is sometimes lost" (Davidson, *Analytical Hebrew and Chaldee Lexicon*, 26).

91. It is suggested that what the Hebrew is recording here is a synecdochical transition from a restricted understanding of 'נפש' to a much more comprehensive concept that includes psychic capacities. In this regard Brotzman acknowledges that "נפש, sometimes found alongside "heart" and sometimes not, is also used to refer to the seat of mental activity in man" (Brotzman "Man and the Meaning," 404). Effectively, the 'נפש' becomes delocalised from its normal locus in the body, but this is not the same as opposing the current "consensus among biblical scholars that the *nephesh* and the body are not separate and detachable entities." Nevertheless, it can be agreed with Overholt that "matters do not appear to be that simple," and that "it is especially important to note that *nephesh* can be distinguished from 'flesh' (*basar* ...)" (Overholt, "Elijah and Elisha," 106–7).

92. Hauser, "Yahweh Versus Death," 62.

93. In the sense of *anima*, (latin = a. air, breath, life and b. mind, soul).

94. White, *Elijah Legends*, 6.

95. Where remarked upon at all, commentators tend to relate the narrator's remark to a political consciousness of the separation of Israel and Judah (Gray, *I & II Kings*, 407 and Wiseman, *1 & 2 Kings*, 172).

emphasizing Elijah's speed of translation[96] within the altered/extended reality. At 'Beersheba' the altered-state momentum is maintained when Elijah leaves his (spirit) servant there, and the (modern) reader's natural inclination is to associate this servant with the servant referred to in 18:43–44. Two points militate against this however: Firstly, Elijah's servant on Mt. Carmel was sent to Ahab and did not return, and secondly, the last spiritual entity to be encountered by Elijah was Jezebel's messenger (*malak*) in the verse immediately preceding this (19:2). Within the context of the ASC/dream the clear inference is that Jezebel's spiritual messenger has been subordinated to the authority of Elijah, that is, the malevolent, projected messenger has now become Elijah's spirit-servant.

Reference has already been made to Gershom Scholem's identification of the position adopted by Elijah on Mt. Carmel ("he bowed himself down upon the earth and put his face between his knees," 18:42) with that of the later Jewish mystics. But it may also be of significance that the Hekhalot texts "prescribe ascetic practices like fasting . . . as preparation, not for ascent, but for other activities like the adjuration of angels,"[97] and the question arises: Is the narrator portraying Elijah anticipating a spiritual attack from Jezebel, and preparing himself by practicing pre-hypnotic autosuggestion prior to entry into an ASC as Scholem appears to be suggesting?[98] Moreover, a further significance of Beersheba may very well lie in the presence there of the wells or cisterns so often used for imprisonment,[99] since Jezebel's defeated and enslaved messenger could be (symbolically) left there—permitting Elijah to 'travel' a further "day's journey into the wilderness" alone (19:4a).

The spiritual journey continues culminating in suicidality, suicidality in which Elijah requests YHWH to take away his נפש, and the two-fold repetition of this latter term may be highlighting the vulnerability of Elijah to death whilst in his extended, ethereal 'body.' Moreover, cross-cultural data indicate that such 'journeys' are extremely dangerous. The healers of the Kung people of Namibia make such 'journeys' during healing sessions, and "God is confronted by the most powerful healers only, whose souls travel to

---

96. Hauser, although pursuing a quite different exposition, also notes that "the threefold use of ו, 'and,' helps stress the rapidity . . . of Elijah's flight, as does the fact that he is immediately seen passing through the fairly distant city of Beer-sheba" (Hauser, "Yahweh Versus Death," 62–63).

97. Himmelfarb, "Practice of Ascent," 127.

98. Scholem, *Major Trends*, 49.

99. Excavations at Tel es-Sebaʿ in stratum III-II (circa mid-ninth century BC) appear to have revealed the use of one such well as a waste water cistern into which contaminated water was channeled from inside the city, thus providing an ideal shaft in which to incarcerate miscreants (Manor, "Beer-Sheba," 643).

his home, at the greatest risk to their very lives."[100] Elijah, the Divine Man, is of course a very powerful healer indeed, as the text of 1 Kings 17:17–24 amply illustrates. The extreme vulnerability of Elijah to death—as a function of 'unworthiness'[101]—may moreover, be reflected in the final words of his prayer: "I am no better than my ancestors." Elijah's perception of his own unworthiness is typical of those suffering from major depression, which "tends to increase sensitivity to rejection, and . . . may be accompanied by a loss of self-confidence and self-regard."[102] The רתם (broom tree, NRSV), which has already been introduced into the story as a part of Elijah's dream imagery, now becomes the storyteller's link between the first and second dreams, thereby helping to bridge the intervening sleep period before the introduction of the second messenger.

Following the narrated interjection of v. 5a, the second dream commences with a sequence in which all of the five sense experiences are recorded. Firstly, the 'angel' touches Elijah, whereupon he hears and obeys, and this is followed by his looking (v. 6) around prior to identifying a cake of bread whose detailed description would seem to connote the sense of smell, before finally Elijah tastes his food and drink. The employment of all five senses—particularly the latter three—within the dream does much more than simply record the fact that dreams are multi-sensorial. It serves to emphasize the vividness of the dream content that derives from Elijah's waking experience of semistarvation.[103] Elijah's experience of famine and its consequences will not be lost on the first readers of this text, for whom starvation would be an all too frequent occurrence and for whom "it can even spill over into dreams, as when a hungry man dreams that he is eating and awakes with his hunger not satisfied (Isa 29:8)."[104] More importantly, however, just as the first dream was labeled with a depression motif, the labeling of the second dream with this starvation motif firmly

---

100. Westerlund, "Spiritual Beings," 158. It should, however, be borne in mind that the Kung healers are operating in a public, dance-induced, trance situation, albeit that these sessions usually involve small groups of people only. The importance of the dangers of 'soul-travel' in ASCs nevertheless still apply.

101. Parallels may also be drawn here with the inherent dangers of Merkabah mysticism. Indeed, "the dangers of the ascent through the palaces of the Merkabah sphere are great, particularly for . . . those who are unworthy of its object. As the journey progresses, the dangers become progressively greater" (Scholem, *Major Trends*, 51).

102. Solomon, *Noonday Demon*, 48.

103. Kramer writes "It is clear that the dream is responsive to a number of affective influences. The dream responds to the emotional experiences of the prior days, the effect of new and continuing experiences . . . (and) important interpersonal situations. . . " (Kramer, "Selective Mood," 175).

104. Jenks, "Eating and Drinking," 251.

links the enforced fasting with its potential, ultimate outcome—an altered state of consciousness.

It is significant that the meal itself is of bread, which had a known effect upon mood, for the Psalmist notes (Psalm 102:4, MT and LXX) that forgetting to eat one's bread causes the heart to become 'smitten' or 'stricken' (*nakah*) like grass, this being somewhat archaic language used to describe grass that has been flattened.[105] Thus, the simile pictures flattened or depressed mood as the direct result of failure to eat bread, and its converse—the lifting of or restoration of normal mood—results from eating bread. Modern findings that "a high carbohydrate, protein-poor meal elevates brain tryptophan, (thereby) accelerating serotonin synthesis"[106]— with consequent amelioration of mood—resonate with these antique observations borne of experience. It is possible that this dream content may be the narrator's way of indicating a symbolic end to Elijah's enforced fast, prior to the third messenger's visit.

In his commentary on 1 Kings, Cogan sees 'watershed' significance in Elijah's two meals (1 Kgs 19:5, 7), but like most other commentators perceives chapter 19 as a real journey to Horeb, and as such he considers that the first meal (v. 5) is provided to end "the self-inflicted fast Elijah had undertaken from Samaria to the wilderness of Beersheba."[107] But the text makes no mention of Elijah engaging in a self-inflicted fast whilst travelling between Samaria (18:46?) and the wilderness of Beersheba (19:4). If Elijah is indeed portrayed as engaged in a fast his condition depends entirely upon his entry into Samaria (18:2) where the "famine was severe," and it was as a consequence an enforced condition held in common with his compatriots. Cogan is, however, right to focus on the 'watershed' nature of the two meals where he notes that the first one relates to the past and the second to the future. A better explanation—in terms of dream symbolism—might be to see the first meal ending an enforced fast shared with others, whilst the second meal may signify the commencement of a holy fast exclusive to Elijah. The symbolism is continued by the typological use of the number 'forty' in the expression "forty days and forty nights" (v. 8), and in which Cogan sees "a legendary aspect to the journey, a long distance into the wilderness."[108] Indeed, the wilderness and (ultimately) the mountain are recognizable from Daur Mongol shamanic possession,

---

105. It is, however, possible to view this verse as indicating failure to eat as the outcome of a depressed condition. So KJV, NRSV.

106. Wurtman, "Ways That Foods," 2. Bread, as quite distinct from meats (protein) of various kinds, has a high carbohydrate content in the form of starch.

107. Cogan, *1 Kings*, 452.

108. Cogan, *1 Kings*, 452.

where "the mountains, rocks and trees were not objects of worship, but rough, cold objects in the wilderness and the 'other world.'"[109] Eliade concurs and in his discussion about 'seeing spirits' he can say that:

> 'Seeing' a spirit, either in dream or awake, is a certain sign that one has in some sort obtained a 'spiritual condition,' that is, that one has transcended the profane condition of humanity. . . . Among the Menangkabau of Sumatra the *dukun* complete their shamanic instruction in solitude, on a mountain; there they learn to become invisible and, at night, see the souls of the dead.[110]

The relationship between solitude and wilderness or mountain experiences on the one hand, and 'hiddenness,' 'darkness,' and 'seeing' on the other is brought out here. The storyteller appears to be aware that the seeking of solitude in wilderness or mountain can result in visionary experiences, and may be using this awareness to illustrate and reinforce the dream or vision quest nature of this epiphany. Eliade can, moreover, emphatically affirm that shamans in pursuit of such vision quests actually become spirits; they are in fact effectively dead.

The point at which Elijah resumes his vision/dream quest is indicated by the use of the verbs קום and הלך, and Hauser draws out the direct correlation between 19:3 and 19:8 wherein these same verbs, ויקם, 'and he rose up,' and וילך, 'and he went,' are used.[111] But he immediately dilutes the import of that relationship by placing wholly different interpretations on the situations in which these verbs occur. In his view הלך,—which is essentially a neutral term meaning 'go' or 'walk'—is effectively colored by its context in v. 3 where וירא is translated as 'and he feared,' with the result that הלך, is often given the meaning 'ran' or 'fled.' This perceived compulsion is absent from v. 8 (and moreover from 19:21 where these two verbs also occur together) and a more restrained English translation results. If, however, these parallels are to have any force at all, then the verbs must relate to the same activity in both sets of circumstances, that is, activity in which the *nephesh* has become delocalized from its normal locus in the body during an ASC.[112]

---

109. Humphrey appears to be describing the simultaneity of physically and literally running away into the 'wilderness' whilst mentally participating in distant events, indeed "the afflicted person ran to them (i.e. the cold objects of the wilderness) hid in them, merged with them" (Humphrey with Onon, *Shamans and Elders*, 220).

110. Eliade, *Shamanism*, 85–86.

111. Hauser, "Yahweh Versus Death," 66.

112. Lindblom appears to have early recognised that the content (speech/action) of this exchange (19:7–9a) took place in a dream (Lindblom, *Prophecy*, 56).

Theophanic Dialogue within the Dreamform

Any demonstration that a passage has a dreamform structure almost invariably suggests that it has retained a single, unified origin in an oral tradition, and that this has largely precluded editorial activity to a significant degree, save where this has served to preserve the traditional culture-pattern. Nevertheless, although it is not the purpose of this present work to examine the historico-literary origins of the various components of the Elijah narratives, some of the comments of Marsha White merit closer attention. White argues that only the drought legend is original to the Elijah narratives and that "this legend was originally independent of the inserted material,"[113] that is, originally independent of 1 Kings 17:2–6; 17:8–24 and 18:2–40. Notwithstanding this she does acknowledge that these stories sitting within their drought "matrix" "are all present to testify to Elijah's status as YHWH's special prophet,"[114] and in this regard at least do have some coherence. White maintains, however, that "the Elijah of the miracle stories is a literary construction . . . as is the Elijah of the theophany (1 Kings 19:1–18), call (1 Kings 19:19–21) and succession legends (II Kgs 2:1–18)."[115] In fact, this literary construction is "designed to make a statement of Mosaic authority, which obscures the historical prophet,"[116] and, moreover, subordinates the narrative coherence of the entire passage (1 Kings 19) to this end.[117] White's belief that chapter 19 has little or no narrative coherence is seemingly based upon a consideration of Elijah as a Moses *redivivus*, which is not borne out by the structural integrity of 1 Kings 19 viewed as the logical trajectory of the themes developed in chapters 17 and 18. To suggest, as White does, that 1 Kings 17–18 is really a preface to 1 Kings 21, and that 1 Kings 19:1–21 is a "written/redactional phase . . . composed and inserted into 1 Kings 17:1—18:46,"[118] is really to admit defeat regarding any meaningful exegesis of 1 Kings 19.

The demonstration in the preceding discussion that 1 Kings 19:2–21 is a dream sequence stands in opposition to White's view that visions and dreams constitute "indirect mediation,"[119] in which Moses—considered as Elijah's model—did not take part. The reference is to Numbers 12:6-8

---

113. White, *Elijah Legends*, 31.
114. White, *Elijah Legends*, 40–41.
115. White, *Elijah Legends*, 15.
116. White, *Elijah Legends*, 11.
117. White, *Elijah Legends*, 4.
118. White, *Elijah Legends*, 32–33.
119. White, *Elijah Legends*, 11.

where Moses is distinguished from other prophets. This latter passage does, however, find accord with the cross-cultural model of all prophets advanced in this study, and makes the point that Moses might expect to experience direct mediation with YHWH within dreams and visions (ASCs).[120] All the prophets—Moses included—could expect to enter altered states of consciousness, but Moses could expect an encounter with YHWH within that condition that included "mouth to mouth" speech (Num 12:8), that is, dialogue. The other prophets can only expect "riddles" from YHWH, that is, either unmediated, symbolic information, or perhaps information mediated by lesser spirits. This is the essential point conveyed by this passage and is entirely in accordance with Eliade's criteria for the common antecedents of the shaman-prophet, any one of which indicates the prophetic vocation:[121] Both Moses and the other prophets exhibit the essential, visionary criteria which allow them all to be so designated as prophets by their contemporaries (or on Auld's view by the post-exilic editors of the text[122]), but the purpose of this passage is to point to the 'clear blue water' between them. In short, Moses engages in direct spiritual encounters with YHWH during altered states of consciousness that involve dialogue, whereas the other prophets do not.

White also notes that Moses and Elijah both share the epithet 'עבד יהוה' (servant of YHWH), and it is this appellation that sits between (and thereby separates) the description of YHWH's relationship with Moses (Num 12:8) and that which he has with the other prophets (Num 12:6). Rather than this term being used to designate Moses and Elijah as intermediaries—with the latter (Elijah) being merely a literary construction based on the former[123]—it interposes more 'clear blue water' between them and the other prophets of their respective times. Moses the prophet has this additional attribute that separates him from the other prophets—he is a

---

120. Numbers 12:6 and 8 are linked by the relationship between the nouns מַרְאָה and מַרְאֶה, where מַרְאֶה "can mean almost anything having to do with outward appearance, the way things look. So the notions of a 'sight' or phenomenon, whether usual ... or unusual (Ex. 3:3) is common." The "nearly identical noun *marʾâ*, (is) distinguished from *marʾeh* only by the second vowel. This related word is used almost exclusively for vision(s) as a vehicle of divine revelation to prophets" (Culver, "רָאָה," 824).

121. In the prophets' case it is only "various revelations" that are received, whereas Moses engages YHWH in 'dialogue.'

122. Auld offers the view "that both parts of the 'prophetic' canon of the Hebrew Bible received much of their distinctive and positively intended 'prophetic' vocabulary over a briefer and in a much later period of the biblical tradition than is regularly supposed.... It was on to these books ... that 'prophetic' and 'visionary' terminology was grafted" (Auld, "Prophets," 16).

123. White, *Elijah Legends*, 11

servant of his spiritual entity, YHWH (v. 7),[124] whereas they are masters of theirs.[125] Elijah is similarly (self) designated as a servant of YHWH in an immediate context (the climax of the contest, 1 Kings 18:36), which has no parallel within the Mosaic narratives, and which precedes the so-called literary construction (apparently modeled on Moses) of 1 Kings 19. This therefore points to the use of the criterion of servanthood to independently designate both Moses and Elijah as being quite separate and distinct from their prophetic contemporaries.

These distinctions—specific dialogical encounter with YHWH and willing servanthood when allied to lifelong (non-trance) possession,[126] that is, symbiotic relationship with divinity (Moses is the 'Divine Man' איש אלהים, Deut 33:1),[127] coalesce to form the vast gulf in attributes between Moses and other prophets alluded to in Deuteronomy 18:15 and 18.[128] The latter term (איש אלהים) is used in 1 Kings 17 as an appellation for Elijah (vv. 18, 24) and although it appears within what White regards as another "insertion," it again occurs in an immediate context without parallel in the Mosaic narratives, and moreover, remains consistent with cross-cultural perceptions of the shaman as healer.[129] All of this is not to argue for 'a factual or historical Elijah' so much as to demonstrate the unique nature of the additional supernatural attributes that define the prophet who is quintessentially both a Divine Man and servant of YHWH, that is, one who has abilities that extend far beyond those of any other prophet. Thus, these very specific concepts of lifelong (non-trance) possession (איש אלהים) and servanthood (עבד יהוה) as distinct from mastery of spirits may very well have become subsumed[130] within the much broader and more general designation נביא (*nabi*).[131]

As already noted, the specific contexts in which Elijah is independently designated as איש אלהים and עבד יהוה have no parallel in the Mosaic stories,

124. Auld also pinpoints servanthood as Moses' key criterion when he notes that "the clue to his (Moses) categorization may lie in the words: 'in all my house it is he who is established/faithful/ trustworthy'" (Auld, "Prophets," 19).

125. Grabbe, "Ancient Near Eastern Prophecy," 18.

126. Bourguignon, *Possession*, 46.

127. Hallevy, "Man of God," 237.

128. "The LORD your God will raise up for you a prophet like me from among your own people" (Deut 18:15).

129. Bourguignon, *Possession*, 45.

130. Auld can say that "It seems unlikely that earlier designations of these figures were suppressed by later tradition. The evidence suggests refinement by supplementation, rather than alteration or suppression of terminology already in our texts" (Auld, "Prophets," 14).

131. Auld posits a "plausible post-exilic context for almost all *singular* uses of 'prophet' in Kings" (Auld, "Prophets," 8).

and this therefore suggests that Elijah is being portrayed as holding these attributes in his own right. Elijah, therefore, like Moses engages in direct spiritual encounters with YHWH during altered states of consciousness that involve dialogue—dialogue that is first encountered at the beginning of the long, final dream in 19:9b. Childs considers that the narrator's main concern in the theophany scene of chapter 19 is related to Elijah's 'feeling sorry for himself,' having already asked God to take his life away. The writer is considered to use the repetition of YHWH's question (vv. 9, 13)—"Elijah, what are you doing here?"—and Elijah's responses (vv. 10, 14)—"I have been very zealous for the LORD, . . . for the Israelites have forsaken your covenant, . . . I alone am left,"—to emphasize Elijah's crestfallen demeanor. Certainly, with Childs it can be agreed that Elijah's mood is brought to the fore here, but this in no way leads to Child's conclusion that Elijah believes he is the only faithful Israelite left. This latter conclusion seems to stem from considering God's assertion that he intends to leave a remnant in Israel (v. 18) as effectively positioned earlier (v. 15). Childs writes:

> God's reply in verse 15 serves as a stern rebuke: "I have left seven thousand in Israel who have not bowed the knee to Baal."[132]

It is rather Elijah's mood—depicted as intruding into this dream in a manner similar to the way in which semistarvation intruded into the earlier dreams (vv. 5, 7)—that is the issue here. Elijah's daytime experience of the 'prophetic condition' (depression) has become the subject matter of this final dream and allows the narrator to produce a grotesquely bizarre parody of the true situation.[133] Indeed, the irrationality of depression is exemplified by Solomon when he writes:

> It (depression) seems to be very much wrapped up in what is about to happen to you. Among other things you feel you are about to die. . . . All that is happening in the present is the anticipation of pain in the future, and the present qua present no longer exists at all.[134]

As already suggested, the metaphorical and symbolic import of 'the cave' is that it is a 'depression motif,' which describes that within which Elijah has withdrawn and from which he cannot escape unless helped. Elijah's 'complaint' of v. 10 is the stereotypical 'cry for help,' for "no one can do anything but beg for help . . . at the lowest depths of a major depression, but once

---

132. Childs, "On Reading," 135.

133. Commentators frequently note the unrelatedness of Elijah's comments to the realities of the previous chapter. See for example Cogan, *1 Kings*, 452–53.

134. Solomon, *Noonday Demon*, 28–29.

that help is provided, it must be accepted."[135] YHWH provides the help (v. 11a) by commanding Elijah to emerge completely from within the cave and stand upon the mountain, but Elijah only stands at its entrance (v. 13), thereby indicating the continuation (albeit somewhat relieved) of Elijah's depression, but resulting in a repetition of the 'complaint' in v. 14.

Between v. 11a and v. 13 lies the long, narrated interjection that comprises the famous 'theophany' of 1 Kings 19, which some have considered to be "a subsequent interpolation"[136] within the 'original' text, but which should more properly be seen as a narrated expansion on the 'דבר־יהוה' (the word of the LORD) in v. 9b. Reference has already been made to the ability of some mystics to experience sound as vision and vice versa, and synesthesia is defined by Cytowic as: "The rare capacity to hear colors, taste shapes, or experience other equally strange sensory fusions whose quality seems difficult ... to imagine."[137] Moreover, he describes the current scientific interest in the phenomenon thus:

> Neuroscience is particularly curious ... because of what synesthesia might reveal about consciousness, the working of non-synesthetic brains, subjective-objective relations, the neural basis of metaphor, and the relationship between reason and emotion.[138]

The removal of the narrated interjection (vv. 11b–12) from the sequence vv. 9b–21 appears to make little difference to the flow of the story, and indeed, the juxtapositioning of vv. 11 and 13 emphasizes the *fusion* of the visual and the aural. Elijah is shown covering and protecting his eyes *rather than his ears* when he 'hears' (v. 13a) the dangerous proximity of YHWH, and thus the narrator is seen to lay stress on the visual nature of this communication. With Cogan it can be acknowledged that the NRSV when translating קול דממה דקה (the sound of sheer silence) gives a "successful approximation of the assonance of the Hebrew text."[139] Indeed, this phrase describes perfectly the silent communication of verbal/aural information through the visual senses, that is, by a synesthetic fusion. In Robinson's view the theophany is a prediction by YHWH himself, which Elijah must emerge from the 'cave' to hear: "There is thus only one *qôl*: v. 12 foretells it;

---

135. Solomon, *Noonday Demon*, 29.

136. See for example Würthwein, "Elijah at Horeb," 161.

137. Cytowic, *Synesthesia*, 2. "The word *anesthesia*, meaning 'no sensation,' shares the same (Greek) root with *synesthesia*, meaning 'joined sensation'" (Cytowic, *Synesthesia*, 2).

138. Cytowic, *Synesthesia*, 2.

139. Cogan, *1 Kings*, 453.

v. 13 narrates it."¹⁴⁰ This conclusion is, of course, highly likely to be the case given the proximity of the two occurrences of קוֹל (*qol*) in adjacent verses (vv. 12b, 13b) and in his résumé of various exegetes' explanations of this term, Robinson synthesizes and theologizes these into a character definition of YHWH over and against the Baals, that is, YHWH remains beyond the natural elements.¹⁴¹ In this review of other work, Robinson dismisses Lindblom's perceptive suggestion that the theophany might represent a tranquil form of prophetic ecstasy in which divine revelation is received in a passive state of mind.¹⁴² Robinson may, however, be right to see 'beyondness' in this scene, but it is possible that the repeated use of אחר, (*achar*, 'after,' 'behind') is atemporal, referring ultimately to the silent sound lying behind, and mediated synesthetically through, the visual components of this 'theophany' scene. Certainly, an understanding of אחר as an adverb referring to 'place' rather than 'time' is acceptable for this common word.¹⁴³ Moreover, if אחר were to be considered to refer to 'place' throughout the 'theophany' then each element of the sequence would represent a progressive increase in danger, behind and beyond all of which ultimately lay the "sound of sheer silence." The acceptance of an atemporal progression in vv. 11b-12 gives better agreement with the use of the participle עבר (*abar*) in v. 11a to represent visual action that is virtually simultaneous. This narrated expansion on the visual nature of the LORD "passing by" is prefaced by הנה,¹⁴⁴ 'behold'—a term which emphasizes the immediacy/simultaneity of the situation—and the insertion of this term in vv. 9 and 13, where the reference is to 'word' and 'voice' respectively (*dabar* and *qol*), argues for the visual conveyance of an aural communication throughout.

In addition to its function as an explanation of the mode of divine communication the narrated interjection serves other purposes. Rather than being an editorial interpolation into an earlier text as per Würthwein, or a part of a larger literary fabrication designed to evince Mosaic authority as White suggests, this commentary serves as a device designed to separate and emphasize vv. 9b-10 and 13b-14. Würthwein is, however, suggesting identification, at least in some measure, of the דבר of v. 9b with the קוֹל of v. 13b, which he considers are part of the repetition of vv. 9b-10 in vv.

---

140. Robinson, "Elijah at Horeb," 521.

141. Robinson, "Elijah at Horeb," 527.

142. "This legend does not condemn orgiastic ecstasy, but aims at defending the more tranquil forms of divine revelation" (Lindblom, *Prophecy*, 49).

143. Alden, "אַחַר," 33.

144. Compare the use of 'הנה' in Genesis 41:17 for relating the visual content of a dream.

13b–14.[145] But it is not necessary to view this repetition as the result of a subsequent (crude?) redaction, if the whole point of the narrated interjection is to feature and reinforce (by repetition) the fact of the dialogue as fundamental to the prophet-deity relationship. Moreover, it is quite plausible that the content of the repetition, at least so far as Elijah's input is concerned (vv. 10 and 14), is the narrator's ongoing illustration of the 'prophetic condition.' In a Western, emic analysis the 'prophetic condition' corresponds to the prophet's continuing depression, which should perhaps be better understood as a character trait that by its very nature can never quite be removed. It is, however, possible at least to alleviate depression by the use of interpersonal therapy (IPT), which "focuses on the immediate reality of current day-to-day life," and in which "the therapist and patient establish a few attainable goals."[146] This IPT pattern appears to be present in vv. 15–18 where Elijah receives a new 'to do' list of jobs from YHWH. Redaction there may have been in 1 Kings 19:1–21, but only in so far as it may have shaped, facilitated and enhanced an already elegant story.

Dialogue with other Nepheshim within the Dreamform

Bergen observes, as others have done, that 1 Kings 19:16 is the only place within Genesis—2 Kings where a prophet is recorded as being anointed, but claims this is readily explained by directing the focus of the verb משח onto the subject of the anointing, that is, Elijah rather than the object, Elisha. Indeed, "anointing is an action done *by* Moses (Exod 28:41; 29:7, 36) or Samuel (1 Sam 9:16; 15:1; 16:3), rather than an action done specifically *to* priests or kings."[147] The whole rationale of the procedure is based on the need to convey authority, and Bergen argues that Elisha is the only prophet to be so anointed because his authority rests on "being the legitimate successor of another prophet."[148] This would, however, be an incorrect reading of the situation, since Elisha's authority—and Jehu's and Hazael's also—rests exclusively upon their election by YHWH, rather than any 'legitimacy' of succession. YHWH's authority is directly conveyed to Elisha by the 'Divine Man,' Elijah, during the continuation of his vision quest in vv. 19–21. Although a break is established after v. 18, a state of altered consciousness

---

145. Würthwein, "Elijah at Horeb," 160–61.
146. Solomon, *Noonday Demon*, 109–10.
147. Bergen, *Elisha*, 47. Author's emphasis.
148. Bergen, *Elisha*, 47.

continues to apply, which the narrator records is at the direction of YHWH himself in 19:15:

לך שוב לדרכך מדברה דמשק

Most English translations of this phrase tend to link the term 'wilderness' (מדבר) with the destination 'Damascus' (דמשק) as a genitive—so the KJV: "Go, return on thy way to the wilderness of Damascus." But the effect of appending a Hē Locale to מדבר is to position Elijah in(side) his previous, wilderness 'way' or 'road,' that is, to embark him upon a further leg or phase of his vision quest. The LXX may preserve some sense of this in its use of "εις την οδον σου," before and separate from "ηξεις εις την οδον ερημου Δαμασκου," which adds 'the wilderness of Damascus' indicating the new direction of the vision quest. The import of the command lies primarily in the stress placed on Elijah's return to his vision questing or spiritual travels, rather than a geographical relocation. Nevertheless, the geographical integrity of the narrative remains firmly in place (i.e. to דמשק, *Demesheq*) and accounts for the apparent reversal of the order of YHWH's commands (vv. 15, 16). Thus, Elisha is the first of the three to be found, and he is found 'ploughing with twelve yolk of oxen' (v. 19), often seen to symbolize the twelve tribes of Israel,[149] and he is with the twelfth, that is, with or in the territory of Benjamin. This is therefore, simply vision or dream symbolism used to locate Elisha within firstly Israel and then secondly Benjamin within Israel. In his vision quest, Elijah comes first to Benjamin just to the northeast of Jerusalem[150] where he encounters Elisha, the implication being that the journey continues in a northeasterly direction traversing the Jordan, and producing further encounters with Jehu and Hazael—in that order.[151] The simultaneity of this new ASC with continued depression is again topographically represented by the change in altitude from the heights of Horeb (10,000 ft.) to the Jordan rift valley (approx. 1,000 ft. below sea level), before Elijah's 'way' passes close by Mt. Hermon (9,232 ft.) *en route* to Damascus.

When Elijah finds Elisha he "passes by" (עבר) him in a manner analogous to the way in which YHWH passed by Elijah on Horeb (v. 11),[152]

---

149. Bergen, *Elisha*, 49. White also notes the "realistic absurdity" of plowing with twelve yolked pair of oxen, but relates the scene to a further Mosaic parallel, that is, Elijah and Elisha's presidency over the twelve tribes in a manner analogous to Moses and Joshua (White, *Elijah Legends*, 8–9).

150. May, *Oxford Bible Atlas*, 61.

151. Bergen is clear that "given the direct movement of the story between YHWH's word and Elisha's call, the reader is likely to expect that the rest of YHWH's commands will be obeyed with similar dispatch" (Bergen, *Elisha*, 54).

152. White notes that עבר is one of four "verbal hooks" linking 1 Kings 19:19–21

and from this we should therefore understand that Elisha too is here experiencing the visual conveyance of information within an ASC. The content of this visual information will be Elisha's own commission from YHWH conveyed by the Divine Man, Elijah. In casting his mantle (אדרת = glory) over Elisha, Elijah has endued him with YHWH's power and authority,[153] and in the ensuing supernatural dialogue between the two of them, Elisha leaves the oxen (Israel) and asks to follow Elijah. Elijah's response includes another of White's verbal 'hooks'—the command to 'go back' (לך שוב, v. 15), but this time the command should be interpreted to mean Elisha must return, rather than accompany Elijah upon his personal vision quest. Thus, there follows a return to the world of Elisha the small farmer, in which he sacrifices a pair of oxen—a symbolic 'burning of bridges' as it were[154]—before setting out to serve Elijah proper. In the final verse (v. 21b) of chapter 19 the verbs ויקם and וילך are applied to Elisha, and these are the same verbs used of Elijah in vv. 3 and 8 to depict the two legs or stages of Elijah's spirit journey in an ASC to 'Horeb'. The use of this form of words may very well be indicating that Elisha has remained in some form of ecstasy throughout, before 'rising up' to resume his spirit journey and become Elijah's spirit servant (cf. 18:43–44), serving beneath (תחת, v. 19:16) Elijah who effectively becomes 'God' to him.

A Dreamer of Dreams

The essence of this somewhat exhaustive chapter has been to establish through the application of the derived methodology that 1 Kings 19: 2–21 is a sequence of dreams, even though none of the terms for dream or vision are mentioned. As a result of the secure mapping of a modern hypnogram to the speech-action/sleep sequences, it becomes incumbent upon the reader to accept that the prophet, Elijah, is indeed a dreamer of dreams, and is dreaming all those sequences. This in turn has implications for the way in which the various encounters are understood, since the dreamform environment

---

with "the preceding theophany and commission of Elijah" (White, *Elijah Legends*, 9). Bergen concurs, but considers that "the impact of the action is certainly less significant," since "Elisha receives his message second hand from Elijah" (Bergen, *Elisha*, 50).

153. White states that the casting of the mantle "*substitutes* for an annointing" (White, *The Elijah Legends*, 9). The reverse is probably more accurate, however, that is, physical anointing with oil substitutes for, or rather symbolises, the spiritual conveyance of the glory/majesty of God. The indwelling of the Spirit/Power of God continues to be associated with clothing in New Testament references e.g. Luke 24:49.

154. Kissling remarks that Elisha "makes a clear and decisive break with the past" (Kissling, *Reliable Characters*, 152).

insists that each of the entities encountered is immaterial in nature. Indeed, commencing with the latter verses of 1 Kgs 18 we find Elijah encounters spirit servants and messengers (both good and bad), before finally engaging with YHWH himself and then Elisha—a fellow 'delocalized' *nephesh*. Every one of these encounters is conducted in the altered or extended reality, and is an aphysical interaction, having no relationship to either sense reality or the so-called 'real' world. The lengthy exegesis of this passage is a necessary preamble to an examination of the creation-paradise story, which itself exhibits a number of qualitatively different encounters at least one of which (YHWH) can definitely be considered immaterial in nature. It follows that if Genesis 2–3 can be successfully shown to have the same dreamform structure as 1 Kings 19, then all of the other entities encountered must likewise be considered immaterial or spiritual in nature.

Such an examination might at first sight seem inappropriate, since the principal character, 'the man', is never described as a prophet in the text, despite being considered as such within Islamic traditions. Moreover, there are no references to either 'personality traits' such as 'suicidality' or anger (listed within the diagnostic criteria for depression by the American Psychiatric Association in DSM IV), or indeed, any inducing physiological state such as famine or fasting. What we do have is the unequivocal presence of one of the terms for sleep mentioned earlier תרדמה (*tardēmā*), and this suggests the possibility that the story may turn out to be a further example of the same enculturated, behavioral pattern found elsewhere. This is, of course, a reasonable supposition on the basis of the authorial link between the Genesis 2–3 story and the Abramic covenant (Gen 15), which displays the same term (*tardēmā*) for sleep, within this behavioral pattern. It is, furthermore, quite reasonable to expect the Yahwistic writer to equate the story of the creation of humanity, with the beginnings of Israel, through the use of the same enculturated template.

The synoptic writers together with John all record a number of comparisons between Jesus and Elijah in their gospels, and in this chapter we have discussed the Elijah story (1 Kings 19:2–21) in psychophysiological terms based on its derived, etic, hypnogram structure. This structure reveals that the longest dream, 1 Kgs 19:9c–21, is (not unusually), the last one of the night, occurring just before dawn, and by way of confirmation this dream features a synesthetic interlude, involving a "mixture of sensory systems . . . common to dream experiences and experiences of the numinous."[155] Certainly, synesthetes have in what for them is 'normal waking reality,'

---

155. Hasan-Rokem, "Communication," 219.

described the "feeling of a presence or the 'visitor experience'"[156]—a feature known to clinical neurology that correlates with lesions in mesiobasal portions of the temporal lobes. The next chapter will accordingly be concerned with demonstrating the presence of the same dreamform structure in the creation-paradise story, by the application of the same derived methodology. Confirmation that the two stories (Gen 2–3 and 1 Kgs 19:2–21) display the same behavioral structure, that is, of depressed prophets, will constitute firm evidence in support of the recorded behavioral comparisons in the gospels between Jesus and Elijah, and the allusion of Paul in Romans 5:14 concerning Adam's sharing of certain traits and characteristics of Jesus (discussed in chapter 6).

---

156. Cytowic, *Synesthesia*, 305.

5

Dreamtime in the Garden of Eden

IN THE DISCUSSION THUS far comparisons have been drawn between the structures of the stories of two prophets (the Abrahamic covenant and the Elijah narratives), and the structure of a modern hypnogram. A surprising match was found in each case enabling the derivation of an etic hypnogram, the validity of which was shown to depend upon cross-cultural psychology as quite distinct from the invalid, modern, Western disciplines of psychology and psychiatry. This demonstration that significant amounts of text in these stories is in fact dreamform has quite profound implications for exegesis, especially where doubt concerning the unity of the stories (e.g. the Elijah narratives) has previously been mooted. This is also true of the story of Adam and Eve, which in addition has its exegetical difficulties compounded by being a foundational text for Christian doctrine. Applying this cross-cultural methodology in practice, we can identify a speech-action/sleep/speech-action sequence in the creation story that corresponds perfectly with the dream/(deep) sleep/dream sequence of the modern hypnogram, and which can be depicted as the derived etic hypnogram shown in fig. 7. This hypnogram can be seen to display the elongated first dream (relative to the second dream), which is so characteristic of the dream of a depressed dreamer.

The story of Adam and Eve runs from Gen 2:4 through to the end of chapter 3, and using this comparison we find a dream/sleep/dream sequence commencing at Gen 2:15 when God first interacts relationally with the man. Adam's first dream concludes at the end of v. 2:20, and during this time God brings the animals to him both to be named and to identify a suitable partner for him. The importance of this passage lies in the fact that we find that God, the man and the animals are all present together in an immaterial environment—a dream, and since God is, of his nature, immaterial we cannot escape the conclusion that for the writer of the story both the man and the animals also have an immaterial component. In short, the man and the animals are both considered by a writer—conscious of the dreamform nature of the oral tradition—as having a spiritual component, which

DREAMTIME IN THE GARDEN OF EDEN

for want of a better expression we should call a 'soul!' After the man's deep sleep (*tardēmā*) and the creation of the woman from the same material, a second short dream ensues running from v. 22 and concluding at the end of v. 23, during which all three characters (God, the man and the woman) interact. As previously noted a narrated insertion (2:24-25) follows, which may extend into 3:1a to produce a bridge between the chapters, and which can be considered to represent a further period of non-REM sleep, before the long dream (3:1b-21) of chapter 3 commences. This dream concludes with God's last interaction with the pair during which he clothes them, and this is followed by a final narrated interlude (vv. 22-23)—the theophanic council and its outcome. Once again, the narrated portion may be considered to represent a period of dreamless sleep, the final one before the dawn.

The final verse of chapter 3 holds in microcosm the very essence of all that has gone before, for contained within it lies the interface between physical sense reality and the realities of the numinous. As the verdict of the theophanic council is enacted, the man experiences ejection from Eden, and undergoes a period of semiconsciousness before waking (labeled hypnopompia in fig. 7), which is familiar to many people as that period of early morning drowsiness when one is unsure whether one is awake or still dreaming. It is at this point that the so-called 'fall' occurs, whether this is considered to be a 'fall from grace' as Christian doctrine has it, or another kind of 'fall' that finds the man (Adam) waking up to full sense reality (in India, as many Islamic commentators would have it).

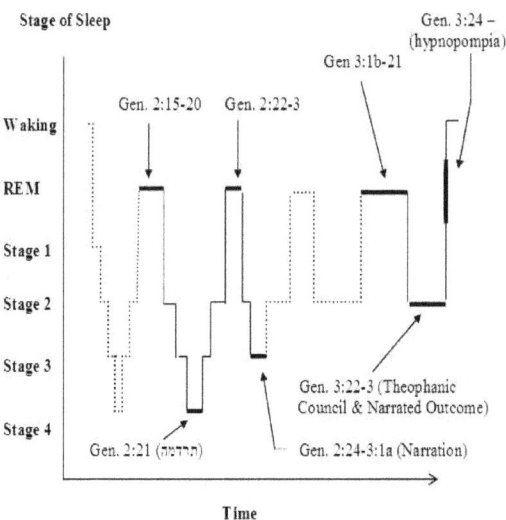

Fig. 7 – 'Derived Etic' Hypnogram of Genesis 2:15 - 3:24

"White Man got no Dreaming!"[1]

Having spent the two previous chapters developing and exegetically supporting the comparison methodology, it seemed appropriate to plunge straight into setting out the derived etic hypnogram for 'Adam' (fig. 7). This will enable reference to be made to figure 7 during the ensuing discussion as it progresses—a discussion that will use the work of the formidable exegete, Phyllis Trible, as a foil in the development of a new perspective on altered state reality in the Garden of Eden. The derived etic hypnogram of the creation account in Gen 2–3 is one of the few Western attempts to illustrate the dreamform nature of this story, and W. H. Stanner's title *White Man got no Dreaming* shows just how difficult it has been for most modern Westerners to reconcile this narrative with an (Australian Aboriginal) understanding of creation as the *Dreamtime*.

Trible, early in her exposition, rightly makes the point that "most interpreters bypass the preface in 2:4b–6,"[2] before she labels the "lengthy introduction" (2:4b–7) as a movement from "cosmos to earth."[3] Moreover, Trible's use of the term 'cosmos' seems to be in agreement with both von Rad[4] and Westermann,[5] who are confident that the term cosmos describes a totality—a physical totality that includes the earth. Thus, the stylistic form 'heavens and earth' comprises the physical universe; all that is. Such a description seems at once at odds with the text itself insofar as it fails to adequately account for the clear reversal of the stylistic form "heavens and earth" (Gen 1.1, 2:4a) to "earth and heavens" (2:4b). Trible continues:

> This tedious sentence (2:4b–7) . . . does not introduce a story about the universe but rather uses cosmic creation as a prelude to the advent and fulfillment of human life on earth. . . . earth and heavens split. The latter passes away; the former leads into the story.[6]

It is at this point that it becomes quite clear that Trible, in common with the vast majority of interpreters, considers that the action in the creation and paradise story of Gen 2:4b–3:24 takes place entirely within/upon the

---

1. This was the title first applied over 30 years ago to a collection of essays written by W.E.H. Stanner about the Australian aborigines.
2. Trible, *God and the Rhetoric*, 72.
3. Trible, *God and the Rhetoric*, 74.
4. Von Rad in his discussion of Gen 2:4b–7 is clear that the introductory clause (2:4b) refers to "the creation of the actual cosmic system" (Von Rad, *Genesis*, 76).
5. Westermann, *Genesis 1–11*, 101.
6. Trible, *God and the Rhetoric*, 75–76.

physical earth, at a location as yet undetermined by biblical exegesis, or indeed any other investigative discipline. In pursuing her literary analysis of the prologue (2:4b-7) Trible notes the parallelism that exists between ארץ (*erets*, 'earth') and אדמה (*adamah*, 'ground'), and this allows her to translate האדם—made from האדמה (the ground), as "the earth creature."[7] This is a perfectly acceptable rendering of a common noun, which arguably never assumes the status of a proper noun/personal name throughout the whole text. Thus, in her discussion of what she describes as the first episode (2:7-8), Trible can say:

> As presented in this first episode, with the definite article *hā* — preceding the common noun *'ādām*, this work of art is neither a particular person nor the typical person but rather the creature from the earth (*hā-'ªdāmâ*)—the earth creature.[8]

Designating the human in this way as "the creature from the earth" permits Trible to further develop her argument, and to claim that this earthling or more accurately groundling is in fact "sexually undifferentiated."[9] But of much greater significance is Trible's illumination of the human's provenance, that is, his derivation from and belonging to the ground, a very specific origin that labels the human as quite distinct from all the denizens of the transcendent heavens—the abode and environs of God.

Trible has little to say about the bulk of what she describes as episode two (2:9-17) of scene one (2:7-24) save to say that the depiction of the garden and the river(s) of Eden (2:9-14) are in "design, context, and vocabulary" necessary to "its final integrity."[10] In moving on to vv. 15-17 she reflects on the differences between the portrayal of God in episode one (2:7-8) and his portrayal in v. 16, since in the earlier verses God is reported in third-person narration, whereas v. 16 shows him in "direct discourse"[11] with the man. This direct interaction is entirely consistent with the dream/sleep/dream structure found in vv. 15-23, a structure within which person-to-person engagement is as likely to occur as voyeurism, eavesdropping or Trible's 'sense' experiences—smell, sight, taste, and hearing.[12] Although the first three of these experiences occur outside of the dream structure, they

7. Trible, *God and the Rhetoric*, 78.
8. Trible, *God and the Rhetoric*, 80.
9. Trible, *God and the Rhetoric*, 80.
10. Trible, *God and the Rhetoric*, 81.
11. Trible, *God and the Rhetoric*, 86.
12. Trible, *God and the Rhetoric*, 86. I have argued elsewhere that 1 Kings 19 is a dream/sleep/dream sequence, and that vv. 5-7 depicts all five senses either overtly (touch, hearing, sight) or by implication (taste, smell) (Wilson, "Significance," 116-17).

are linked to the first dream (2:15–20) by the generally accepted doublets of 2:8/15, 2:8/9, and the continuity of the narrated discourse in 2:7–8. The clear implication of this linking is to highlight the other-worldly nature of the bulk of vv. 8–14, and the largely earthly nature of what preceded them (vv. 5–7). Thus the introduction to the story (v. 4b) is an entirely factual statement insofar as it tells of the time when "the LORD God made (both) the earth and the heavens," that is, made the physical earth and the aphysical or immaterial heavens. The remainder of Gen 2 following v. 4b flip-flops between the two abodes (the earthly and the numinous as previously outlined in chapter 2), with the expansion of v. 8, that is, v. 9 describing the means of access or portal from one to the other. Although it is clear that the man is instructed/ commanded in v. 16–17 not to eat "of the tree of the knowledge of good and evil," Trible seems unsure whether "these words of death (are) a threat or a consequence."[13] Any decision between either of these two interpretations must have major implications for the way in which virtually the whole of chapter 3 is viewed.

Trible's interpretation continues with episode three (2:18–20) where she notes that another creation, the animals, are made from the same material as the man (האדמה, the ground).[14] No comment is made about the 'bringing' (בוא) of each animal/bird to the man, but it is significant that this verb may (primarily) be translated 'to enter' enabling ויבא to have the meaning 'and he caused (*hiphil*) them to enter into.' This carries much the same sense as the earlier use of ויקח (v. 15) and in both cases the object of the verb is the living *nephesh*, suggesting that this term has the same meaning for both man and beast, but only in the sense of its separability from the physical body. Importantly, this clear statement of the belief that animals also possess a separable and immaterial 'spirit/soul,' testifies to the very great antiquity of the story. Trible correctly points out that the creation of the animals (2:19) accurately replicates—with the exception of the word dust (עפר, *āpār*)—the first stage in the creation of the man,[15] she fails, however, to draw any comparison between the creation of the animals and the second stage in the creation of the man, other than to note that:

> . . . the phrase *"living nephesh"* is particularly striking, since it is the same phrase used to describe the earth creature after it received the breath of life (2:7).[16]

---

13. Trible, *God and the Rhetoric*, 87.
14. Trible, *God and the Rhetoric*, 88.
15. Trible, *God and the Rhetoric*, 91.
16. Trible, *God and the Rhetoric*, 92.

Thus, the clear implication is that the animals have also undergone a second stage creation, whether by similar means or not, to produce an immaterial and separable component capable (with divine assistance) of "entering into" (בוא) the man's dream, in the same way he himself did. On this point it should be noted that the second use of the verb 'call' (קרא) in the naming of the animals is to emphasize by repetition that they all have an immaterial living *nephesh*. Indeed, each of the three uses of the verb is for different purposes, and although they indicate the subordination of the animals to the man, they are not used primarily for this purpose. Consequently, when Trible argues that "the repeated emphasis on naming underscores the subordination of the animal world ... and thus demonstrates the unsuitability of the animals for humanity,"[17] it is the very negation of the author's intent. Hence, it is precisely the very great similarity between the man's living *nephesh* and those of the animals, which suggests at least the potential for finding a suitable companion for the man. It is significant that Trible concludes her translation of episode three (2:18–20) in the following way:

> But as for ʾādām, it did not find a companion corresponding to itself.[18]

The import of this perfectly valid translation lies in the fact that, although narrated, it describes the man's active looking for, yet not finding a counterpart, and thus it concludes the speech/action of the first dream of the dream/sleep/dream sequence.

Trible's conclusion to scene one (2:7–24) is made up of the four verses 21–24, of which v. 21 is perhaps the single, most important verse in the entire narrative. Importantly, the sleep (תרדמה) that is deliberately specified here is deep, dreamless (stage 4) sleep; sleep which is the complete antithesis of the dreaming (REM) sleep that is depicted in the dreams on either side of this term. Trible herself correctly emphasizes the nature of the sleep with her description of it as "unconsciousness,"[19] albeit in pursuing her argument about the man's resumed passivity—his animation from dust. In this description of the 'deep sleep' she is supported by Lipton who (as previously noted in chapter 2) suggests, "the term (*tardēmā*) may refer to a certain quality of sleep that was achieved, without waking, during the night."[20]

17. Trible, God and the Rhetoric, 92.
18. Trible, God and the Rhetoric, 89.
19. Trible, God and the Rhetoric, 95.
20. Lipton, Revisions, 191. In a similar vein, Robinson argues that Zechariah 4:1 where the prophet describes being awakened 'like a man that is awakened out of his sleep' could refer "to an awakening to a revelation during the sleeping state" (Robinson, "Dreams in the Old Testament," 16).

Moreover, Lipton whilst acknowledging with McAlpine the "divinely-given" nature of "this particular form of deep sleep," notes in passing that *Genesis Rabbah* describes it as the torpor of prophecy.[21] Such a description finds agreement with von Rad for whom "'*Tardēmā*' is a deep sleep in which the natural activities of spirit and mind are extinguished."[22]

Trible's conclusion to scene one (2:7–24) is made up of the four verses 21–24, which she labels episode four and entitles "human sexuality,"[23] and which for Trible are dominated and delineated by the Hebrew word בשר (*bāśār*, 'flesh'). Certainly, on the face of it this passage does appear to be about the physical creation of a female counterpart to the man, and although this may be taking place simultaneously on the ground (האדמה, *hā-ʾadāmâ*), vv. 22–23 must be considered in the knowledge that these two verses comprise the second dream of a dream/sleep/dream sequence. Significantly, the building of the woman makes use of the verb בנה (*bānâ*, 'build') which is used nowhere else in the entire story, but which has other applications where forming/fabrication in the heavens (the immaterial abode of God) takes place (Am. 9:6). Consequently, all the action in these two verses is taking place in the extended reality, where the woman is 'built' from the same immaterial substance as the man, a fact which he acknowledges through the largely symbolic statement "bone of my bone and flesh of my flesh" in v. 23. Thus, the man's exultant cry—albeit dream symbol—is a cry of identity with his new counterpart whose immaterial, living *nephesh* is not merely similar to his own, as were those of the animals, but rather identical. In short, the man had literally been given a 'soul mate,' together with whom he was identical, forming a single and indivisible whole. It is at this point that we must part company with Trible by affirming that the creation of the woman is not about the creation of human sexuality, but rather the completion of a single, indeed the same creation. Neither does the use of "raw material from the earth creature" make the woman "unique in creation,"[24] and it is my intention to show that it is the completion of the same creation that is the issue here. In the development of her argument, Trible feels able to say:

> To be sure, continuity exists in the oneness of humanity, but here (v. 23) stress falls upon the discontinuity that results from sexual differentiation.[25]

---

21. Lipton, *Revisions*, 191.
22. Von Rad, *Genesis*, 187.
23. Trible, *God and the Rhetoric*, 94.
24. Trible, *God and the Rhetoric*, 96.
25. Trible, *God and the Rhetoric*, 97.

The insistence on sexual differentiation would not be at variance with the oneness of the humans were it not for the fact that the action in this pericope is taking place in an asexual environment, that is, the action is taking place quite literally 'soul' into 'soul.'[26] It is the very 'material' of the *nephesh* that permits, indeed, facilitates the oneness, but in this extended reality environment sex and/or sexuality is, by definition, precluded by the lack of a physical body.[27] The normal usage of words fails to cope with this ethereal situation, and although איש (*'îsh*) and אשה (*'ishshâ*) can in context mean male/female, man/woman or man/wife, it may be more important to concentrate on the assonance of the Hebrew to get a proper feel for the integrity of the new creature(s). Thus, it is suggested that these words struggle to convey a profundity, which might be better expressed as ομοουσιος (*homoousios*),—an identity of substance between things generated of the same substance.

Explained in this way, that is, within a transcendental context the terms *'îsh* and *'ishshâ* are incapable of adding a sexual aspect to האדם as Trible would have it,[28] rather the latter term retains its initial meaning, continuing to point to the provenance of the man as being quite distinct from the denizens of this spiritual realm. Moreover, as Trible points out, there is no naming of the woman taking place here (v. 23),[29] and all reference to her is by the oft-repeated use of the adjective 'this' (זאת), except where the man observes that "it is called woman." This latter observation is entirely understandable given that within his dream, the man was transcendentally present[30] to the 'building' of (and presumably the naming of) the woman by YHWH God, as related in v. 22. Finally, the immaterial context demands that the rib or side from which the woman was built is dream symbol for the 'substance' of the *nephesh*, rather than "raw material comparable to dust from the earth."[31] In this context, it is the second component of the original creation (2:7) that is used to 'build' the woman, who is created a 'soul' from a 'soul,'[32] complete with a full and identical compliment of intellectual

---

26. The term 'soul' is placed in quotation marks to distance it from any connotations of immortality, although this aspect of the 'soul' will be discussed at a later stage.

27. On this point, it is interesting to note Jesus' words concerning marriage in heaven (Mat. 22:30, Mark 12:25).

28. Trible, *God and the Rhetoric*, 98.

29. Trible, *God and the Rhetoric*, 99–100.

30. Contra Trible, the man is indeed a spectator, or rather a voyeur during the building of the woman. As soon as the unconscious sleep of v. 21 is replaced by the action of v. 22 the man is again present as voyeur (Trible, *God and the Rhetoric*, 102).

31. Trible, *God and the Rhetoric*, 100.

32. This is consistent with Islamic, or rather Arabic, traditions, which consider

attributes and memories—memories which will have bearing on the joint culpability of the couple later in the story.

It has already been noted in fig. 7 that vv. 22–23 comprise the second dream of the sequence, beyond which the narrated interlude of vv. 24–25 occurs, and clearly, these verses could be considered to convey information important to any theological interpretation of Gen 2–3. Structurally, however, they serve as a closure to the dream action of chapter 2, and together with 3:1a form a narrated break[33] between the two chapters of indeterminate length, before the dream action in Eden resumes at 3:1b. As can be seen from the derived etic hypnogram of Gen 2:15—3:24, this break probably consists of two further periods of deep (stage 3/4) sleep interrupted by a third dream, which is not utilized by the author. Most interpreters would agree that vv. 24–25 function as a narrated interlude, and many would argue that they form a 'bridge' rather than a break. Indeed, it can be agreed with Westermann that "the narrative would be quite complete,"[34] if it ended at v. 23, since this is the point at which the second dream ends. Moreover, he contends that v. 25 is a narrated link verse, one whose function "is to form a bridge from the creation narrative to the narrative of the expulsion from the garden."[35] It stands repetition, however, that structurally vv. 2:24—3:1a constitute a break in the night-long sequence of dreams, which only reaches closure in the hypnopompia of 3:24. Although these verses (2:24—3:1a) should be understood as a narrated break between dreams, it is essential to see them also as the link between the dreams of chapter 2 and those of chapter 3.[36] This link is made manifest by the "clear play on words between the cunning (ערום) nature of the snake, and the word 'naked' (עירם) applied to the human pair,"[37] and this device performs the function of welding the two chapters together into a single, unified, nocturnal experience.

The conclusion of chapter two (v. 25) corresponds for Trible with the commencement of her second scene (2:25–3:7), and in her estimation the new meaning of האדם as a synonym for 'male' is taken forward,[38] and clearly, in a context where sex and/or sexuality is the issue this is a very valid interpretation. But, as previously explained, the context here is asexual insofar

---

'Eve' was created a 'soul from a soul.'

33. Consistent with her own interpretation, Trible sees v. 24 terminating "scene 1," and v. 25 commencing "scene 2" (Trible, *God and the Rhetoric*, 105).

34. Westermann, *Genesis 1–11*, 232.

35. Westermann, *Genesis 1–11*, 234.

36. Though not strictly a 'dream,' the hypnopompia of 3:24 is certainly an altered state of consciousness.

37. Barr, *Garden of Eden*, 69.

38. Trible, *God and the Rhetoric*, 107.

as the action from which the narrator draws his inferences has taken place in an immaterial and transcendent environment, requiring a more nuanced rendering of the verb (בוש) usually translated as 'ashamed.' Consequently, it would not be inconsistent with the indivisibility or oneness of the humans to suggest that they were not disconcerted by their nakedness. Put simply, the humans remained united, and were not in any way troubled, flustered or ruffled by their new condition.

Dreamtime in the Garden

Right from the presentation of the woman to the man in v. 23 Trible has been able to maintain what is essentially an incongruous position, that is, to uphold the oneness of the couple whilst insisting on a sexual differentiation into two separate, gender-based beings, and in referring to the exchange with the serpent she writes:

> Although the divine words of prohibition were addressed to the earth creature, she assumes responsibility for obeying them. Clearly, this incident shows continuity between the earth creature and both human sexes.[39]

Rather than being clear, Trible fails to explain how such continuity has come about within the unity she insists on maintaining. Moreover, any assumption of responsibility by the woman must imply a degree of autonomy that is entirely inconsistent with the supposed oneness of the couple. On the view expressed here, however, although the two may be deemed separate beings they act—as the narrator said in 2:25—completely in concert at all times, since they are composed of identical 'material.' This is the reason why one can know what the other knows (the prohibition 2:17), why one can stand in the stead of the other (3:1b-6), and why the man hearkened to (eavesdropped upon) the voice of his woman (3:17). In short, the man and the woman were, at least up to the point of eating the fruit, continuously present to each other, and contra Trible, undifferentiated. Indeed, up to and including the point of decision (3:6) both the man and the woman are acting completely in concert, and as a result both must assume full responsibility for obeying the divine words, together with all that ensues from their transgression.

On a literary view, Trible suggests that the story of the serpent is neither about a villain, nor is it about evil, but rather she suggests that in his posture of 'surrounding' the woman he behaves as:

---

39. Trible, *God and the Rhetoric*, 110.

... a literary tool used to pose the issue of life and death, and not a character of equal stress. A villain in portrayal, he is a device in plot.[40]

Certainly, this is a very acceptable way to view the serpent's role in this pericope, and it is possible to agree with Trible here, but for quite different reasons. Indeed, applying the enculturated view suggested here this passage may be understood on two separate levels. Firstly, at the cultural level the speech/action is still taking place within what for the ancients is the extended reality, and as such, is a real exchange between the *nephesh* of the serpent and that of the woman, which is as already suggested identical with that of the man. Secondly, from the author's viewpoint it would be entirely appropriate to depict the serpent in this reality as a dream symbol—equivalent to Trible's "device in plot," which would therefore give every appearance of being a "literary tool." Such tools would be essential to an author's craft in the conversion of an enculturated, oral, revelatory pattern into written form.

At risk of laboring an earlier point, the human couple's condition is that of having identical *nepheshim*, that is, of being 'clones' or perfect copies of each other in an asexual environment. This removes support for Trible's multiple inferences from silence concerning the man's apparent non-participation in the discourse with the serpent, which culminate in her (bizarre?) conclusions that he is "belly-oriented, passive, brutish and inept."[41] As already noted, the man has been fully involved in this discourse from outset, albeit as voyeur, eavesdropper, and support,[42] rather than simply being at hand when the woman gave him the fruit (3:6). Accordingly, and contra Trible, it may be asserted that his (non) depiction in this pericope does "reflect his position of equality with the woman in creation,"[43] showing him to be equally responsible for the encounter with the serpent, and everything that eventually transpired from it.

Much now turns on precisely what the couple knew after eating the fruit (v. 7), and in this regard we must again remind ourselves of the immaterial and asexual nature of the environment in which the action is taking place. If being ashamed in respect of their nakedness was not the issue in

---

40. Trible, *God and the Rhetoric*, 111.

41. It may be noted that the pronoun 'it' has now been abandoned in favour of the gender specific pronoun 'he.' Trible, *God and the Rhetoric*, 113.

42. On this point it may be noted that should the identical nature of the human couples' *nepheshim* be denied, then the man would still be present and party to the woman/serpent dialogue on the simple grounds that it is the man's dream in which the encounter takes place.

43. Trible, *God and the Rhetoric*, 113.

2:25, but rather the absence of any disconcertedness, then the knowledge of the presence of this feature now becomes the issue in v. 7. Thus, it is the awareness of knowing others and therefore of being known in the same way that prompts the later desire to hide. As 'one flesh' they were in concert, now they are separate, different, exposed and vulnerable and they see and know as God, that is, from without. Having previously had a single, indivisible identity they have now acquired the knowledge that is the basis of their quite separate personal identities—fundamental to which is gender difference. This latter knowledge is basic to all other knowledge and resonates with the contention—attributed to Socrates—that knowing oneself is absolutely foundational to the pursuit of wisdom. At this point it is possible to view the sewing together of fig leaves as a reaction to the new knowledge of—and responsibility for—their separate personal identities, that is, as an attempt to return to their previous shared identity. In short, the fig leaves serve as a crude device to restore that which has been lost, rather than a covering up of nascent sexuality.

Trible in moving to what she considers to be scene three (3:8–24), and part one (3:8–13, labeled Trial), progresses the view of increasing discord between the human couple:

> Although scene three opened with both the man and the woman hearing the divine voice, this voice first addresses only the man. Such individual treatment increases tension within the unity of the couple. . . . The man answers only for himself.[44]

Despite the attempt at girdle making, the inadequacy of the fig leaf device is as apparent to the human couple as it will be to God, and so they hide amongst the trees where they hear the divine voice addressed only to the man. It is perhaps at this point that YHWH God's debriefing begins based perhaps on an assumption, shared with the serpent, that the man and the woman still stand in each other's stead, that is, as an undivided whole. Contra Trible, the unity of the couple is a thing of the past, rather than simply an increase in tension within that unity, as the man answers for himself personally (v. 10). This is later followed by the woman who likewise answers for herself personally (v. 13), a feature which Trible also acknowledges for other reasons. Indeed, Trible considers the man to have "betrayed"[45] (v. 12) the woman, when the emphasis of the whole exchange lies more appropriately on the man's (and the woman's) newly recognized personhood.

---

44. Trible, *God and the Rhetoric*, 117.
45. Trible, *God and the Rhetoric*, 120.

Having described part 1 (vv. 8–13) as a "trial" Trible proceeds to part two (vv. 14–19) labeling these verses "judgment," and this breakdown of scene three continues with part 3 "the aftermath" (vv. 20–24), which for her subdivides into "human sexuality in disarray" (vv. 20–21) and "the punishment" (vv. 22–24). Although interpretations differ, many scholars consider that Gen 3:8–24 comprises the components; trial, judgment, and punishment, but much depends, as Trible notes,[46] on how the original prohibition of 2:17 is viewed. If 2:17 is viewed as a threat then it is valid to appraise the better part of chapter 3 in terms of trial and punishment, but if the verse proves to be a statement—however forcefully expressed—of the consequences of disobedience, then there arise other interpretative possibilities. Certainly, for Trible vv. 14–19 comprise judgment rather than punishment,[47] which she considers to be the pronouncement of the divine council and subsequent expulsion(s) of vv. 22–24. In this, she shares common ground with Westermann, who from a tradition-history analysis would suggest that vv. 14–19 are an inserted tradition,[48] with the true punishment[49] being the expulsion from the garden.

Beginning her discussion of part two with the fate of the serpent, Trible rightly picks up on the significance of the term 'dust,' which immediately refers the reader back to the formation of the "earth creature"[50] in 2:7. Indeed, this term (עָפָר) forms the boundaries of this portion of scene 3 for Trible (or in Westermann's view, this insertion into the main story), but the reference to 'dust' at both ends of the pericope (3:14 and 19) is vital to the story on the view posited here. Despite noting that the woman is "surrounded by curses," Trible fails to see the full significance of the term 'dust,' but instead maintains that the woman is "never cursed, directly or indirectly."[51] A better understanding of the passage and the woman's part in it might be expressed by saying that the woman is surrounded by 'dust,' and is thus surrounded and categorized by the very stuff from which the man is formed. The man, the groundling, is made from the dust of the ground, and the serpent will be obliged to "go upon his belly" throughout life, thus having the most intimate of relationships with the ground of all YHWH God's creations. This scene then, describes the consequences of transgression for all three of its actors, and it does this so very aptly as three prophecies, since the structure of the

---

46. Trible, *God and the Rhetoric*, 87.
47. Trible, *God and the Rhetoric*, 123.
48. Westermann, *Genesis 1–11*, 256–57.
49. Westermann, *Genesis 1–11*, 270.
50. Trible, *God and the Rhetoric*, 124.
51. Trible, *God and the Rhetoric*, 126.

entire story (2:4b–3:24) represents the dreams of an archetypal prophet. The consequences for the man, the serpent and the surrounded woman comprise the enforced eviction from (this part of) the transcendent realm, and the return to 'the ground.'

Two curses are, however, present in this passage, neither of which pertains to the man or the woman, but which instead relate specifically to the serpent and the ground. With regard to the first of these it has already been noted that the serpent may be regarded as dream symbol, and in a similar manner so may 'the ground,' since it does not play any 'real' part in this immaterial realm—the realm of ideas. More importantly, as Trible has demonstrated, 'the ground' האדמה, is interchangeable with ארץ, the earth, and thus stands as dream symbol for the whole earth. Interestingly, this presents us with two symbols, the first of which could be seen to represent personified or moral evil, whilst the second might signify natural evil. These suggestions are presented here as the developmental consequences of the methodologies employed, which insist that the complete, single, and unified story is a sequence of dreams that include theophanic interaction with the principal characters of the created order. Moreover, because the storyteller/writer would have considered dreaming to be a perfectly valid part of his reality, however bizarrely expressed, it may, indeed must, follow that this passage is intended to be both a prediction and an explanation of the way things are.

Having reached the end of chapter 3 as a fellow traveler with Phyllis Trible, it is interesting to note that other scholars, who oppose her views on the garden story, still fall foul of the view advanced here. Mettinger is a case in point, and in his discussion of the characters in the narrative Mettinger makes mention of his difficulty with her position on the creation of the woman. Mettinger hears Trible to argue that "the woman should be less of an earth creature than the man because she is not said to have been created out of dust,"[52] as the man is in 2:7.[53] In critique, Mettinger responds with the statement:

> If man is dust and woman is created out of man, then she is dust as well. Humanity at large, represented by the man and the woman in the Eden Narrative, shares the human condition of transience and death.[54]

---

52. Trible, *God and the Rhetoric*, 102.
53. Mettinger, *Eden Narrative*, 31.
54. Mettinger, *Eden Narrative*, 31.

In terms of the thesis advanced here Mettinger is wrong insofar as the events taking place in Eden are taking place in an altered state of consciousness: Eden is in the extended reality. Thus the events described are in an 'immaterial realm,' and it is the primacy of the immaterial over the material that is being emphasized by the writer in 2:22. Indeed, despite the making of the woman being described in anatomical terms (2:22–23) the essential point is that she is made of the same (immaterial) 'stuff' as the man. Hence Mettinger's extrapolation concerning dust must be considered speculative. In this regard, Trible is pointing in the right direction, however unknowingly, and in spite of pressing her own agenda regarding the woman being "less of an earth creature."[55] Certainly, it may be said that on expulsion from Eden, the woman would have been obliged to return to a material locus, doubtless made of dust, to become presumably more of an earth creature. Finally, on this point, Mettinger is clear that the wording of 2:7 "does not imply eternal life,"[56] and in agreement with Barr considers that immortality was forfeited in Eden.

The Tree of Life

Regarding the antiquity of the story, Mettinger concludes a discussion of the 'two trees' by noting a recent trend towards treating the narrative as dating from late post-exilic times, and "even to the Persian period."[57] Mettinger's discussion of the two trees in the Garden likewise notes the recent trend toward the acceptance of the final text as we have it, irrespective of how it came to be that way. As a result of his survey, he observes that both literary-critical and tradition-historical approaches consider the tree of life to be a later development.

It has been successfully demonstrated, however, that Gen 2:15–23 is a two-dream sequence, and it therefore follows that both the tree of life and the tree of knowledge (and on this point Mettinger is clear that 'good and evil' or rather 'good and bad' equate to universal[58] knowledge or wisdom) are essential to the logical integrity of the story. That this is so depends on a progression initially commenced by YHWH, and beginning with man's creation as a two-component entity. YHWH's placement of the man within a dream or altered state of consciousness precludes the first component, that is, the component 'formed from the dust of the ground,' simply be-

55. Kawashima, "Revisionist Reading," 46–57.
56. Mettinger, *Eden Narrative*, 31.
57. Mettinger, *Eden Narrative*, 11.
58. Westermann, *Genesis 1–11*, 243. Mettinger, *Eden Narrative*, 63.

cause it is impossible to place a material or physical being in an immaterial environment! Thus the logical sequence presented in the story runs continuously from v. 2:7 as follows:

- v. 2:7 (creation of the immaterial component of man).
- vv. 2:8/15 doublet (placement of the immaterial and separable component of man within the extended reality).
- vv. 3:6,7 (the acquisition of all knowledge/wisdom).
- v. 3:22 (the potential acquisition of immortality).

In summary, therefore, an immaterial man existing separately from the created, contingent, and material world, possessing both (all) knowledge/wisdom and immortality would on any definition be God, not merely similar to God as 3:22 appears to have it. Hence the measures taken in 3:23–24 to prevent this outcome. Consequently, on the view advanced here both trees are essential to the plot, a plot which therefore effectively spans the whole story (Gen 2:7—3:24), and which depends on the demonstrable existence of a greater reality than the modern, Western purview will admit of.

This discussion about the two trees appears to be central to Mettinger's entire understanding of the narrator's literary strategy, indeed the whole purpose of the story. Thus, he is able to state at a key point in his narratological analysis:

> In his literary strategy, the narrator has God plant two trees and arrange a test—a test of obedience. God denies one tree to the humans. The reader may infer that the outcome of this test somehow decides the humans' access to the other tree—the tree of life. It is then interesting to note that *there is no sign that the man and the woman knew anything about the existence of a tree of life.* And apparently *they did not know* that *they were passing a test and that obedience to the commandment would be rewarded with the gift of eating from the tree of life.*[59]

Despite his emphasis Mettinger is only able at this point (his narratological analysis) to suggest that the denial of the tree of knowledge to the humans is a test, since nowhere is this idea mentioned in the text. If, and only if, it is such a test may "the reader" draw the inference that it determines access to the tree of life, but see below. What seems certain is that without the 'knowledge of everything'—whether obtained by illicit means or not—the pair may well have been unable to locate and partake of the tree of life. Nevertheless, it does seem clear that immortality was always ever in YHWH's gift, since

---

59. Mettinger, *Eden Narrative*, 37.

he is able to remove the potential for access to the Garden (3:24), and also presumably, to restore it. In terms of the thesis offered here, however, one is obliged to agree with Mettinger when he concludes that the consequences of their disobedience are "transience and death."[60] But the death in question is the death of the separable and immaterial component of mankind, and this is of course, why the lack of an immediate (physical) death has puzzled many generations of scholars. It follows that if such a death was to have been avoided, then YHWH did indeed intend to give access to immortality via the tree of life. In any event, it seems that the two trees were mutually exclusive[61]; it was never intended that the humans should have both. On this point we probably need to remind ourselves that the knowledge of 'good and bad' is a wide spectrum spanning all knowledge, and therefore the human transition is not from ignorance to knowledge, but rather from some knowledge (note tilling and keeping in 2:15, and naming of animals in 2:20) to all knowledge.[62]

Returning to the theme of a divine test, Mettinger's view that the denial of the tree of knowledge was a divine test is predicated upon Deuteronomistic theology, and upon covenant theology in particular. He cites passages in Deuteronomy (11:26-28, 30:15-20), which speak of choice,[63] and others (Deut 8:1-3) that link obedience with life.[64] This idea is continued by citing individual examples (Abraham in Gen 22, and the book of Job) where the satisfactory performance of the test leads to a later and as yet unknown reward. Indeed, in comparison with the book of Job, Mettinger suggests that:

> The Eden Narrative tells about an analogous case. Not knowing about the potential reward—being allowed to eat from the tree of life—the two humans are asked for obedience, obedience that is not contingent on reward. They are asked for what will ultimately be disinterested piety—just as in the case of Job.[65]

---

60. Mettinger, *Eden Narrative*, 41.

61. The tree of knowledge served as the test case; the tree of life was the potential reward if the humans passed the test. The accent is slightly different: to attain divine knowledge by an illicit act, or to receive immortality as a gift. See Mettinger, *Eden Narrative*, 60.

62. Blenkinsopp concurs: "He (Adam) has the knowledge and wisdom necessary for naming the animals, somewhat in the manner of Solomon, the paradigm of onomastic wisdom" (Blenkinsopp, *Treasures Old and New*," 94).

63. Mettinger, *Eden Narrative*, 52.

64. Mettinger, *Eden Narrative*, 53.

65. Mettinger, *Eden Narrative*, 55.

Thus, in overview, Mettinger sees the Eden poet amalgamating a preliterary Adamic myth involving the components; sin as hubris, wisdom, and immortality, together with expulsion (based on Ezekiel 28, Job 15:7–8), and a Deuteronomistic theology that contributed blessings and curses that were contingent upon obedience.[66] The Eden Narrative that results from his pen is considered to be a very skillfully crafted, fictive creation that is heavily dependent on the 'developed theology' of the late post-exilic period. Fundamentally, in this view, the Eden Narrative results from the imposition of the Deuteronomistic value system on a pre-existing oral tradition(s) to leave the unified, albeit late, narrative that has come down to us. Whilst holding that this narrative is an integrated whole, it remains possible to posit a different route to the finished story.

Given that there is no word for test (*nsh*) in the Eden Narrative, Mettinger rightly points out similarities of language such as the curses of 3:14–19, which are of course very reminiscent of Deuteronomistic passages. But it is equally likely that a preliterary story about Creation and Paradise, fixed in an enculturated, revelatory pattern came into the written record at a relatively early period in the formation of the Hebrew canon. Thus an Eden Narrative that entered the written record complete in almost every detail would be quite indistinguishable from that produced by Mettinger's holistic analysis—his 'final text as we have it' approach. The identified motifs of sin, testing, blessings/curses, and obedience/ disobedience may indeed be there, merely requiring development and codification into Deuteronomistic theology, and of course, particularizing to YHWH's covenant relationship with Israel. None of this detracts from the skill of an author whose primary task was to convert an oral creation story into written form, since the two media require the application of wholly different techniques for their transmission.

The Genesis account of the expulsion of the man from the Garden of Eden concludes by saying that the man "was sent forth from the garden of Eden to serve the ground from which he had been taken," (Gen 3:23). There is no mention here of a 'fall' of any description, and this is at variance with the much fuller description of the 'fall of Adam and Eve' attributed to the Quranic commentators by Wheeler and listed below:

1. *Tabari*: Adam fell in India.
2. *Tabari*: It is said that . . . Adam fell to earth . . .
3. *Ibn Abbas*: Adam was cast down in India, and Eve in Jeddah.
4. *People of the Torah*: Adam fell to India . . . Eve fell to Jeddah . . .

---

66. Mettinger, *Eden Narrative*, 125.

5. *Ibn Abbas*: Adam was made to fall to earth, to a place called "Dahna" between Mecca and Ta'if (near Jeddah).

6. *Hassan al Basri*: Adam was made to fall in India, Eve in Jeddah . . .

7. *Suddi*: Adam came down in India . . .

8. *Abu al-Aliyah*: Adam left Paradise and . . . He fell to India.[67]

If, for the moment, we leave aside the locations cited here, the commentators are unanimous in their assertion that Adam fell from Paradise to earth. Thus the clear implication is that Paradise is higher than the earth, which in a physical sense is simply not possible, unless some high, Asian fastness (the Hindu Kush?) is claimed as Eden's location. Moreover, given that the Quranic commentaries offer no theological explanation of this fall (e.g. fall from grace as per Christian theology), and that a physical fall from a geographical location may be ruled out on the basis of the forlorn, 1,500 year old quest to find such a place,[68] then another solution to this enigma must be found. Here, we must remind ourselves of the implications of understanding the Eden story as dreamform, and that movement into and out of Paradise, that is, heaven takes place along (i.e. up and down) the Tree of Life (Axis Mundi), within that dreamform. Effectively, heaven and earth are linked as planes of (spiritual) existence by the Tree of Life or World Tree, which acts as a bridge between them.

Intriguingly, the Quranic commentators add an apparent geographical location for Adam's fall, which they almost unanimously agree took place in India, and this in itself is remarkable for a religious tradition that regards Mecca as its most holy place. Put simply, it seems anomalous to find an Arabian religious tradition that cites India as the 'location' of the fall of its first prophet. Moreover, we find that three of the commentaries add that Eve—who is explicitly stated to have fallen with Adam by the Prophet, Muhammad, himself[69]—fell to Jeddah in the province of Mecca. There is a certain cultural inconsistency in Adam falling to earth hundreds of miles from Arabia, whilst Eve, who is arguably a member of the inferior and subordinate gender in the tribal culture of sixth century CE Arabia, falls to earth near 'holy' Mecca. This suggests that what we appear to have here is

---

67. Collected commentaries on the 'Fall of Adam and Eve' in Wheeler, *Prophets in the Quran*, 25–26.

68. In the conclusion to his exhaustive reference work, Alessandro Scafi, writes: "It is clear that no surviving biblical earthly paradise will be found or mapped" (Scafi, *Mapping Paradise*, 371).

69. See Wheeler, *Prophets*, 28. It should be noted that it is only the expulsion of 'the man' that is explicitly recorded in the Genesis account (Gen 3:24).

a very ancient (oral) tradition, which is quite consistent with the primeval origins[70] of the biblical story, and which recounts approximately where the dreaming took place. With this in mind it might be instructive to remind ourselves of the diaspora from Africa (chapter 1): ". . . the initial dispersal was from Ethiopia, across the mouth of the Red Sea, and then either northward through Arabia or eastward along the south Asian coastline to Australasia—the so-called "southern" or "coastal" route."

Death in the Garden

Positing an other-worldly or numinous environment for the garden of/in Eden poses even more fundamental questions than those raised concerning the created status of woman, for we are obliged to consider the implications of the prohibition in v. 17. If the threatened consequence of eating fruit from the tree of the knowledge of good and bad was death, what should we understand death to mean in this environment, and how, if at all, does such a death relate to normal physical existence? In the previous discussion we have briefly touched upon the prohibition of eating the fruit of the tree of the knowledge of good and evil (Gen 2:17), and the apparent failure to exact the penalty (death) for this transgression. In thinking this through James Barr brings a clarity to bear on the story, which is better expounded in his own words, which I make no apology for reproducing. When Barr talks about immortality, he is essentially speaking of the immortality of the soul, and in the first few pages reviews the opposition to this idea as it was at the end of the C20th. Barr traces the opposition through this period in the writings of a number of influential scholars who beginning with Cullman[71] suggest that a tension exists between the immortality of the soul and bodily resurrection. Support for this argument was derived from the supposed contrast between Hebrew and Greek ideas, a contrast which held that in Hebrew thought "there is no separation of body and soul: body and soul are a unity."[72] Indeed:

> The idea of an immortal soul comes not out of the Hebrew heritage upon which Christianity was built, but out of Platonic philosophy, and it is a severe distortion of the New Testament if this foreign idea is read into its teaching. The immortality of the soul, then, in so far as it has been part of the Christian tradition, has entered into it through a mistaken infiltration of

70. Westermann, *Genesis 1–11*, 195.
71. Barr, *Garden of Eden*, 1–2.
72. Barr, *Garden of Eden*, 3.

Greek philosophical ideas into the quite different idea-world of the Bible.[73]

Barr's basic thesis argues that:

> Taken in itself and for itself, this narrative is not, as it has commonly been understood in our tradition, basically a story of the origins of sin and evil, still less a depiction of absolute evil or total depravity: it is a story of how human immortality was almost gained, but in fact was lost.[74]

Continuing at length:

> The story (Gen 2:4b—3:24) nowhere says that Adam, before his disobedience, was immortal, was never going to die. The natural cultural assumption is the opposite: to grow old and die with dignity. . . . To die was human; only gods—generally speaking—lived for ever. Conversely, however, the problem that Adam's disobedience created—a problem for God himself above all—was not that he brought death into the world, but that he brought near to himself the distant possibility of immortality. This alone is the reason why he and his wife have to be expelled from the Garden of Eden.[75]

Although the present study does not concern itself with sin, it is important for the discussion to note in passing that sin, within traditional Christianity was underpinned by Paul's understanding (as expressed in Romans 5:12), that is, "sin came into the world through one man, and through sin, death." Clearly, however, if it can be agreed with Barr that mankind was not, and never was, immortal, then natural physical death cannot be the outcome of any supposed sin on Adam's part. As Barr points out:

> Nowhere in all the books of the Hebrew canon is the existence or the profundity of evil accounted for on the grounds that Adam's disobedience originated it or made it inevitable. It is not clear that the Old Testament is interested in knowing or finding one universal cause or origin of evil. Indeed, far from taking the universal sinfulness of humanity as an obvious and ineluctable fact, the Old Testament seems to assume the possibility of *avoiding* sin.[76]

---

73. Barr, *Garden of Eden*, 3.
74. Barr, *Garden of Eden*, 4.
75. Barr, *Garden of Eden*, 5–6.
76. Barr, *Garden of Eden*, 6.

Thus, if there was no change in mankind's mortal condition following expulsion from Eden, then it must be concluded that sin did not bring about physical death, and we must look for some other way of understanding God's warning in Gen 2:17. If indeed it was the case that natural physical death was not the outcome intended by God in Gen 2:17, then another explanation of this verse must be found, and this apparent failure by God to give effect to his warning will be expanded upon as the ensuing discussion unfolds. The same problem presents itself to Barr, that is, Adam did not die, a problem that he explains in terms of the manner of his dying: Adam will die in frustration and unfulfilment brought about more by the manner of his living—a living wrested from an unforgiving land after the expulsion from Eden. Barr concludes by conjecturing that "the manner of his (Adam's) dying was the consequence of his disobedience, but his dying in itself was not."[77]

> Adam and Eve were mortals, as human beings normally were, . . . (and) they came near to the achieving of eternal life. The importance of this for our subject is great, for it means that in the structure of biblical ideas immortality does not come in at the margin, at the latest point, or through the intrusion of Greek philosophy. It is present, at least as an idea, at the earliest stages, and is a force that thereby has an effect on much of the thought of later times. That this sort of interest in immortality, in the sense here implied, is ancient in the Old Testament seems highly probable. It is something that goes back to, and links up with, a wider and older mythological background, only part of which remains alive in Israel of biblical times.[78]

Barr reaches the conclusion of the presentation of his thesis by arguing with conviction that the Hebrew understanding of immortality in the Eden story has been colored by later theological ideas:

> In particular, our story does not speak of 'life after death', nor about the 'immortality of the soul'. The 'living for ever' which Adam and Eve would have acquired had they stayed in the garden of Eden is a permanent continuance of human life.[79]

Acceptance of this understanding of immortality, which as Barr points out is entirely in accordance with Hebrew thinking, must necessarily pose a number of questions about the very nature of Eden. Added to the conundrum of death failing to materialize—at least immediately—is the

---

77. Barr, *Garden of Eden*, 11.
78. Barr, *Garden of Eden*, 14–15.
79. Barr, *Garden of Eden*, 19.

difficulty that immortality, in the sense of the avoidance of death, is to be found in this strange 'land' about which so little is known. The 'what,' 'where,' and 'when' of Eden has been much debated, and without a great deal of success, but it is the very nature of Eden that is central to the story. It is to this issue that we now turn.

Barr acknowledges in his discussion about Hebrew 'totality thinking' that he himself has at times talked about the disparity between this oft-rehearsed view of Hebrew thinking and the analytic study of the Greeks and of modern times. It would be only natural to do this, that is, to espouse the views of the cultural and scholastic milieu within which one lives and works. But on reflection, Barr poses the questions:

> Is it even remotely plausible that ancient Hebrews, at the very earliest stage of their tradition, already had a picture of humanity which agreed so well with the modern esteem for a psychosomatic unity? How did they manage to get it all so perfectly right, when the Greeks apparently, so thoroughly misunderstood everything?[80]

The key expression, *nephesh ḥayyah*, for the study of our passage occurs in 2:7 where God forms Adam from the dust of the earth/ground before breathing into the man 'the breath of life.' In Barr's view[81] Adam is initially made out of mud—a point that he repeats three times in about as many sentences—and a point with which Westermann disagrees.[82] For Barr, however, and notwithstanding this distinction between dust and mud, the creation process in 2:7 is "obviously dualistic: there are two ingredients in man, the mud and the breath."[83] While accepting that the meaning of *nephesh* in 2:7 is not 'soul,' Barr seems to suggest that soul-like qualities result from the "breath that comes from God, which is quite distinct from the mass of mud out of which Adam is made."[84] Barr is clear that:

> What cannot be done is to argue, as countless presentations have argued, that the *nephesh ḥayyah* of the text tells us that the 'soul' of Hebrew thinking is the totality of the human person.[85]

---

80. Barr, *Garden of Eden*, 36.

81. Barr, *Garden of Eden*, 37.

82. Westerman finds no evidence for any "moistening" of the dust of the earth in order to make it suitable for moulding, finding instead that the event is "inexplicable, indescribable and wonderful" (Westermann, *Genesis 1–11*, 205).

83. Barr, *Garden of Eden*, 37.

84. Barr, *Garden of Eden*, 37.

85. Barr, *Garden of Eden*, 37.

Continuing to counter the so-called 'Hebrew totality view,' and citing the references 1 Kings: 21 and 1 Samuel 18:2, Barr can assert:

> The soul seems to extend itself beyond the frontiers of the person.... This extension and mobility of the soul is an important reality which should not be explained away.[86]

Moreover, for Barr "there are few or no ... cases" where it is said "his *nephesh* died,"[87] and he goes on to suggest the possibility "that the soul might extend itself beyond bodily death."[88] Taken together, the extendibility, mobility, and separability of the *nephesh* (by death, but not necessarily implying immortality), indicate that the human person acts as a locus wherein resides a component or ingredient that looks remarkably like a soul. Therefore:

> It seems probable that in certain contexts the *nephesh* is *not*, ... a unity of body and soul, a totality of all these elements: it is rather, in these contexts, a superior controlling centre which accompanies, expresses and directs the existence of that totality, and one which, especially, provides the life to the whole. Because it is the life-giving element, it is difficult to conceive that it itself will die.[89]

Crucially, if the nature of Eden turns out to be immaterial, that is, numinous or other-worldly we are again forced to contemplate what death might mean in such an environment, and perhaps more importantly what a permanent continuance of human life there might mean? What seems clear at the very least is that the immaterial or numinous environment of Eden is no longer accessible to the man following his expulsion (the 'fall'), either in dream/vision quest or on death. Certainly, ideas on the survival of physical death by the soul are very widespread, and those of the Daur Mongols seem to correspond well with Hebrew concepts of the נפש, in so far as the *sumus* (soul) was normally fully integrated with the body and as such was not discussed as a separate entity. However, in those circumstances where the *sumus* was discussed (suffering, dreaming, death, and near-death) it is clearly "an overarching concept that implied a human existence both in and beyond the confines of the body."[90] This brings us back to Barr's view on the possibility "that the soul might extend itself beyond bodily death,"[91] but it is perhaps the quality of

---

86. Barr, *Garden of Eden*, 40.
87. Barr, *Garden of Eden*, 40.
88. Barr, *Garden of Eden*, 41.
89. Barr, *Garden of Eden*, 42–43.
90. Humphrey with Onon, *Shamans and Elders*, 213.
91. Barr, *Garden of Eden*, 41.

that continued existence that is at issue here. In later Hebrew thought death meant incarceration in Sheol, that is, in the underworld—the place furthest removed from heaven—and therefore from God, which is surely a kind of death given the way in which 'life' in Shoel is described as being a grey and wraithlike existence, a mere shadow of the former life.

Access to Eden was definitely blocked, as later vision questers were to find, indeed it was dangerous in the extreme as the *Hekhalot* practitioners,[92] and their Kabalistic heirs were to discover. But the way to God—at least according to the Christian understanding of this creation narrative—is not completely barred, and depends as the apostle, Paul, writes in Romans on another 'man.' Indeed, Paul says of Adam that he "is a type of the one who was to come,"[93] and although we know that Paul is talking about Jesus, we might still ask how this statement should be understood.

---

92. Davila considers that the Hekhalot literature records actual 'ascetic' practices and visionary journeys by practitioners, rather than being merely literature. Thus, he offers a full description of the practices recorded in the Hekhalot, comparing these with shamanic practices in other cultures (Davila, *Descenders to the Chariot*).

93. Romans 5:14, NRSV.

6

"The One Who Was To Come"

HAVING CONCLUSIVELY SHOWN THAT Adam is a prophet by demonstrating the dreamform structure of Gen 2–3, and noting that Paul considers Adam to be a "type of the one who was to come" (Rom 5:14), that is, Jesus, leaves us to conclude that Adam and Jesus were both prophets. This is not surprising, since Jesus was certainly regarded as a prophet by the people of his day (Mat. 14:5, 21:11, 43; Mar. 6:15, Luk. 7:16, 24:19), but is Paul also alluding to Jesus sharing Adam's depression, as indicated by the characteristically elongated first dream (Gen 2:15–20) in Genesis 2? Certainly, the Greek-speaking world knew that prophetic-types generally were depressed if only from the work of Aristotle,[1] and the methodology employed in this present work indicates that most if not all the prophets found in the Hebrew Bible (including Adam) were likewise clinically depressed. Thus, in the socio-cultural background (both Greek and Aramaic) of the first-century, Roman-ruled Levant, the psychophysiological 'make-up' (personality traits) of the prophetic type would be well-known and easily recognizable. In such circumstances, it would have been unusual for the Gospel writers not to have recorded some instance of Jesus addressing the matter, if only from his personal experience as a 'prophetic-type,' and to this we now turn.

The Beatitudes—Matthew 5:3–12

The Matthean beatitudes are considerably more elaborate than the Lukan account, and can be considered as a prelude to what follows in the remainder of chapters 5 and chapter 6 of his gospel. It may therefore prove beneficial to examine the Matthean narrative in detail, using other examples of this type of writing—in particular the Dead Sea Scrolls (4QBeatitudes from cave 4 at Qumran)—to both reveal and elaborate on the structure found

---

1. Aristotle observed that Sibyls, soothsayers and the divinely inspired (that is, prophetic types generally) were drawn from the ranks of "those who naturally possess an atrabilious (melancholic) temperament" (Forster, *Works*, 954[a]).

therein, before the multidisciplinary methodologies previously introduced are again utilized. While it has long been recognized that psychological factors are a feature of the lives of the prophets,[2] attempts to reveal meaningful information by the application of psychological methods to particular texts in the Hebrew Bible have met with only limited acceptance amongst biblical scholars. This is in part due to the difficulties inherent in endeavoring to apply the tenets of what is in essence a modern, empirical, 'scientific' discipline to 'inert' historiographical material produced by a pre-modern people group. One of the purposes of my own cross-cultural, comparative studies was to examine the part played by psychophysiological factors in the generation of altered states of consciousness, and to consider how these are related to spiritual encounter. In what follows it will be suggested that the psychophysiological disposition of "the prophets" mentioned in Matt 5:12 may play a more significant part in the structure of the Matthean beatitudes than has previously been revealed.

Harrington in his exposition of 4Q525—more commonly known as 4QBeatitudes writes:

> The five beatitudes (actually macarisms) most fully preserved in 4Q525 2 ii form a series—a phenomenon best attested previously in Matthew 5:3–12 and Luke 6:20–23.... Unlike the New Testament macarisms which are highly eschatological ("Happy are you poor, for yours is the kingdom of God"), the macarisms in 4Q525 are sapiential (which is the usual case in the Hebrew Bible and Sirach). Indeed, the 4Q525 macarisms declare happy or fortunate those who seek and find wisdom (which is identified as the Torah).[3]

The first point to note here is that Harrington is clearly acknowledging that both 4Q525 and the NT texts are the same type of writing—they are macarisms—a transliteration of the Greek word μακαριος meaning 'fortunate.' Secondly, he designates the Matthean and Lucan texts as highly eschatological and quite distinct from the sapiential 4Q525 text, quoting only Luke 6:20 rather than the (more esoteric?) Matthean correlate. It is, moreover, implied that most of the macarisms found in the Hebrew Bible, for example, those found in Proverbs 3, 8 and 28, and also in Ben Sira (Sir 14, 25, 26, 28, 48 and 50) are similarly unlike the Matthean macarisms.

But a closer look at 4Q525 reveals a very similar structure to that found in Matthew, one which George Brooke argues[4] mirrors the 8 +1 structure

---

2. See for example; Wiener, Elijah, and also Lacocque and Lacocque, *Jonah*.
3. Harrington, *Wisdom Texts*, 68.
4. Brooke, *Dead Sea Scrolls*, 221.

found there. This view depends upon the substitution of the conjunction that commences the second line of each couplet in 4Q525 with the "Blessed" formula, thus producing "four pairs of macarisms."[5] The similarities continue when it is noticed that these four pairs are "alternating opposites" of positive and negative statements,[6] which may be compared with three pairs of opposites found in the central six macarisms of Matthew (vv. 4–9), and comprising non-social vs. social contexts. 4Q525 and the Matthean text are, moreover, alike with regard to the ninth macarism, indeed:

> The ninth element in both develops what precedes it. In Matthew the ninth beatitude is a development of what is described briefly in the eighth concerning persecution. In 4Qbeatitudes the ninth beatitude describes the one who has obtained wisdom, the natural development from the description in beatitudes 7 and 8 of those who seek and search for her.[7]

Most importantly, Matthew's ninth macarism, which at this point changes tense to second-person plural, "may also be connected with the first through the eighth, heaven being mentioned in all three."[8] At this point in his argument, Brooke draws out a possible alternative/additional structure for 4Q525, wherein the eight beatitudes may be considered to be comprised of an initial couplet followed by two triplets, and with the introduction to the ninth as an originally independent unit. A triplet structure is then plausibly demonstrated for vv. 11 and 12 of the Matthean passage, culminating in "a comparison with the prophets which is presumably meant to be positive and encouraging for the audience."[9]

Thus far we have somewhat exhaustively followed Brooke's argument regarding structure, but must part company at this point where the comparison with the prophets is said to be "positive and encouraging." Accepting that Matthew's ninth macarism points backwards to all that has gone before, and to v. 3 in particular, it becomes necessary to draw out the implications of Brooke's concluding comments, namely that on the basis of 4Q525 Matthew's text must be "recognized as just as Semitic."[10] It is precisely Matthew's Semitism that underlies his use of προφητης (*prophétés*), which equates to the Hebrew *nābî'* and from which the denominative verb *nb'* 'to prophesy' is derived, thus, 'to prophesy' (נבא) is characteristically what prophets (and

5. Brooke, *Dead Sea Scrolls*, 222.
6. Brooke, *Dead Sea Scrolls*, 222.
7. Brooke, *Dead Sea Scrolls*, 222.
8. Brooke, *Dead Sea Scrolls*, 223.
9. Brooke, *Dead Sea Scrolls*, 223.
10. Brooke, *Dead Sea Scrolls*, 224.

shamans[11]) do.[12] Significantly, however, the earliest attestations of the verb's use (listed by Fleming)[13] are indicating mainly one of two types of behavior, that is, reflexive behavior as opposed to interpersonal behavior. Reflexive behavior is characterized in Hebrew by the use of the *hithpael* or reflexive stem of the verb, which indicates private, internal, and quiescent behaviors that resonate with Brooke's classification of three of the six central beatitudes as non-social. But what does this mean in practice, how and in what manner does one prophesy reflexively?

Insights from anthropology may prove helpful here. Quiescent, private altered states of consciousness are brought about by non-ordinary physiological states such as dreaming, drunkenness, fasting, mental illness, and sleeping, which may be considered to "form a group on account of their common symbolic reference."[14] If, however, dreaming and mental illness are removed from the group on the grounds that they are involuntary, then the remaining non-ordinary states will be seen to be self-induced. Thus, one gets drunk, fasts or goes to sleep—all voluntary and more importantly reflexive activities, which are done to the self. The link between the involuntary and the voluntary states in the eyes of pre-modern people groups lies in the identity of these physical states with their visionary results. These non-ordinary states symbolize their visionary outcomes to the extent that they "are conceived of as modes of dissociating the soul from the body,"[15] thus enabling contact with the spirit world. Consequently, the altered states of consciousness (ASCs) resulting from such voluntary activities are themselves deemed to be reflexive in nature. It follows that supernatural encounter and dialogue are similarly considered to be reflexive in nature, and all the more so because they ensue from voluntary, self-induced actions that affect the heart,[16] the place where the possessing spiritual being is said to reside.[17]

Returning to the Matthean macarisms we may now note that the fourth one (v. 6) is linked to the eighth through the use of the word righteousness

11. See 2 Kgs 14:25, 2 Kgs 9:36, 1 Kgs 12:15, Ahijah the Shilonite

12. Fleming, "Etymological Origins," 222.

13. Num 11:25–27; 1 Sam 10:5–6,10–11,13; 18:10; 19:20–21,23–24; 1 Kgs 18:29 and 1 Kgs 22:8,10,12,18 (Fleming, "Etymological Origins," 222).

14. Hamayon, "Are 'Trance,' 'Ecstasy,'" 22.

15. Hamayon, "Are 'Trance,' 'Ecstasy,'" 22.

16. Drunkenness and fasting have to do with ingestion or non-ingestion into the heart or centre of being. So with sleeping considered as a 'mini-fast.'

17. Reference is here made to Eliade's observation that the shaman often has his "internal organs and viscera" renewed during the visionary states that accompany the initiatory "vocation sickness" (Bourguignon, *Possession*, 45).

(δικαιοσυνη, *dikaiosuné*), and through v. 10 to προφητης (*prophétés*) via the linking use of 'persecution.'[18] Nolland, in his discussion of v. 3 also points up the possibility that the term 'poor in spirit' may be linked with "a state of depression,"[19] and v. 3 is, of course, likewise linked to v. 10. On the basis that depression is a known outcome of fasting—one of the voluntary, reflexive activities previously referred to—it is also possible that the "hunger and thirst" of the fourth beatitude is a straightforward statement referring to fasting. Indeed, fasting has been shown by the famous Minnesota experiment[20] to induce depression in up to 40 percent of people, but only a tiny proportion of these go on to experience audio-visual imagery—categorized medically as psychotic depression.[21] In psychiatry, such imagery is classified as delusional, and until comparatively recently, "strong religious belief" was categorized as "a mental disorder."[22] But it could be precisely this tiny proportion of his hearers, that Matthew has Jesus address as 'fortunate,' and for them the generation of ASCs through fasting-induced depression may be much more than simply a technique. The anthropologist, Rouget, in his discussion of trance and possession states expresses it in this way:

> It would be a fundamental error to reduce these various forms of trance to no more than various forms of corporeal technique. . . . The technique operates only because it is at the service of a belief, and because trance constitutes a cultural model integrated into a certain general representation of the world. Here we have an essential intellectual datum, which underlies both the psychology and physiology of trance. . . . Entry into trance always seems to depend upon a kind of restrictive clause: however well prepared one may be, physically and psychologically, one must still be prepared intellectually, and have made the decision (more or less unconsciously) to succumb to the trance state.[23]

This is precisely the point of the fourth beatitude. The fortunate one must do more than simply 'hunger,' or fast, which even though it is likely to produce a depressed condition favorable to audio-visual imagery, it still requires

---

18. Nolland, *Gospel of Matthew*, 208–9.

19. Nolland, *Gospel of Matthew*, 199.

20. Early studies such as the "Minnesota Experiment" indicated that depression, although a noted result of fasting, was not present in every case (Fichter and Pirke, "Starvation Models," 83).

21. Coryell, "Psychotic Depression," 49.

22. Newberg et al., *Why God Won't Go Away*, 130. This latter citation refers to the American Psychiatric Association, *DSM-IV*, 1994.

23. Rouget, *Music and Trance*, 320–21.

the seeker to earnestly desire engagement with God. Such an engagement or encounter with God cannot be achieved by fasting alone, and physical thirsting adds nothing to the technique, but would rather initiate a more abrupt termination of the fast. Consequently, 'thirsting' is here used metaphorically to describe the earnest desiring, indeed the intellectual will, to encounter and engage with God within an altered state of consciousness. Put simply, the fourth macarism appears to be a prescription for the attainment of righteousness (understood as relationship with God), as achieved through encounter with God within an ASC. Certainly, this appears to be the understanding in Matthew. "The fact that the basic relationship to God is always in view, and that it is related to the *event of revelation*, . . . links it firmly with the OT,"[24] and the usage of צְדָקָה (*ṣᵉdāqâ*, 'righteousness').[25]

The foregoing interpretation of the fourth beatitude as referring to fasting-induced depression finds a resonance with the first two macarisms, which may now be understood as respectively referring to endogenous and reactive depression. The endogenous depression of the first macarism is linked to the fourth macarism via the 'kingdom of Heaven-righteousness' expressions found in v. 10, and through v. 10 to the prophets of the ninth beatitude. In absolute terms, however, it has not proved possible to find an exact correlate to the expression 'poor in spirit,' either in OT usage or at Qumran and Nolland points out that:

> In Qumran usage no discernible difference in meaning is created by the addition of 'of spirit', which serves only to point beyond any more restricted sense for *ʿnw*.[26]

This leads Nolland inexorably in the same direction as Harrington in the opening quotation, that is, towards the accepted conclusion that the first Matthean macarism, and much of what follows it is thoroughgoing eschatology. But for the fortunate few who are able to access the kingdom of Heaven through altered states of consciousness the accent is definitely on the 'now' rather than the 'not yet.' Moreover, a direct equivalence has been set up between the fortunate few and "the prophets who were before you"[27] in terms of their abilities to enter such states. The implied exhortation to the audience is to find such people whether they are marginalized

---

24. Schrenk, "δικαιοσύνην," 198.

25. Genesis 15:6 could be considered as the *locus classicus* for the use of צְדָקָה. In commenting on this verse, Von Rad describes it as *"an event of believing"* (Von Rad, *Genesis*, 77).

26. Nolland, *Gospel of Matthew*, 200.

27. See Nolland who considers Jesus' hearers were on the scene more or less at outset (Nolland, *Gospel of Matthew*, 196).

by their own natural psychophysiology, by bereavement or sorrow or by self-induction through fasting, and herein perhaps lies the need for the use of the future tense.

The ninth macarism has been described as backward looking towards the preceding eight, in accordance with the reflexive nature of prophecy, but what of the other more widely understood aspect of prophecy—the prophet as a mediator who communicates divinely-sourced messages to recipients?[28] Viewing v. 12 as a watershed based on Matthew's use of προφητης would appear to satisfy both 'types' of prophesying and the latter type is immediately addressed in the four verses that follow it. These verses are the famous 'salt and light verses,' and they represent two ways of understanding the same property—that of quantity—for it is ratio that is the issue here, with the fortunate being weighed or measured relative to the mass of humanity (or more probably the mass of believing Israel), by Matthew's use of metaphor. Indeed, the fortunate are *few* relative to the larger body of humanity in the way that salt is small in mass relative to the larger mass of food, and the lamp-lit city is tiny relative to the vast blackness of the night. There is much more that can be brought out here in a more thoroughgoing exegesis, but the essential point concerning the intended vocation of Jesus' hearers is, I think, clear and the immediate admonition to the fortunate few (v. 13) should they fail to fulfill their vocation is noteworthy.

I would, therefore, wish to argue that the Matthean beatitudes are correctly couched as wisdom, and as such would be recognizable in that format to Matthew's readers, despite their highly structured form and esoteric nature. Unfortunately, the psychophysiological nature of this wisdom is nowadays difficult to express in other than medical language, and perhaps, as previously noted, Aristotle conveyed it best when he observed that:

> "Sibyls, soothsayers and the divinely inspired (that is, prophetic types generally) were drawn from the ranks of those who naturally possess an atrabilious (melancholic) temperament."[29]

Consequently, and notwithstanding its highly structured form, it is entirely appropriate to present this wisdom in the traditional manner, that is, using the same forms found not only at Qumran, but also in the Hebrew Bible and Ben Sira. Immediately, however, a problem presents itself, since the appeal of these opening verses of the Sermon on the Mount is neither to ancient sapiential traditions nor to the Torah; it is instead to the phenomenon of prophecy generally, and pre-exilic prophecy in particular.

---

28. Shields, "Wisdom and Prophecy," 877.
29. Forster, *Works*, 954ª.

Fundamentally, the problem lies with the slow, yet inexorable formation of the Mosaic Torah in the second temple period. The books of Exodus to Deuteronomy were viewed as the books of Moses, and eventually as written by Moses. Since the book of Genesis had become linked with that story of national origins, the authorship of the whole of the amalgamated book of Genesis was likewise attributed to Moses.[30] This scenario had largely become established by the early second century BCE, since Jubilees (Jub. 2:1) attributes the authorship of the whole of Genesis, including the primeval narratives, to a divine instruction to Moses.

Put at its simplest the 'new' Mosaic Torah had become a theological interloper in an environment imbued with an ancient and venerable sapiential tradition, one which had been invigorated by the Persian and Hellenistic influences of the exilic and post-exilic periods. Sanders writes: "Ben Sira was surely Torah-devout. . . . But he could not imagine, could not conceive that its morality could be other than his traditional sapiential morality."[31] A similar purview is found at Qumran, where Sanders especially notes in 4Q525 the "personification of Torah brought about by its (her) identification with Wisdom."[32] Moreover, "4Q185 (4QSapiential Work)" displays "a blending of Wisdom and Torah" that witnesses to the creation of a new entity— "Torah-Wisdom . . . very much the same kind of personification of Torah" seen in 4Q525.[33] The *Wisdom of Solomon* in Sanders view represents an even "more deliberate attempt to accommodate the Mosaic Torah to the sapiential tradition,"[34] but one which blends or fuses the two together. He draws an analogy with the conflict between secularism and theology in the latter third of the C20th, but points out that in the "Pentateuchalism" of the second temple period Wisdom and Torah were not mutually exclusive.

Consequently, in circumstances where Torah-Wisdom had become the entrenched philosophical incumbent of the mid-first century CE, the radical nature of the Matthean appeal to the practice of ancient prophesy may readily have been seen as revisionism. This would be especially so where that appeal was delivered in a known and accepted wisdom formula, and the macarisms of Matt 5:3–12 and their practical outcomes in vv. 13–16, might be seen to threaten the accepted tenets of Torah-Wisdom. In order to pre-empt any suggestion that this might be so the Matthean narrative moves smoothly into a defense of the Law and the Prophets in vv. 17–20. Again,

30. Ulrich, "From Literature to Scripture," 8–9.
31. Sanders, "When Sacred Canopies," 125.
32. Sanders, "When Sacred Canopies," 126.
33. Sanders, "When Sacred Canopies," 126.
34. Sanders, "When Sacred Canopies," 129.

without recourse to any extensive exegesis, it can be seen that both the Law and the Prophets might require such a defense. The former because of its accommodation to traditional sapiential wisdom, and the latter perhaps because of the esteem in which they were held by the people at large.

The Matthean beatitudes when seen in the light of a revisionist view of the dominant genre of the time (Torah-Wisdom) display and promote an ongoing dependency on prophecy, and are effectively an appeal for a new generation of prophets. Matthew's elaboration on, and expansion of, the four macarisms found in Q are shot through with connections designed to make this latter point. Indeed, it is well established that Matt 5:3 and 5:10 are connected,[35] and through that connection v. 3 is related to vv. 11–12 (all of a piece with v. 10), a fact apparently acknowledged by Harrington who considers that the Matthean beatitudes comprise 5:3–12, rather than 3–10.[36] Certainly, those who are sad, who sorrow or mourn could be described as low in spirit, and it may be noted that 'low in spirit' (cf. 5:3) features in Proverbs 16:19 (שפל־רוח),[37] in the construct case, i.e. as a single, unified concept that describes, in this instance, one particular human condition. Interestingly, this verse also features both 'poor' and 'meek' ('ānî, 'ānāw) adjacent to each other. Moreover, 4QInstruction, or Sapiential Work A, also from cave 4 at Qumran, is preserved in seven separate fragments, one of which (4Q417) appears—depending on translation—to combine these first two macarisms (vv 3 & 4) into one: "Has not rejoicing been appointed for the *contrite of spirit* and for those among them who *mourn* eternal joy?"[38] Clearly, although 'contrite of spirit' and 'mourn' may not be exact equivalents of the terms found in the first and second Matthean macarisms, they do appear to be addressing a similar emotional condition.

The connectedness of the passage continues, and France points to the shared OT root of 'poor' and 'meek' ('ānî, 'ānāw) in the "Psalms and elsewhere,"[39] which would seem to suggest that vv. 3–5 share a common theme. This theme may continue into v. 6, also linked to v. 10 by the use of δικαιοσυνην (righteousness), which itself is linked back to v. 3 by the use of "βασιλεια των ουρανων" (kingdom of heaven). If it is argued that there is a direct connection between the "the poor in spirit/those who mourn" and access to the kingdom of heaven/righteousness (vv. 3,4, & 10), then

35. France notes "the correspondence of the second clause in the first and last beatitudes" (France, *Gospel According to Matthew*, 108).

36. Harrington, *Wisdom Texts*, 68.

37. Proverbs 16:19 (LXX). "Better is a meek-spirited man with lowliness, than one who divides spoils with the proud."

38. Harrington, *Wisdom Texts*, 50.

39. France, *Gospel According to Matthew*, 109.

this connection extends all the way through to v. 12. In short, some kind of relationship exists between "the poor in spirit," "the prophets" and indeed Jesus himself, comprising access to the kingdom of heaven/righteousness in the present, that is, in this life (On this point see Matthew 6:31–33, where v. 33a is present tense).

Consequently, the question that must be asked is: What feature of the human condition is shared by "the poor in spirit," "the prophets" and Jesus himself? Firstly, we can begin with our examination of the prophets where we have found, almost without exception, that to be a prophet means to be depressed, and this view is supported by the observations of Aristotle, together with other observations of ancient and contemporary premodern people groups. As to Jesus, we find Paul relating him directly to the prophet 'Adam,' (considered as such in pre-Islamic tradition), whom we find can demonstrably be shown to have been depressed. This leaves the "poor in spirit" to whom the 'kingdom of heaven,' is accessible should they choose to "hunger and thirst" for it, becoming in the process, a new generation of prophets.

The significance of the beatitudes (concluding at v. 12) moving seamlessly into the 'salt and light' verses commencing at v. 13 has already been noted, but it may also be pointed out that the 'salt' analogy gives good agreement with the genetics of schizophrenia/bipolar disorder. Indeed, it was suggested that these verses were concerned with ratio, the ratio of those who were depressed to the rest of the body of believing Israel, and which mirrored the proportion of salt added—relative to the mass of the food being salted. This resonates well with the persistence of schizophrenia/bipolar disorder at a prevalence of approximately one percent across all human cultures. Now a figure of one percent added salt may seem high to modern, Western eyes, but this reckons without the much greater use of salt for preservation (and therefore cooking) in ancient cultures, with the result that the metaphorical analogies found in Matthew appear to be very accurate indeed.

The Transfiguration—Luke 9:28–36

Thus far, our discussion has suggested that Jesus (the man) was a prophet, and as such, has the personality trait(s) of, (to use modern medical language) clinical depression, this being the plain import of Paul's comparison, supported as it is by the depressive, dreamform structure of Genesis 2–3. This perhaps begs the question; does Jesus himself take part in any dreams in like manner to Adam? One passage in particular presents itself

"THE ONE WHO WAS TO COME" 121

for examination, the transfiguration, which includes a period of sleep in both the Matthean and Lucan versions. Matthew's narrative (Matt 17:1–9), however, displays the sleep period at the end of the speech-action, and features the lone figure of Jesus rousing the three disciples from their sleep. The Lucan account (Luke 9:28–36) is much more interesting and displays the sleep period in a central position, producing a speech-action/sleep/speech-action sequence readily equatable with the dream/sleep/dream sequences encountered in the prophets.

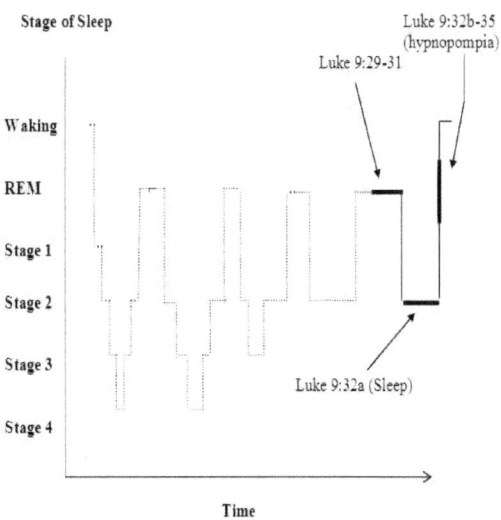

Fig. 8 'Derived Etic' Hypnogram of Luke 9:29-35

Significantly, however, the Lucan passage displays so much more, insofar as v. 32 may be read quite differently to the translation presented normally in the versions, indeed v. 32b is usually rendered "but when they became fully awake" (NIV). But in the context of a dream/sleep/dream sequence where the final 'dream' could be a hypnopompic experience,[40] a more appropriate translation might read "Now as they were awakening out of sleep." On the basis that no timescale is given for this narrative, that is, from when the four of them head off up the mountain, until when the lone Jesus rejoins the three disciples again, it may be that the body of the story takes place towards the back end of a night's sleep, and can be represented by the derived etic hypnogram shown in fig. 8.

40. Hypnopompia, is the condition between dream and full wakefulness, experienced by many people usually towards the end of a night's sleep just before dawn.

The Greek participle διαγρηγορησαντες (*diagrēgorēsantes*, 'to awaken thoroughly,' aorist tense) is here qualifying a finite/main verb (ειδον, 'they saw'), and because this is also aorist, it can be considered to be contemporaneous with that main verb rather than preceding it[41]. Thus, the interactions presented in the next three verses take place in a hypnopompic state, before leading finally to the fully awake condition where Jesus is found alone (v. 36) in 'normal' sense reality. This is the most probable reason for Peter's inability to know what he said, although this in itself raises questions, especially when it is considered in the light of Peter's later-recorded (Acts 10:10 ff)[42] predilection for dream/vision activities. Once again an examination of the Greek is illuminating, since the word usually translated as 'knowing' (ειδος), is strictly speaking, better translated as 'having seen,' which produces the seemingly nonsensical statement; "not having seen what he said." However, we have previously referred to the condition known as cross-modal perception or synesthesia,[43] which for a prolific dreamer like Peter in a dream/vision situation may have ('normally') caused him to see his own words. On this occasion (v.33) it was apparently remarkable that it did not happen.

Another aspect of this passage that might seem puzzling to modern, Western eyes is the shared nature of these dreams, since we find all three of the disciples engaging in the speech-action, at least insofar as concurrent visionary activity (vv. 30, 32) is concerned, and they were certainly all afraid (v. 34). But this too has precedent, with other examples including 'Adam' and 'Eve' (of course, see chapter 5), Elijah/Elisha in 1 Kings19:15 ff (see chapter 4) and also Samuel/Saul in 1 Sam 9:19–26.[44] Thus, in a surprising number of cases, we find the 'souls' (*nepheshim*) of the living meeting, and at the very least, coordinating with each other within altered states of consciousness outside the confines of the body. What then about meeting the 'souls' of the long-dead (Moses and Elijah) in an ASC: Is there precedent for this? Well, perhaps, since Saul even though estranged from God seems able to raise Samuel if only via the prohibited arts of the witch of Endor (1 Sam 28:7 ff). What does seem clear, however, is that there are no

---

41. Wallace, *Greek Grammar*, 623–27.

42. This visionary experience is of itself relevant to the discussion, since there would simply be no reason to mention Peter's hunger unless it was to convey that the vision was fasting-induced, as in "hunger and thirst for righteousness" (Matt 5:6).

43. "Synesthesia is the transmutation of sensory modalities, where sound may be seen or color experienced by the sense of smell and so on" (Goodman, "Serotonergic System," 265).

44. I have previously shown that this passage takes place primarily in an altered state of consciousness (Wilson, "Significance," 210–20).

occasions found anywhere else in scripture where both the *nepheshim* of the living and of the dead meet with each other.

In answer to the question originally posed, however, we may say that Jesus does take part in a dream (although not in the same way as Adam), albeit that this is the shared dream of the three disciples. Moreover, the disciples seem to be merely observers, with Peter unable to obtain a response to his offers of service, other than the final words spoken from the cloud. Jesus, later joined by Elijah and Moses, is portrayed entering Peter's dream God-like to be confirmed as such by the voice from the cloud, and in this regard Jesus is shown to be utterly different to every other prophet.

The Temptation—Matthew 4:1–11

The first thing we should note about this passage is that it takes place in the wilderness—often mistranslated in some versions (NIV and others) as the 'desert' and although the Judean desert can serve as a wilderness in the prophetic/shamanic understanding of this word, it is not desertification that is at issue here. Indeed, the wilderness and (ultimately) the mountain (Matt 4:8) are recognizable from Daur Mongol shamanic possession, where "the mountains, rocks and trees were not objects of worship, but rough, cold objects in the wilderness and the 'other world.'"[45] At this point I make no apology for re-introducing Eliade's comment—found in chapter four, since this is pertinent to the temptation narrative:

> 'Seeing' a spirit, either in dream or awake, is a certain sign that one has in some sort obtained a 'spiritual condition,' that is, that one has transcended the profane condition of humanity. . . . Among the Menangkabau of Sumatra the *dukun* complete their shamanic instruction in solitude, on a mountain; there they learn to become invisible and, at night, see the souls of the dead.[46]

The relationship between solitude and wilderness or mountain experiences on the one hand, and 'hiddenness,' 'darkness,' and 'seeing' on the other is brought out here. Indeed, the gospel writer appears to be aware that the seeking of solitude in wilderness or mountain can result in visionary experiences,

---

45. Humphrey with Onon, *Shamans and Elders*, 220. Humphrey appears to be describing the simultaneity of physically and literally running away into the 'wilderness' whilst mentally participating in distant events, indeed "the afflicted person ran to them (i.e. the cold objects of the wilderness) hid in them, *merged* with them" (Humphrey with Onon, *Shamans and Elders*, 220).

46. Eliade, *Shamanism*, 85–86.

and may be using this general, cultural awareness (shared with his readers) to illustrate and reinforce the dream or vision-quest nature of this encounter. Eliade can, moreover, emphatically affirm that shamans in pursuit of such vision quests actually become spirits; they are in fact effectively dead, and herein lies the significance of the temptation, for had Jesus, in the spirit, thrown himself off the temple pinnacle he would in all probability have remained dead, and being unable to return to his physical body his earthly mission would, as a consequence, have been aborted.

Secondly, and contemporaneous with his presence in the wilderness, we find Jesus fasting in the Matthean account for "forty days and forty nights," which may be viewed as a formulaic expression introducing or signifying a period of numinous encounter, and this is certainly the meaning of the term where it is found elsewhere in the Old Testament. The phrase appears twice in the Genesis account of the flood (Gen 7:4, 12), yet there appears to be little or no reference to dream/vision states. However, in the Gilgamesh Epic[47] account of the flood, Utnapishtim, Noah's counterpart, receives his instructions in a dream, and this is consistent with Islamic tradition which considers Noah to have been a prophet. Additionally, there are several occurrences of the 'forty days and forty nights' expression in Exodus and Deuteronomy most of which recount Moses in numinous experiences, with many of them featuring 'the mountain' of shamanic vision quest experience, together with fasting. The only other appearance of this phrase (apart from the Matthean account of the Temptation), is in 1 Kgs 19:8, and this also features 'the mountain (of God)' after Elijah takes his leave of the angel just prior to his long encounter with the LORD.

None of this is particularly new, the story of Jesus' testing having been cited as a shamanic vision quest before,[48] but the fasting does provide a pointer towards Jesus' depression, in the apparent absence of any depressive dreamform text (featuring Jesus as the dreamer). Depression, as previously outlined (chapter 3) is known to be a function of serotonin deficiency in the brain, and the production of serotonin is dependent on the non-destructive, absorption of the amino acid precursor, L-tryptophan by the stomach, followed by the subsequent, efficient, enzymatic processing of the absorbed amino acid in the brain. Clearly these processes will vary between individuals, and there is evidence to suggest that variations (abnormalities?)

---

47. Cuneiform Tablet 11/Gilgamesh Epic—1 of 12 tablets dating from 650 BC found in the ruins of Nineveh.

48. "The experience and successful passing of this test is . . . another step toward becoming a shaman: Jesus demonstrates that he has acquired the necessary ritual skills to deal with and control the spirit world" (Pilch, "Altered States of Consciousness," 109).

in serotonergic systems can occur from individual to individual.⁴⁹ Thus, it would be only natural to expect those who possess such an abnormal serotonergic 'make-up,' to be exceptionally prone to extreme physiological regimes (fasting) that can exacerbate such serotonergic deficiencies. Viewing depression as a natural propensity innate in human nature, but affecting some individuals more than others is therefore perfectly consistent with the genetic research on schizophrenia/ bipolar disorder reviewed in chapter one. In extreme cases, fasting-exacerbated depression can turn into what medics would label as psychotic depression,⁵⁰ leading to the numinous experiences characterized formulaically as "forty days and forty nights."

Jesus has therefore in this pericope been grouped with prophets who are fasted and arguably psychotic, and in the case of Elijah demonstrated to have been clinically depressed, by the cross-cultural methodology employed in this present work. Structurally, however, the Temptation story does not appear to display the dream/sleep/dream sequence of a depressed prophet, *unless this has been purposely omitted*, simply because it does not need restating in a cultural milieu that expects depressive dreaming to be present in a fasted, 'prophetic-type.'⁵¹ Consequently, if another means of linking this passage to the Elijah narrative could be found it would imply that the same depressive dream/sleep/dream sequence found there was likewise present in the Temptation story. In terms of content—apart from featuring both stones and bread—the two passages appear to bear little resemblance to each other, they do however, show great structural similarity. The Elijah story features three angelic visitations (albeit by 'angels' of different persuasions) or more properly messengers (Hebrew, mal'āk), the first one being the demon sent by the witch, Jezebel, to Elijah (1 Kgs 19:2), and this was followed by the sequential appearance of two angels of the LORD (vv 5, 7).⁵² This pattern is repeated in exactly the same, 3-part sequence in the Matthean narrative, where the devil ('fallen' angel) initiates Jesus' temptation, and this is followed by a reference to angels of (specifically) the Lord, before the passage closes with a visitation by ministering angels, which again implies (a second provision of bread⁵³ by a (third) angel, as in 1 Kgs 19:7. For the

49. Leonard, *Fundamentals*, 38.

50. See Fig. 1, 'Normality'/Psychosis Continuum, Chapter 1.

51. "All language derives its meaning from the social world. . . . Since these authors and their original readers (or listeners) shared this social world and were intimately familiar with it, there was no need for an author to spell out the obvious. . . . It is important to realize that . . . far more was left unsaid than in a modern Western context" (Pilch, "Transfiguration," 50).

52. See chapter 4.

53. Twelftree, "Temptation of Jesus," 825.

contemporary hearers or readers of this story the conclusion would seem to have been inescapable—Jesus was an archetypal prophet—a depressed dreamer just like Elijah.

Having begun this chapter by drawing attention to Paul's typological equation between Adam and Jesus, we were able to suggest from the methodology applied to Genesis 2–3 that Jesus was a prophet like Adam. It was noted that this would not have surprised many in Jesus' day, or indeed the later adherents of Islam who consider Jesus (*Isa*) to have been an important prophet. Moreover, Paul's comparison suggests that Jesus was also depressed, but it was unclear, whether this implication could be shown conclusively, despite that being the case with Adam, and most, if not all, of the prophets. An examination of the Matthean beatitudes in the light of certain Qumranic texts further revealed that Jesus was fully aware that depression was, indeed should continue to be, a much sought after feature of prophetic psychophysiology, and those who 'suffered' from it should consider themselves fortunate ($\mu\alpha\kappa\alpha\rho\iota o\varsigma$, *makarios*). The following 'salt and light' verses then went on to graphically illustrate the relative proportions of depressives to non-depressives within believing Israel. This ratio approximated to one percent giving good agreement with modern genetic research on the incidence (then as now) of schizophrenia and bipolar disorder, and dateable to approximately 80,000 years BP.

Next an examination of the transfiguration was undertaken in an attempt to seek supporting information concerning depressive dreaming in respect of Jesus. This was unsuccessful for two reasons: Firstly, Luke's precise information established that despite being dreamform, the derived, etic hypnogram produced did not include an elongated first dream, which is characteristic for the dreaming of a depressive. Secondly, and more importantly, the dreams are not those of Jesus who featured in them as, or in the place of, God, and were more properly the dreams/hypnopompic experiences of the disciples, chiefly that of Peter.

Finally, the temptation revealed Jesus engaging in a wilderness vision-quest, which featured a long period of fasting—acknowledged to be an ascetic practice known to "create a physical precondition for mystical states in the context of spiritual practice."[54] Serotonin deficiency resulting from a failure through fasting to absorb the serotonin precursor, L-Tryptophan (only available to the body by the ingestion of food, especially carbohydrates), can give rise to entry into vision and encounter with the denizens of the extended reality. All this occurred in classic prophet/shaman manner to an individual, Jesus, who like the prophets before him,

---

54. Clarke, "Psychosis and Spirituality," 139.

may have been genetically pre-disposed to 'benefit' from it. Although, the Matthean account of the Temptation does not feature depressive dreaming as such, it was found to closely follow the sequence found in 1 Kgs, 19:2–8, where Elijah has three numinous encounters. Indeed, both accounts were found to contain three angelic (messenger) encounters, the first of which was demonic/diabolic, followed by two further encounters with, or reference to, angels of the LORD/Lord, and this suggests that the Temptation story is intentionally patterned on Elijah's dream sequence. Moreover, each of Elijah's angelic encounters takes place in a separate dream—the first of which is characteristically that of a depressed dreamer—further suggesting that this pattern is also true for the Temptation narrative, and that Jesus was likewise depressed. Significantly, however, we find Jesus in a situation never previously encountered in the prophets, for Jesus contends with and vanquishes beelzebul (the devil) directly, as quite distinct from Elijah's encounter with and suppression of Jezebel's demon. In summation we can say that Jesus has been compared by Paul and Matthew respectively to two depressed dreamers (Adam and Elijah) from Israel's scriptures, and if a third such comparison can be found it must surely amount to conclusive evidence that Jesus was a depressed dreamer or—in modern medical parlance—clinically depressed.

7

"One Greater Than . . ."

IN THE PREVIOUS CHAPTER the comparative discussion of the Matthean beatitudes produced a number of interesting insights, amongst which was the suggestion that Jesus himself was not unfamiliar with depression and its mystical and spiritual outcomes. Indeed, the suggestion that Jesus was amongst the 'fortunate' few who were personally familiar with ascetic physiological practice (fasting) and its mystico-spiritual effects was supported and reinforced by the Temptation passage found in both Matthew and Luke. Moreover, Peter's proclivity for altered state experiences (dreams) was also demonstrated in our examination of the Transfiguration (Luke 9:28–36), and his acquaintance with fasting-enhanced (depressive) dreaming was noted by reference to the passage beginning at Acts 10:10. Thus, collecting these thoughts together we are compelled to ask: Is it possible to conclude that Peter was also one of the 'fortunate few' and can we find any evidence in support of such a proposition?

Interestingly, Matthew records Jesus applying to Peter the exact same accolade used in the beatitudes ($\mu\alpha\kappa\alpha\rho\iota o\varsigma$, 'fortunate'), in a passage (Peter's declaration about Jesus, Matt 16:15–20) subsequently used to support the "claim to the primacy of the bishop of Rome."[1] This claim, emblazoned as crossed-keys on the armorial bearings of the Vatican, suggests that whatever attribute Peter had that made him 'fortunate' was subsequently the sole preserve of the church of Rome. But perhaps a better explanation of Peter's 'fortunate' status might be in terms of fasting-enhanced, mystico-spiritual, altered states—dreams in particular, and here we are presented with a clue. It comes in the form of the address (Matt 16:17) given to Peter by Jesus: "Blessed are you, Simon son of Jonah!" Previously, this address has been explained in a number of different ways: Firstly, and straightforwardly on the basis of Peter's patriarchal origins, that is, his father's name was Jonah, Jona or John. Secondly, it is mooted to be an idiomatic form of Jewish address, presumably something similar to 'John Doe,' but amongst all the

---

1. France, *Gospel According to Matthew*, 253.

explanations there are few attempts to explain the expression either on the basis of some attribute shared by Peter and the Hebrew prophet, or (and this amounts to the same thing) an 'inherited feature' of Jonah's life.

Certainly, whatever this attribute is it allows Peter to receive direct revelation from God (v. 17), and it will apparently enable Peter to be the 'rock,' or foundation of the church (community), although it does not refer to physical, intellectual or volitional strength (v. 18), as this is roundly refuted by Peter's later exploits. It seems to involve Peter's receipt of the "keys of the kingdom" (v. 19), which has previously been understood to mean divinely delegated authority in the church to 'bind' and to 'loose,' terms better expressed as forbid or allow. Perhaps the best insight into the meaning of these terms is the final one in France's commentary on this verse, where he can say "Peter will pass on decisions that have already been made in heaven."[2] This is tantamount to saying that Peter is a prophet, a dreamer of dreams who encounters God, and perhaps this is the attribute that renders Peter 'fortunate?'

The Sign of Jonah: Luke 11:29–32

The 'sign of Jonah' sits uneasily amongst the "Q" sayings transmitted by Luke and must of necessity require an explication in terms of the material recorded in the book of Jonah, and in pursuit of this aim understand how and in what way Peter may be confirmed a prophet in Jonah's mould. More importantly, however, the book of Jonah holds the key to how Jesus may be better understood relative to the prophet Jonah. Accordingly, we will attempt a fresh look at that material following a brief excursus into the Lucan preamble (Luke 11:27–28) to the pericope proper, and the request for a sign (Luke 11:16). The results of that examination can then be applied to the comparison drawn by Luke between Jesus and Jonah, with a view to 'fleshing-out' what an implied and hypothetical 'sign of Jesus' might comprise.

In attempting an exegesis of the 'sign of Jonah' passage (Luke 11:29–32) it may prove illuminating to examine firstly Luke's seemingly motiveless insertion of non-"Q" material (vv. 27–28) immediately before the pericope proper. Fitzmyer suggests that the 'word of God' (τον λογον του θεου) found in v. 28 is to be identified with Jesus' preaching and wisdom,[3] and Luke certainly appears to have equated Jesus' 'word' with the 'word of God' (cf. Luke 5:1). This material (vv. 27–28) is peculiar to Luke and some have considered it to be a "possibility, and even a probability, that

---

2. France, *Gospel According to Matthew*, 256.
3. Fitzmyer, *Gospel According to Luke*, 934.

the expression "Word of God" was introduced here by Lk.," rather than drawing the "conclusion that Jesus Himself actually used the word and applied it to His own preaching."[4] An acceptance of this view demands that an attempt be made at understanding the motivation for Luke's insertion of these verses here, about which Fitzmyer acknowledges that they are a puzzling interruption of Luke's use of the previous "Q" material.[5] The λογος sayings in the New Testament are generally based on LXX perceptions of the Hebrew equivalents, and the LXX uses λογος and ρημα as synonyms in a manner that "can be fully understood only against the background of the Hebrew דבר"[6] Thus, "τον λογον του θεου" is to be understood in terms of its relationship to the Hebrew equivalent דבר אלהים (Word of God) and its counterpart the דבר והיה (Word of YHWH).[7] The idea conveyed by these underlying, construct, Hebrew expressions is considerably stronger than the simple, genitive found in the Greek phrase, indeed the use of the construct state is effectively a statement that a single, unified concept or entity is in view here. Understood in terms of the force of the underlying Hebrew, 'τον λογον του θεου' is indicating that 'Word' is inseparable from 'God,' and as a consequence both terms—as a single, unified concept—are inseparable from, and originate in the person (Jesus) who utters the 'Word.' In short, Luke could be suggesting from his use of this phrase that God is present to Jesus, or to put it another way, Jesus is (a man) possessed[8] by God, that is, he is a 'man of God,'[9] and Luke may be presenting this as a possibility in order to expand on it in what follows.

Thus the prospect presented to Luke's readers (by v. 28) is that Jesus could be such a "Divine man"—an identification which, if correct, the content of the following pericope should support. If indeed the full force of the Hebrew expression דבר יהוה underpins "τον λογον του θεου" then Fitzmyer's suggestion that Jesus' wisdom is equivalent to the 'word of God,' rings true, and resonance with the terms דבר יהוה and איש אלהים—especially

---

4. Kittel, "Word and Speech," 121.
5. Fitzmyer, *Gospel According to Luke*, 926.
6. Procksch, "Word of God," 92–93.
7. Ames, "דבר," 913.
8. Bourguignon's cross-cultural research acknowledges the existence of lifelong (non-trance) possession, that is, a symbiotic relationship with divinity that is distinct from shamanic possession trance (Bourguignon, *Possession*, 46).
9. The Hebrew term 'man of God' (איש אלהים) is another construct state expression the force of which fails to be conveyed by the English genitive. Indeed, in Hallevy's estimation an איש אלהים possesses "something of the nature of the divinity," enabling him to describe Elijah as a "Divine Man . . . endowed with superhuman, divine qualities and powers" (Hallevy, "Man of God," 237).

the latter—ought to be found in the pericope proper. On examination, however, the term 'man of God' is clearly not found, and Solomon despite being endowed with the gift of wisdom is only a man, whilst to Matthew alone falls the task of labeling Jonah "a prophet" (Matt 12:39). At this point it may be observed that the Hebrew term for 'prophet' (נביא, *nabi*) is most frequently translated as προφητης—the word used by Matthew, but the term נביא is in many cases used as a supplementary, post-exilic, editorial overlay for much older terms such as איש אלהים.[10] Clearly, a more thoroughgoing examination of the person of Jonah is required—a task that is made all the more difficult by the fact that neither נביא nor איש אלהים are mentioned in the book of Jonah!

Fitzmyer suggests that the 'sign' requested by the onlookers (11:16) was some kind of "flamboyant manifestation"[11] similar to the description of Jesus' third temptation in Luke 4:9–11. But any such sign would only have to combine the two essential factors of a sign (σημειον, *sémeion*), that is, "sense perception and confirmation," such that "those who observe it may draw assured conclusions."[12] These criteria would have to apply to both the observers' expectations and Jesus' own 'sign of Jonah,' in order to comply with this generally accepted understanding of *sémeion*.[13] To put it another way a sign (*sémeion*) on either view would have to be a visual, or perhaps aural phenomenon. Many scholars have elected for the latter sense perception, as for example Marshall, who's view from the outset is that the two statements in vv. 31 and 32 contrast the preaching of "two OT preachers" (Solomon and Jonah) with "the message of one who is superior,"[14] and therefore that the 'sign' consists in preaching. But can one look elsewhere for the essential difference between what the crowd expected, what Jonah was, and what Jesus will be (or has already been?) displaying?

---

10. Auld can say that "It seems unlikely that earlier designations of these figures were suppressed by later tradition. The evidence suggests refinement by supplementation, rather than alteration or suppression of terminology already in our texts" (Auld, "Prophets," 14).

11. Fitzmyer, *Gospel According to Luke*, 933.

12. Rengstorf, "σημειον in the New Testament," 231–32.

13. Nolland has suggested that Luke had already shown Jesus demonstrating such a sign in his exorcism, which was visible, subject to confirmation and manifestly unambiguous insofar as it was "against the interests of the forces of evil" (Nolland, *Luke 9:21—18:34*, 638).

14. Marshall, *Gospel of Luke*, 483.

The Sign

As an aural phenomenon the preaching of Jonah seems unlikely because of its very brevity to qualify as a sign, and although Landes favors treating Jonah's judgment proclamation in 3:4 rather than Jonah's sojourn in the fish (Jonah 2) as the "more likely definition of the 'sign of Jonah' in Luke,"[15] he observes that many scholars believe the latter on the grounds that Jonah must have been authenticated in some way prior to arrival in the city. Indeed, "why else would the Ninevites—both instantaneously and unanimously (Jonah 3.5)—believe Jonah when he predicted their demise within forty days?"[16] Clearly, this interpretation has the advantage of having a measure of agreement with the material in Matthew 12:40, but fails to account for how the Ninevites had acquired information about Jonah's piscatorial adventures. If, however, the preaching of Jonah as an aural 'sign,' and the fishy sojourn as divine validation are both discounted, but the idea of Jonah's prior authentication is still retained, can the text of Jonah offer an alternative aural/visual phenomenon capable of serving as the σημειον Ιωνα? Moreover, if the idea of prior authentication is allied to the view that Jonah himself is the 'sign,' then the text (Jonah 3) should be searched for some behavioral (audio-visual) feature of Jonah that would serve as a sign. Luke's simile then leads us naturally to look for a similar behavioral/audio-visual feature of Jesus' future (or past?) activities that would lead his hearers to draw assured conclusions. Certainly, a number of scholars seem compelled to the view that 'σημειον Ιωνα'—a genitive of apposition—is indicating that "the sign is Jonah himself,"[17] or that v. 30 as it originally "stood in "Q" . . . would have to refer to the person of Jonah."[18] Indeed, "taking the text of Lk. 11.30a at its face value, . . . would seem to convey that Jonah himself, in his own person and presence, was a sign to the Ninevites."[19] Thus, it will be necessary to closely examine the text of Jonah 3 (with special emphasis on 3:1–5a from a cross-cultural viewpoint), in order to demonstrate that behavioral aspects of the person of Jonah are of paramount significance to any satisfactory exegesis of Luke 11:29–30. The text of Jonah 3 will therefore be examined from a number of other disciplinary perspectives in furtherance of this aim.

15. Landes, "Jonah in Luke," 158.
16. Landes, "Jonah in Luke," 136.
17. Swetnam, "Some Signs of Jonah," 76.
18. Fitzmyer, *Gospel According to Luke*, 933.
19. Landes, "Jonah in Luke," 141.

Any examination of the text of Jonah 3 should be set in the context of the structure of the book as a whole, which has been regarded as divided into three segments by the insertion of two scribal marks (*setûmā'* [ס]) in the text. Indeed, the threefold, Masoretic division of Jonah's narrative predates the medieval division of the book into four chapters, and because of its duplication at Qumran, this suggests to Sasson a textual tradition that antedates the second century BC.[20] In Sasson's view the first division of the Jonah narrative (1:1—2:10) corresponds with a downward movement, the second division (2:11—4:3) being horizontal and the third having "no spatial movement,"[21] but this view fails to fully account for what is effectively the isolation of 2:11 within the narrative. The latter verse is bounded on either side by scribal marks; at the beginning by the first *setûmā'*, and at the end by a another scribal mark (a *petûḥa'* [פ])—the only one of its kind in the book. It has been argued elsewhere[22] that 2:11 corresponds to a hypnopompic, altered state of consciousness,[23] which is experienced by Jonah just prior to becoming fully awake after a night spent dreaming. Thus, in the ejaculation from the fish (v. 11) Jonah is in fact undergoing the slow process of exiting his dreamy state, and one may imagine him finally jerking awake in a cold sweat following his harrowing experiences of the night.

The significance of viewing the first two chapters of *Jonah* as a sequence of dreams lies in the relationship between dreaming and other psychophysiologically related altered states of consciousness—in particular (yogic or transcendental) meditation.[24] Support for the contention that yogic or transcendental meditation is related to dreaming can be found in some modern studies on meditation, as well as traditional teachings, and the dreams of meditators. The latter were found to contain "significantly more archetypal elements (reflecting universal moral themes), than those of the non-meditators, which were characterized by personal and everyday

---

20. Sasson, *Jonah*, 270–71.

21. Sasson, *Jonah*, 271.

22. See Appendix.

23. It may be helpful to enumerate the various different altered states of consciousness and a useful list is reproduced by Pilch from Krippner (1972) including: "dreaming, sleeping, hypnagogic (drowsiness before sleep), hypnopompic (semiconsciousness preceding waking), hyperalert, lethargic, rapture, hysteric, fragmentation, regressive, meditative, trance, reverie, daydreaming, internal scanning, stupor, coma, stored memory, expanded consciousness, and 'normal'" (Pilch, "Altered States," 106).

24. It is pertinent in this regard to note that the meditative states employed by mystics are said to involve deafferentation, in which the brain's orientation area is deprived of neural input—effectively a serotonergic/ aminergic deficit condition (See Newberg et al., *Why God Won't Go Away*, 114). Serotonin (5HT) deficit is likewise a feature of REM (rapid eye movement) or 'dreaming' sleep (Leonard, *Fundamentals*, 175).

issues."²⁵ In this regard it seems clear that the 'poem' of Jonah 2:3–10, despite its more bizarre features, depicts the serious matter of Jonah's relationship with YHWH, set against a background in which the entire cosmology of the Ancient Near East²⁶ is drawn. Thus, on the basis that these two altered states of consciousness (dreaming and meditation) are related, two questions present themselves to the reader: Firstly, does Jonah meditate, and secondly, does he do so at the beginning of chapter three? Effectively, these two questions condense to a single question the answer to which lies in demonstrating that the early part of chapter three shows Jonah to be in an altered (meditative) state of consciousness.

Acceptance that Jonah 1:1—2:10 is a dream/sleep/dream/sleep sequence that culminates in a hypnopompic ASC (2:11) invites the idea that Jonah never left home, and awoke to find himself at home in Gath-Hepher in northern Israel (2 Kings 14:25²⁷), yet still apparently receiving from YHWH within an altered state of consciousness (ASC). This invites the question: What would be the nature of this third type of ASC that immediately follows the dreaming and hynopompia of the previous two chapters? The first sure indication that Jonah is in a meditative ASC does not come until 3:3b where the reader finds a parenthetical insert by the narrator. Certainly, in Sasson's view v. 3b is a parenthetical inclusio²⁸ in a sequence of activities spanning vv. 2–4—a sequence that should not in his view be arrested or disturbed.²⁹ The first of the two couplets in this inclusio tends to be treated by some scholars as an indication of the size³⁰ or importance³¹ of Nineveh, but it is the second of the two that has commanded the most scholastic attention. This couplet 'a three days journey' (מהלך שלשת ימים) is the more difficult to interpret, and most commentators consider it refers in some way to the

---

25. Murphy and Donovan, *Physical*, 141. Parenthesis added.

26. Marinatos, "The Cosmic Journey," 391.

27. A significant body of opinion favours treating the *Jonah ben Amittai* of 2 Kings 14:25 as related to the book of Jonah. Indeed, Sasson asserts "it is beyond probability that in Scripture two different individuals would bear the same names and patronyms" (Sasson, *Jonah*, 342).

28. So also Wiseman, "Jonah's Nineveh," 36.

29. Sasson, *Jonah*, 228.

30. Marcus thinks a superlative is in play here, which may render עיר־גדולה לאלהים as "an exceptionally big city" or more colloquially as "a godawfully big city" (Marcus, *From Balaam to Jonah*, 101–2).

31. Stuart argues that the phrase indicates Nineveh's importance to God (Stuart, *Hosea–Jonah*, 483).

dimensions of Nineveh, either the city's diameter,[32] circumference[33] or layout.[34] Stuart, following Wiseman favors the view that "a walk of three days" refers to the total duration of Jonah's visit to Nineveh, and includes one day each for arrival, purpose/business, and departure.[35] It is probably correct to accept with Sasson that the latter, minority view has "no merit," whilst noting that Sasson still finds common ground with Stuart on the nature of מהלך as a measure of duration or time, observing that "*mahalak* is not a standard linear measure."[36] Thus far, the narration has indicated Jonah's compliance with YHWH's instruction (v. 3a)—perhaps locating the prophet in Gath-Hepher at the beginning of his journey,[37] followed by a brief parenthetical excursus on the nature of Nineveh and some 'measure' of duration or time associated with it (v. 3b). This appears to be followed by Jonah's actual transit to, and entry into Nineveh (v. 4a), since the Hebrew expression ויחל יונה לבו בעיר (began to enter the city) normally connotes arrival[38]—in this case Jonah's. The content of the parenthesis (v. 3b), therefore, appears to be providing a reference point with which Jonah's subsequent behavior (vv. 4–5) may be compared—the reader being invited initially to compare the normal transit time to Nineveh (v. 3b) with Jonah's ability to "cover this great distance "lickety split" or in an exceptionally short amount of time"[39] (v. 4a). To put it a little more succinctly the reader is being invited to draw a comparison between a long transit time and a short transit time to Nineveh,

---

32. Both Wolff and Sasson translate in this way (Wolff, *Obadiah and Jonah*, 143; Sasson, *Jonah*, 224).

33. A typical day's walk of about 17 miles gives a circumference for the city of over 50 miles—a figure wholly inconsistent with Sennacherib's enlargement (assumed to give a circumference of 7.5 miles). Moreover, Wiseman observes; "I do not know of any description of the size of an ancient city by the circuit of its walls" (Wiseman, "Jonah's Nineveh," 37).

34. Simon exemplifies the view that מהלך שלשת ימים refers to the duration required to cross the city street by street repeating the proclamation of v. 4, which implies that Jonah "proclaimed his message in only one third of the city" (Simon, *JPS Bible Commentary: Jonah*, 28).

35. Stuart, *Hosea–Jonah*, 487.

36. Sasson, *Jonah*, 230.

37. Marcus writes, "The language indicating Jonah's compliance is formulated precisely like that of the command (קוּם לֵךְ אֶל־נִינְוֵה v. 2 // בִּדְבַר יְהוָה v. 3; דְבַר־יְהוָה v. 1 // וַיָּקָם יוֹנָה וַיֵּלֶךְ אֶל־נִינְוֵה v. 3). The force of this statement of Jonah's departure to Nineveh is that of an anticipatory exposition common with descriptions of departure elsewhere in the Bible (e.g. Gen 22:3; 24:10; 28:5; 1 Kgs 17:10). These verses describe reports of departures to a place before the individual arrives there" (Marcus, "Nineveh's 'Three Days' Walk,'" 48–49).

38. Marcus, "Nineveh's 'Three Days' Walk,'" 44.

39. Marcus, "Nineveh's 'Three Days' Walk,'" 47.

where the phrases "a three days' walk" and "a one day's walk" are here being used "figuratively,"[40] that is, in a general or non-quantitative manner.[41]

In Marcus' view *Jonah* is written as a satire and the import of Jonah's fast transit to Nineveh lies in it being a "parodic emulation"[42] of the fast transit (run) of the Divine Man, Elijah (an 'אישׁ אלהים', 1 Kgs 17:18, 24), from Mount Carmel to Jezreel—a distance of eighteen miles. But Elijah's feat can be explained in terms of *lung gom pa*[43] or 'trance' running, where the subject takes "extraordinarily long tramps with amazing rapidity," but which consist in "wonderful endurance rather than . . . momentary extreme fleetness."[44] Such 'trance' runs[45] are invariably undertaken in a state of possession wherein the subject tramps "at a rapid pace and without stopping during several successive days and nights."[46] These runners are able to cover immense distances in a swift, leaping gait whilst alone and in a quiet, ASC that cannot be interrupted.[47] It is interesting that David-Neel's informant avers that to break into their meditation would cause the "god who is in them" to escape, with the result that "he shakes them so hard that they die."[48] Clearly, an immense distance could be covered in this manner, and even the distance between Gath-Hepher and Nineveh (approximately 500 miles) could be accomplished, especially if a more direct, overland route was taken. Jonah's arrival in Nineveh at the end of such a 'trance' run[49] might

---

40. Marcus, "Nineveh's 'Three Days' Walk,'" 45.

41. M. Sæbø acknowledges that the plural (ימים), which is introduced in the parenthesis (v. 3b) before the singular of v. 4a, can "move in the direction of a general (and abstract) notion of time" (Sæbø, "יום," 22). If it is accepted that a notion of 'time' in a general sense is intended here (v. 3b), then it could be seen to be qualified in construct with שׁלשׁ relative to the phrase immediately following (מהלך יום אחד) in v. 4a.

42. Marcus, "Nineveh's 'Three Days' Walk,'" 47.

43. David-Neel, *Magic and Mystery*, 184.

44. David-Neel, *Magic and Mystery*, 184.

45. David-Neel affirms that 'trance' or *lung gom pa* running is a meditative state (David-Neel, *Magic and Mystery*, 186).

46. David-Neel, *Magic and Mystery*, 185.

47. This may well be at the root of Obadiah's expressed fears about Elijah in 1 Kings 18:12: "As soon as I have gone from you, the spirit of the LORD will carry you I know not where."

48. David-Neel, *Magic and Mystery*, 186.

49. Clearly, this is to take the position that *Jonah* 3 actually treats with an historical event, yet it is often pointed out that the very title 'king of Nineveh' is invalid in the context of an Assyrian empire. But this objection can be overcome if one accepts with Ferguson that the 'king' of Nineveh was one of a number of provincial governors "paying lip service to the Assyrian king," in a politically unstable period (781–745 BC) during which the "Assyrian empire almost passed out of existence" (Ferguson, "Who Was the King," 311). See also Lemanski who concurs with Brinkman in restating that

be seen by the 'religious' Ninevites as a sign of his possession—a sign giving divine authority to any subsequent utterances. Indeed, the appearance of Jonah seen 'running' towards the city walls from afar at an unnatural pace would be behavior indicative of an altered (meditative) state of consciousness—the very essence of a (visibly) possessed Divine Man (איש אלהים).[50] Such behavior would help to explain the otherwise curious efficacy of his brief announcement: "Forty days more, and Nineveh shall be overthrown!" Consequently, it is suggested that it is the behavior of Jonah (running in 'trance'), which constitutes the 'sign of Jonah'—an unnatural, visible phenomenon first perceived from afar by the men[51] of Nineveh (v. 5a) as they sat debating in the gate. Presented with this sign of the presence of God in a possessed man the men of Nineveh would quite naturally believe/trust God (v. 5a), as quite distinct from Jonah (the man), or even God's word.[52]

The 'Sign of Jesus'

As noted earlier, Luke, in the seemingly motiveless preamble to this pericope (the non-"Q" material of vv. 27–28) appears to be suggesting that Jesus is a man possessed by God—a Divine Man (איש אלהים) who speaks the 'Word of God.' This idea is then substantiated and reinforced on entry to the pericope proper if the "sign of Jonah" (v. 29) is understood (cross-culturally) as a reference to another Divine Man, Jonah, who displayed all the features of possession by 'God'[53] to the Ninevites. We know that comparisons had al-

---

"this (772–745 B.C.) was a period of local autonomy in Assyrian regions as well as in Babylonia" (Brinkman, "Political History," 218 and Lemanski, "Jonah's Nineveh," 46).

50. "Someone endowed with superhuman, divine qualities and powers: possessing something of the nature of the divinity" (Hallevy, "Man of God," 237).

51. Nolland makes the comment that "the use of the term ανδρων, "men," rather than ανθρωπων," "people/ human beings," is a linguistic reflection of the male domination of public life in the ancient world" (Nolland, *Luke 9:21—18:34*, 654). But the use of ανδρων merely reflects the 'matter of fact,' topographical use of אנשי in the original Jonah story (Jonah 3:4-5), since it would be the אנשי נינוה 'the men of Nineveh' who would be the first to see Jonah from afar as they sat in the city gate. The city gate had for long (from village times in fact) been a place of counsel, debate and judgement (see Prov 31:23) by the local elders, and as such the men of the town/city would be the first to see any newcomers (Borowski, *Daily Life*, 21). Quite simply, it was only the men of Nineveh who saw the sign of Jonah! Significantly, the narrator of Jonah changes this to the more generic (and thereby inclusive) term for mankind, 'אדם,' in Jonah 3:7 when this is topographically more appropriate.

52. "We are not told that the Ninevites believed "the word"" (Wolff, *Obadiah and Jonah*, 150).

53. The term אלהים (Jonah 3:5) may simply be the application of a designatory or titular status to the Ninevites' own personal deity. Ringgren cites Micah 4:5; and Jonah

ready been made between Jesus and another איש אלהים, Elijah, (Luke 9:19) who likewise appears also to have been equated with John the Baptist. Luke's readership entering v. 30 with these equations firmly in place, and knowledge of the full significance of the "sign of Jonah"—as contended above—are met immediately with a further equation between Jesus and Jonah. But now, having established these equations, Luke records Jesus' own deconstruction of them (Jonah in particular) as categories for his own self-understanding and for the understanding of his hearers.

Jesus' deconstruction of this equivalence with the divinely, possessed man, Jonah, begins in v. 31 where the order of the 'queen of the South' saying is different to that found in Matthew (12:42). Fitzmyer observes that the "saying about the Queen of the South is found in both Matthew and Luke" and must therefore have been in "Q," but he adds that "it is intrusive in the story about the sign of Jonah," before going on to moot the likelihood that "it could have been uttered independently by Jesus on another occasion,"[54] after which it was brought into topical alignment when "Q" was being formed. Nevertheless, he accepts the possibility that the topical arrangement may stem from Jesus himself.[55] The order can only be of importance if the emphasis of the reports of the two evangelists lies in different places. In Luke's view there appears to be an escalation of superlatives involved, and this begins in v. 31 with Jesus' statement that "something greater than Solomon is here" (NRSV), since the "something greater" is not only greater than a king, but a king of legendary greatness who was gifted by God. This progression of superlatives continues as Luke returns to Jonah (v. 32), where the great and God-gifted king is surpassed by the Divine Man, Jonah. It seems that for Luke the "something greater" has surpassed both the greatest of men and (arguably) one of the greatest of Divine Men.[56] Significantly, "the twice repeated "here" (*hōde*) even hints at a geographical interpretation of the passage," insofar as these sayings (vv. 29–32) may have originated with Jesus and his early followers in the Galilee, where "it is likely that Jonah was venerated . . . as a local hero."[57]

In recording the deconstruction of the presented equivalence of Jesus with Jonah, the איש אלהים, Luke has created something of a *non sequitur* for his readers, and has compelled them to address the question: How is it

---

1:5 as examples of 'אלהים' used in this sense (Ringgren, "אלהים," 276).

54. Fitzmyer, *Gospel According to Luke*, 931.

55. Fitzmyer, *Gospel According to Luke*, 931.

56. This requires something of a re-evaluation of the status of Jonah within the Hebrew canon. See Appendix.

57. Reed, "Sign of Jonah," 136.

possible to be "something greater" than a divinely (and permanently) possessed man? Since Jesus exceeds Jonah—to whom God was present—the only way to exceed the presence of God (in a man) would seem to be the presence of God as a man, and the statement in 11:32 is effectively a Lucan parallel to the Johanine "making himself equal with God" (John 5:18). Thus, in terms of the categories of this pre-modern culture v. 32 is a comparatively clear statement of Jesus' divinity, but this begs the further question of how that divinity is displayed: What was the 'sign of Jesus?' In this regard, it has been said that "no one should attempt to use . . . the miracles as proof of Jesus' divinity . . . similar miracles have been attributed to many besides Jesus,"[58] and this is certainly true, but it may be that the 'sign of Jesus' had much more to do with the scope, prolificacy, and magnitude of Jesus' miracles compared to those of the men of God (אנשי אלהים). This may be the point that Luke is making in 9:19 when Elijah is introduced as a potential 'category' within which Jesus may be classified. In this verse Elijah, John the Baptist and the ancient prophets are reported as alternative models for Jesus in "the general public opinion of him,"[59] and the reader knows that Elijah—the feeder of three (1 Kgs 17:11–16)—has clearly been introduced at a point in Luke's account immediately following Jesus' feeding of five thousand. Elijah is an איש אלהים (1 Kgs 17:18, 24)—a status claimed here for Jonah, and he is likewise relegated in status (relative to Jesus) by his seeming equivalence to John the Baptist who was 'not worthy to untie the thong' of Jesus' sandals (Luke 3:16).

Returning to the theme of a possible 'sign of Jesus,' and having already mooted the possibility that this may involve superlatives by comparison with the earlier prophets one is still left somewhat dissatisfied. Indeed, the foregoing discussion of Landes' suggestion[60] that Jonah himself was the sign to the Ninevites would seem to point to any 'sign of Jesus' likewise consisting in Jesus' own person and presence. But how, and in what way might that sign be given, as Luke reports Jesus plainly states it will (or indeed, might be suggesting may already have been given, v. 29?)? Is it possible that Jesus' sign would consist in *lung gom pa* or spirit running as claimed here for Jonah?[61] Certainly, a comparable (and surpassing) feat may have occurred when the walk across the Sea of Galilee (recorded in Mark 6:48) took place, but this happened in private, and would by no means satisfy Jesus' hearers on this occasion. But a sign of a similar ilk to Jonah's would most definitely have

---

58. Dunn, *Jesus and the Spirit*, 74.
59. Wright, *Jesus and the Victory*, 529.
60. Landes, "Jonah in Luke," 141.
61. See Appendix: "The Second Mission."

been in the minds of his hearers (v. 29) when Luke has him proclaim that no sign would be given save the "sign of Jonah."

Having previously suggested that Jesus may already have given such a sign, it might prove helpful at this point to revisit the Temptation narrative, but this time to take a close look at the Lucan account. In terms of its structure Luke's account agrees closely with Matthew's, if only insofar as it features the same 3 sequences of speech/action, which closely parallel the first three dreams in the Elijah narrative.[62] There are of course four speech/action sequences or rather dreams found in I Kgs. 19:2-21, and both the Lucan and Matthean accounts mirror these with the exception of the fourth dream. Elijah's fourth dream involves direct encounter with God on Horeb, and both of the fuller (i.e. excluding Mark) Temptation accounts appear to be making the point (by omission) that the divine prophet, Jesus, is not as other prophets, insofar as encounter with God is redundant! Thus, for both Matthew and Luke Jesus' dream sequence ends after the third dream, at which point Matthew concludes his account.

Luke, however, follows the final dream of this (Elijah modeled) dream sequence in a surprising way by recording that Jesus immediately commences a spirit-run of 60-80 miles from the Judean wilderness to Galilee. In so doing, Jesus is replicating another great spirit-run, that of Jonah, which began immediately after Jonah's final dream (Jonah 3:1ff),[63] and which involved a transition from one ASC (dream) to another ASC (meditative spirit-run). In like manner to Jonah, this spirit-run manifestly establishes Jesus' authority as a prophet (a man of God), throughout all the surrounding region, and prior to entry into the Galilee. Here we may note that most commentators consider this verse (Luke 4:14) all of a piece with v.15, and therefore concerned with Jesus' teaching in the synagogues, rather than it recording a visible sign in his own person pre-establishing his authority throughout Samaria and the Galilee, prior to his teaching ministry.[64]

Interestingly, Matthew's account of the 'sign of Jonah' has Jesus speaking of Jonah's three-day visit to the underworld (Matt 12:40), with its veiled allusion to his own anticipated experience. Clearly, Jesus' death and resurrection would qualify as a 'sign of Jesus' in his own person and

---

62. See chapter 4.

63. See Appendix: "The Second Mission."

64. Turner in paralleling Luke 4:14 with 4:36-37 where "the power of Jesus is immediately followed by an affirmation that report of him went out into the whole surrounding countryside," is implicitly confirming that in 4:14 a visible sign enabled by Spirit-empowerment, immediately resulted in news of Jesus spreading, and prior to the commencement of his teaching ministry in the Galilee (Turner, *Power from on High*, 210-11).

presence, whilst any implied allusion to Jonah's running might amount to one component of an intentional and elegant *double entendre* that could prevent any premature, public release of that information. In support of the Matthean account, one is obliged to say that Jesus' resurrection from the dead is the only 'sign' that could exceed that of Jonah, since Jonah's *lung gom pa* or spirit-run far exceeded that of Jesus by nearly 500 miles! It follows that Jesus' words, "and behold, a greater than Jonas is here" (Luke 11:32 KJV), would of course, only serve to confound and confuse (some of) his hearers even further! For the purposes of this present work, however, Luke's comparison between Jesus and Jonah provides a final piece of evidence to add to that of Paul and Matthew, in full confirmation that Jesus was a depressed dreamer—this time in like manner to Jonah, on the basis that Jonah like Adam and Elijah has been shown to be clinically depressed.[65]

---

65. See Appendix: "The Proclamation of a Fast."

8

Conclusions: Depression and the Divine

IN THE FIRST CHAPTER of this book a number of possibilities, even probabilities, concerning the prehistory of early modern humans following the 'out-of-Africa' diaspora were mooted. It was suggested that formulaic oral traditions begun in the mists of prehistoric antiquity could have reached the earliest stages of the compilation of written texts, without significant deformation having taken place. Indeed, those early oral traditions could have included vivid depressive dreams, since the genes associated with schizophrenia and bipolar disorder were in place at this time (65–80,000 years BP), and the co-development of fully fluent human speech meant that dream content could be passed on intergenerationally, formulaically, and without error. Thus, the possibility was raised that the Genesis 2–3 account could be a single, unified account of a very ancient dream or dreams, and that this was at least (anecdotally) consistent with the Australian, aboriginal accounts of creation—'the Dreamtime.' It was, however, noted that form or structural evidence of depressive dreaming would be needed before this view could be supported.

Past approaches to the text of Genesis 2:4b—3:24 have recognized a unified story in the paradise/fall narrative only on a literary level, and irrespective of the mooted tradition history of the received text it is only with considerable difficulty that the 'irregularities' within the narrative can be reconciled to each other. It was suggested that the overall context was numinous and consistent with dreamform, and that those irregularities could be eradicated in a dreamform context. The essential problem with viewing any or all of Gen 2–3 as dream was identified as deriving from a failure to address the relationship between sleep and dream, both within the modern West and the Ancient Near East. Thus an argument was presented for viewing most of the direct and reported speech/action in Gen 2–3 as dream, and that this is entirely consistent with other theophanic encounters found in dream/vision elsewhere in the Hebrew Bible.

CONCLUSIONS: DEPRESSION AND THE DIVINE   143

The development of a suitable methodology for establishing the dreamform structure of the Genesis 2–3 account, or indeed any other prophetic account in which such a structure is suspected, is dependent on demonstrating the presence of an overall sleep pattern within the text under examination, rather than simply showing the presence of a single dream, even if such a task was possible. Treatment of an alternate speech-action/sleep/speech-action sequence as a dream/sleep/dream sequence is valid on the basis that such an overall sleep pattern is a universal behavior common to all cultures at all times. It was, however, suggested in the early days of this research that this was only true where the text in question explicitly stated the presence of dream or vision. But usually such statements are to be found at the outset of a passage, and are invariably present to confirm the primacy of the synesthetic nature of the experience, rather than to confirm the passage as dream or vision experience. Subsequent application of this methodology was found to show that the prophets concerned were experiencing the dreams of those who suffered from depression, as indicated by the relative length of the (first two) dreams to each other, which is known to be characteristic for depressives. The hypnograms produced, as is the case with the Abrahamic covenant, were designated derived etic hypnograms to indicate that there had been little, if any, reliance on the support of invalid, modern, Western disciplines in either the development or application of the methodology.

The Abrahamic covenant is bisected by the Hebrew term, *tardēmā*, meaning 'deep sleep,' but there are other Hebrew terms for sleep such as those displayed within 1 Kings 19: 2–21, where Elijah has a number of numinous experiences. These sleep 'punctuations,' three in all, are consistent with a dream/sleep/dream sequence lasting throughout the night, and which comprises Elijah's wilderness, vision quest. Elijah has encounters with three denizens of the spirit world before a final synesthetic engagement with the LORD on the mountain of God (Horeb)—one in each of the four dreams displayed in the derived, etic hypnogram. The first three encounters are with messengers (*malakim*, 'angels'), the first one an evil being sent by the witch, Jezebel, and the second two are with angels of the LORD. This three-angel structure is found to be overtly followed by Matthew in the Temptation narrative, that is, the two narratives display a pattern wherein one evil 'angel' (albeit present nearly throughout the Temptation narrative) is twice followed by the introduction of angels of the LORD/Lord. In Matthew's story the second (potential) angelic visitation is, however, declined by Jesus. The omission of any reference to sleep, or the display of a dream/sleep/dream structure, simply does not require restating in this much later Temptation story, for an audience fully conversant with such enculturated, prophetic, vision quests. Identification of Jesus with Elijah for contemporary hearers or readers of this story would have been a foregone conclusion, in these vision quest circumstances. Neither would it have been difficult for contemporary readers/hearers to appreciate that Jesus was likewise a 'prophetic type'—a depressed dreamer of dreams through this association.

1 Kings 19:2–21 is typically considered to be part of a group of 'Elijah narratives' in the general biblical consensus, principally because of so-called 'irreconcilable difficulties' between the various sections, or supposed Mosaic analogies. The unity of the complete Elijah narrative (1 Kgs 17–19 and beyond) is, however, much easier to understand in terms of altered states of consciousness (ASCs) exacerbated by severe, ascetic, psychophysiological regimes. Similarly, Genesis 2–3 has often been viewed as a compendium of irregularities, flaws, insertions, links, and amalgamations, to which can be added the exegetical difficulties due to it being a foundational text for Christian doctrine. Notwithstanding these problems, which derive from a failure to acknowledge the dreamform context, I have used the derived cross-cultural methodology to identify a speech-action/sleep/speech-action sequence in the creation story that corresponds perfectly with the dream/(deep) sleep/dream sequence of the modern hypnogram. Moreover, the derived, etic hypnogram of the creation-paradise story displayed the characteristically, elongated first dream typical of a depressed dreamer of dreams. In Paul's comparison Adam is compared with Jesus, indeed he says of Adam that he "is a type of the one who was to come,"[1] and this careful use of language (Greek, $\tau \upsilon \pi o \varsigma$ rather than $\pi \rho o \varphi \eta \tau \eta \varsigma$) is probably designed to avoid relegating Jesus (and perhaps even the pre-fall Adam), to the status of a (mere) prophet. Nevertheless, in the light of the applied methodology, Jesus—whatever else he may be—is demonstrated by analogy to be a 'prophetic-type,' that is, a depressed dreamer of dreams. In this regard Paul and Matthew are shown to be in good agreement.

In the last chapter we examined the passage in Luke (11:29–32) where Jesus compares himself with Jonah for the benefit of his hearers, and in response to their request for a 'sign.' In his reply Jesus invites comparison with Jonah, stating that only the 'sign of Jonah' will be given, and suggesting that both Jonah and Jesus was/is able to display a 'sign' in their own person and presence. On the basis that Jonah has been shown elsewhere (see Appendix) to have delivered such a visible sign to the Ninevites, a passage was sought in which Jesus—under similar circumstances—gave such a visible sign in his own person. In Jonah's case the sign was given just prior to his announcement (prophecy) to the Ninevites, by means of *lung gom*

---

1. Romans 5:14, NRSV.

CONCLUSIONS: DEPRESSION AND THE DIVINE 145

pa or spirit running, as he approached the gate at Nineveh. Jonah's spirit or meditative run began immediately after his last dream had finished, and a parallel situation was then sought in which Jesus featured. Luke's version of the Temptation narrative, is similar to the Matthean version, at least insofar as it too models Elijah's three dreams in 1 Kgs 19:2–8, but differs in that the last dream is immediately followed by Jesus' return to the Galilee in Luke 4:14, thus making an overall sequence in which three dreams morph seamlessly into a meditative run. This overall pattern precisely mirrors the picture shown in Jonah, where the prophet begins his spirit run shortly after the completion of his first dream sequence. In this manner Luke, in line with Paul and Matthew is also confirming Jesus to be a 'prophetic-type'—a depressed dreamer of dreams, albeit this time by analogy with another depressed prophet—Jonah.

Through the application of the derived etic methodology presented here, Jesus has been shown to have been compared with three different prophets by two of the gospel writers and the apostle, Paul. In each case he has been shown to be a depressed dreamer of dreams, an archetypal prophet, who classifies within modern medical categories as one who suffers from clinical depression. In every passage examined, however, there appears to be something slightly different going on that differentiates Jesus from other depressed prophets. In the Beatitudes Jesus was found to give a careful, lucid, and cogent explanation of depression in all its various forms, and most importantly to be making an appeal to his hearers to find such 'fortunate' people. But is this the behavior of someone who is clinically depressed? "Major or severe depression, also known as clinical depression . . . is disabling,"[2] and in addition to "diminished interest or pleasure" the depressed person displays an "inability to think or concentrate."[3] The picture displayed by Jesus is of an outgoing, commanding, peripatetic teacher giving an intellectually consistent, yet fully understandable explanation of his own condition, whilst at the same time extolling the 'attributes' of the 'fortunate ones' his hearers should be seeking. This is not a picture of an archetypally depressed prophet, and it suggests that something more is happening here!

The next passage to be (briefly) examined was the Transfiguration, which in Luke's account may be seen as the back-end of a night's sleep. Indeed the derived etic hypnogram produced from the passage displays a hypnopompic interlude in which the three disciples experience a state of consciousness somewhere between dreaming and normal wakefulness. The bulk of the speech/action takes place in this hypnopompic interlude (Luke

2. Wolpert, *Malignant Sadness*, 1.
3. See *DSM IV criteria* (American Psychiatric Association, *DSM IV*, 356).

9:32b–35), and largely consisted of observation by the disciples. These are not the dreams of Jesus, but rather those of the disciples, chiefly Peter, with Jesus featuring as God in this theophany accompanied by the souls of the long-dead Moses and Elijah. The important point to note is that Jesus is found in the role of God—a feature never before seen in any other prophetic or theophanic encounter. A similar inference may be drawn from both the Lucan and Matthean accounts of the Temptation, which have been seen to closely parallel the characters featured in the four dreams of Elijah in 1 Kgs 19:2–21. Of course, the salient point here is that the fourth dream of Elijah (in which he meets with God) is missing in both of the gospel writers' accounts, and the clear implication is that Jesus is standing in God's stead, having full authority to counter the devil in this diabolic encounter. Even though both gospel writers terminate their narratives after the third testing by the devil, Jesus may have continued his night's sleep in much the same manner as Abraham or Jonah did.

In Matthew 12:38–42 we find the evangelist giving his account of the 'sign of Jonah' pericope, an account in which he gives 'the sign of Jonah' "a different interpretation by inserting the death-resurrection comparison in Matt 12:40."[4] Harrington does, however, consider that the 'sign of Jonah' consists in preaching, and that this is shared by Q, Luke and Matthew, and is in addition to the death-resurrection comparison, which is peculiar to Matthew. Indeed, Matthew is said to have retained "this element of the Jonah-Jesus typology by his inclusion of Matt 12:40."[5] However, in the cultural milieu of the first-century Galilee it is very likely that Jonah's spirit-run was well known in local oral tradition, and Matthew's insertion of 12:40 deliberately introduces another quite different potential category for "the sign." This Jonah-Jesus typology although introducing "a kind of death and resurrection"[6] comparison where Jonah (actually) undergoes a rebirth[7] experience, in no way compares with Jesus' own (real) death and resurrection. This may be Matthew's point leading up to Matt 12:41 ("and behold, a greater than Jonas is here" KJV), and where once again, we find Jesus portrayed as surpassing any previous (prophetic) feat, by entering the underworld itself.

To find these words in the mouth of Jesus the depressed prophet is remarkable indeed, since such a resolute and definite goal (as distinct from the mere contemplation of death) is not found amongst similarly depressed

---

4. Harrington, *Gospel of Matthew*, 189.
5. Harrington, *Gospel of Matthew*, 189.
6. Harrington, *Gospel of Matthew*, 189.
7. See Appendix: "YHWH Controls "The Vertical" (The Psalm)—Jonah 2:1–11."

CONCLUSIONS: DEPRESSION AND THE DIVINE

prophets, such as Jonah or Elijah, rather they are typically found asking God to take away their lives (Jonah 4:3, 1 Kgs 19:4) without, that is, having to (potentially) endure pain. Indeed, for the depressed person the thought of having to endure further pain—further that is—to a life spent in constant suffering can often be what prevents suicide. Wolpert as an erstwhile sufferer puts it this way:

> Though I am a biologist, I did not know of a fail-safe way to kill myself. I did not want to suffer any pain . . . and I did not want to end up even worse off, if such a thing were possible.[8]

Thus, for Jesus to effectively stand outside himself in making this pronouncement seems to go far beyond what is endurable for a human being tormented by the depths of depression, and suggests it is spoken from the very interface with the divine. In many ways this is comparable with the beatitudes, where Jesus delivers such a rational and insightful appraisal of depression and its psychophysiological consequences, whilst at the same time suffering its worst effects in his own person.

We have, so far, in these concluding comments listed a number of instances where Jesus' divinity can be glimpsed, where it seems he goes beyond what it is to be a prophet, and indeed beyond what it is to be human, whilst simultaneously enduring the very depths of that human condition with his fellows. But there is perhaps one, slightly clearer instance of Jesus' prophethood that stands cheek by jowl with his divinity, and this consists in the pericope in John 1:47–51 where Jesus meets Nathanael. At their meeting Jesus greets him as a "true Israelite" whereupon Nathanael responds asking Jesus how he knew him. It is at this point that Jesus reveals he has seen Nathanael "under the fig tree before Philip called" him (John 1:48), even though Jesus was not present[9] to him either before or at the time when Philip called him. The clear implication of this exchange is that Jesus is acting as a 'seer/prophet,' and is experiencing special, enhanced, second 'sight,' that is, seeing action(s) taking place at a distance elsewhere, in like manner (citing only one example) to Saul in 1 Sam 19:20. In this verse the reader is struck by the way in which Saul's messengers and the prophets come together, that is, they do not meet or encounter each other, but rather the messengers 'see' (ראה) the prophets—or so the reading in the LXX (and indeed, most subsequent English versions). But the Hebrew (MT) has 'and *he* saw' (וירא) at this point—clearly referring to Saul as a 'seer/prophet' who appears to

---

8. Wolpert, *Malignant Sadness*, 64.
9. Keener, *Gospel of John*, 486.

be envisioning the whole of the proceedings at a distance in an ASC[10]—a feature attested in numerous shamanic/yogic cultures.[11]

It is the realization by Nathanael that he has been envisioned in this way that causes him to express the Messianic accolades "Son of God" and "King of Israel," since "if he (Jesus) is a true prophet he cannot be a false messiah."[12] In this, of course, Nathanael puts together the sign (second sight) of prophethood, in which Jesus sees him under (υπο, hupo) the fig tree, and the witness of Philip to arrive at his realization of Jesus' divinity.[13] Notwithstanding this entirely logical interpretation of the scene, the immediacy of Nathanael's outburst suggests it has much more to do with the fig tree than any words of Philip. This fig tree is not just any fig tree, or even a fig tree specific to a particular location, it is rather *the* fig tree, which throughout the Middle East and even as far as India was venerated as the Tree of Life.[14] The allusion then—the unspoken, culturally-embedded reality behind the text—is to the ancient Tree of Life that connects Heaven and Earth, which Nathanael was not-so-much sat under, as transcendentally ascending the 'tree' in a meditative state. Confirmation of this is found in the next verse (v. 50), where Jesus states he 'saw' Nathanael underneath *(υποκατο, hupokato)* the fig tree from above, since *υποκατο*—used only eleven times in the New Testament—is almost invariably used where a person relates to someone or thing, which is at or beneath their feet. Thus, the clear implication is that Nathanael within an altered state of consciousness is at the foot of Jesus, who is the Tree of Life, and the bridge between Heaven and Earth, which of course correlates well with the analogy of the following verse (v. 51) referring to the Genesis (28:12) account of Jacob's ladder.[15]

In terms of the thesis offered in this book as encapsulated in its two-part title we find four witnesses giving support in their writings, and all four (Mathew, Luke, John and Paul) are clear in their appraisals of Jesus—Jesus was a prophet! Beyond that we can also know from Paul, Matthew and Luke

---

10. Auld writes, "the regular Hebrew for 'seeing' (*rʾh*) is used not infrequently in the Bible of special, enhanced, second 'sight.' Quite exacting exegesis may often be necessary before deciding that such a sense is appropriate in any given occurrence of the *qal* theme" (Auld, "Prophets," 10).

11. Eliade notes that remote vision is a feature of the yogic practices of the Indian subcontinent, as well as featuring in Artic and North Asiatic shamanism (Eliade, *Yoga: Immortality and Freedom*, 136).

12. Keener, *Gospel of John*, 488. Parentheses added.

13. Keener, *Gospel of John*, 488.

14. Many ancient people groups had one special tree, which symbolised the Tree of Life, World Tree or *Axis Mundi*. For some it was the Ash, known as Yggdrasil in Norse mythology, for others it was the Oak (Leeming, *Oxford Companion*, 404–7).

15. "Jesus is Jacob's ladder" (Keener, *Gospel of John*, 489).

that Jesus was a depressed prophet, because of their respective comparisons between Jesus and Adam, Elijah and Jonah, all of whom were depressed. In short, we may say that the second part of this thesis (Was Jesus Clinically Depressed?) has been adequately demonstrated. Addressing the first part of our theme (Depression and the Divine) is perhaps a little more difficult, since some of the evidence of the passages examined derives from omissions (the Temptation—Luke and Matthew), where the replication of the fourth dream (of Elijah) is found to be missing. Other passages (the Transfiguration) reveal a Jesus present in a dream theophany who stands in the place of God, and in both this passage and that of the Temptation the received message depends on the culturally-embedded knowledge of the hearers and readers of the narrative. Still other passages of Matthew (the Beatitudes, and the Sign of Jonah), reveal a depressed Jesus who simply should not have been able to function as depicted. In the Beatitudes he accurately (and clinically) describes his own condition, in what is effectively a 'recruitment plan' for his followers, and in the 'sign of Jonah' he contemplates his own cruel death. The Johanine passage examined (John 1:47–51) similarly confirms Jesus as a prophet, but goes much further when the cross-cultural significance of the fig tree is weighed together with the perspective from which it was viewed. Moreover, the context of the passage in closing a parenthesis that begins with the equation of the *logos* with God (John 1:1) points directly at Jesus' divinity, and the *logos* connection does of course bring this study back full circle to 'Adam' in the Garden—with its central Tree of Life.

Thus we may say that there is ample evidence to show that Jesus was a prophet, and a significant amount of additional evidence, which goes considerably beyond the category of the 'prophetic-type.' The methodology advanced here has shown in terms acceptable to both ancient, Mediterranean and modern, Western culture that Jesus was a clinically depressed prophet, but the central enigma of the person of Jesus—being fully man yet fully God—still remains partially obscure. What may be said with certainty is that Jesus' depression—which has been clearly demonstrated in these pages—was not able to distract, divert or above all debilitate him in the performance of his teaching ministry or in the willing acceptance of its cruel and fatal consequences. Consequently, there remains a deep mystery at the interface between the human and the divine in Jesus, which enabled him to surmount clinical depression when others (Elijah and Jonah) succumbed to its worst effects. Jesus' followers knew, however, that although God was present to the prophets—even to the extent of permanent possession—this was entirely different to the situation with Jesus, where they were obliged to conclude that he was literally God with them.

Appendix

The Making of a Divine Man —The Book of Jonah

THE CLASSIFICATION OF THE book of Jonah as to the type of literature (genre) it represents has been the subject of much speculation in modern scholarship. Salters isolates seven broad areas of interpretation that he labels history, fable, allegory, legend, parable, midrash, and didactic story respectively,[1] each of which cross-fertilizes with the others to produce numerous subgenres. Latterly, other scholars have suggested a more esoteric genre for Jonah, as for example Sherwood, who has emphasized the "dialogic" qualities of the text, a feature which resonates with this present study.[2] Similar consternation prevails in the not unrelated question of what comprises the book's main theme(s), and where the possibilities include repentance, divine compassion, "the universality of God's concern, and . . . the inability of a prophet to avoid his mission. All of these ideas are present in Jonah, but none is, in and of itself, the main point of the book. All are secondary aspects of the central problem—the nature of prophecy and its effect on the prophet."[3] In her consideration of the place of the book of Jonah amongst the rest of the prophetic literature, Van Wijk-Bos observes that this dual issue has "caused commentators numerous headaches."[4] In particular, she contrasts the dissimilarities between Jonah—included amongst the latter prophets[5]—and the other members of that 'fraternity,' with the similarities between the material in Jonah and that in the Elijah/Elisha stories. Indeed, she seems resigned when she comments that: "It is hard to make

---

1. Salters, *Jonah & Lamentations*, 41–48.
2. Sherwood, "Cross-Currents," 61.
3. Berlin, "Rejoinder," 230.
4. Van Wijk-Bos, "No Small Thing," 222.
5. "The books of Kings are the last of the Former Prophets in the Hebrew Bible." The latter prophets comprise "Isaiah, Jeremiah, Ezekiel and 'the Twelve'" (Howard Jr., *Introduction to the Old Testament*, 171).

Jonah, both prophet and book, fit interpreters' understandings of prophets and prophecy."[6] Significantly, however:

> The canonizers of the Hebrew Bible had apparently no difficulty with placing the book in the midst of the prophetic literature. So we may do best to understand the teaching of Jonah in the context of prophecy in ancient Israel.... The "reality" of the eighth-century setting is significant insofar as it provides a background for the reality of prophecy in Israel, embodied in Jonah.[7]

Van Wijk-Bos sees the emphasis of the book of Jonah placed firmly on a didactic function conveyed through a paradigmatic narrative,[8] which she considers has little to do with historicity and much more to do with theology.[9] But without necessarily accepting the story of Jonah as a theological lesson, it may be agreed with Van Wijk-Bos that Jonah (both prophet and book) *embodies* the reality of prophecy in ancient Israel—even though this book contains neither the root נבא nor any of its derivatives.

In terms of the thesis advanced in the present study the reality of prophecy as it is portrayed in the book of Jonah has to do with a number of altered states of consciousness, which include characteristic depressive dreaming, hypnopompia, and meditation. It may even be the case that so-called 'normal' (sense experience) reality does not figure in the book at all, and that the narrator is recording a smooth, almost seamless transition between several, different kinds of altered state experience. Indeed, the interrelationship between these ASCs as they are recorded in *Jonah* (in terms of the culture-based experience of the behavior of prophets) may very well serve to obscure both the genre and the main theme of the book. In terms of socially embedded, prophetic behavior it is contended that one part of the book may be depicting meditative behavior (Jonah 3:1—4:3), but that this is sandwiched between two periods (Jonah 1:1—2:11; 4:4–11) of nocturnal (dreaming) behavior. All of this would not be inconsistent with a world-view that did not discriminate overmuch between dreaming and 'normal' reality, and presumably therefore between the various different forms of altered consciousness.

Literature produced by such a culture would simply record all of these states as 'real' experiences, with the mundane, the exotic and the bizarre seamlessly juxtaposed in a way not easily comprehended by the modern,

---

6. Van Wijk-Bos, "No Small Thing," 222.

7. Van Wijk-Bos, "No Small Thing," 223.

8. Compare Stuart, who describes the book as "*didactic* prophetic narrative" (Stuart, *Hosea–Jonah*, 435).

9. Van Wijk-Bos, "No Small Thing," 218.

Western mind. On the view advanced here the author of *Jonah* is relating a continuous stream of 'real' behavior, and although it might appear that a work of fiction has been crafted (and this is certainly a possibility) the broader concept of 'reality' employed in this pre-modern culture cautions against taking too restrictive a view on genre. It may still be observed, however, that in the "almost uniform judgment of scholars . . . the Jonah story is closer in type to the stories of the prophets . . . in the book of Kings"[10] including those about Elijah (1 Kgs 17-19), to which the methodologies derived in this thesis have already been applied. Thus, in what follows those same methodologies are applied to the text of *Jonah*.

Jonah's First Altered State(s) of Consciousness—Jonah 1:1-2:11

Eliade in his foreword to *Jonah: A Psycho-Religious Approach to the Prophet* sees in Jonah's flight an example of "the resistance of the future shaman against his "call," his election by supernatural beings."[11] In Eliade's estimation that flight appears to encompass the whole of the first two chapters up to the point where Jonah is ejected from "the whale" (Jonah 2:11), but he does not expand on the shamanic components of the flight. Regarding these first chapters it is important to note that English translations of the book follow a different pattern of verse enumeration to that followed by both the MT and the LXX. It is important, therefore, to state at the outset that this study will adhere to the format of these ancient texts which conclude chapter one at 1:16 and ascribe eleven verses to chapter two (2:1 [1:17]—2:11). A majority of commentators have held to this arrangement and many have further subdivided their observations on these chapters into three, discrete sections (1:1-3; 1:4-16; 2:1-11)[12]—a practice which will be followed in this study, albeit with special attention paid to 1:1. These three, broad subdivisions appear to correspond very largely to the three phases of classic, shamanic/mystical flight, in which "the shaman's spirit may enter into any of three classic worlds (lower, middle, and upper) during flight,"[13] and thereby give the impression that Jonah is exhibiting archetypal shaman-prophet behavior. Careful exegesis will be required in order to demonstrate this analysis of the text, beginning with Jonah 1:1-3,

---

10. Stuart, *Hosea-Jonah*, 433.
11. Eliade, "Foreword," in Lacocque and Lacocque, *Jonah,* xiv.
12. So, Stuart, *Hosea-Jonah*, x; Limburg, *Jonah,* 7; Salters, *Jonah,* 17; Simon, *JPS Bible Commentary Jonah*, v.
13. Winkelman, *Shamanism*, 61.

which contra Eliade cannot be seen as the commencement of a shamanic initiation, because it neglects the important relationship between Jonah 1:1 and the information conveyed by 2 Kings 14:25. The ensuing sections elaborate on the controlling effect of this latter verse on both the flight pericope and the book as a whole.

Jonah Ben Amittai—Jonah 1:1

"The book of Jonah begins with a converted apocopated imperfect verb (ויהי) usually thought to indicate the continuation of a narrative, rather than the beginning of a passage or book."[14] It is with these words that Stuart opens his discussion of the form/structure/setting of the book of Jonah, before going on to dismiss the possibility that the book once formed part of a larger work. Thus, he concludes that the book is "self-contained" and that "ויהי is for Jonah the functional equivalent of 'Once upon a time . . .'" Notwithstanding the discrete nature of the book, continuity of some kind should be factored into this opening verse and thereby the entire book, if only because of the near unanimity amongst scholars concerning the relationship between Jonah—the subject of the book—and the Jonah ben Amittai of 2 Kings 14:25.[15] Indeed, in Allen's view "the obviously intended identification of . . . (Jonah) with the prophet of 2 K. 14:25," leads to the conclusion that "there may be a historical nucleus behind the story."[16] Pearson is clear that Jonah's "name and patronym . . . is taken from a reference to 'Jonah, son of Amittai' in 2 Kgs 14:25,"[17] and Limburg goes so far as to state an identity between the two prophets.[18] Although it is extremely likely that the appellation 'Jonah son of Amittai' would have evoked such an identity in the minds of the "small community of the faithful,"[19] during the exilic and post-exilic periods, it is only necessary for the purposes of this study to agree with Bolin that the book of Jonah "draws upon . . . the story of Jonah found in 2 Kings,"[20] and finally to note with Ben Zvi that:

---

14. Stuart, *Hosea–Jonah*, 444.
15. Watts, *Books*, 72. Stuart, *Hosea–Jonah*, 447.
16. Allen, *Books of Joel, Obadiah, Jonah and Micah*, 179.
17. Pearson, *In Conversation with Jonah*, 63.
18. Limburg, *Jonah*, 38.
19. Limburg, *Jonah*, 39. Moreover, Sasson asserts "it is beyond probability that in Scripture two different individuals would bear the same names *and* patronyms" (Sasson, *Jonah*, 342).
20. Bolin, *Freedom Beyond Forgiveness*, 151.

When the primary community/ies of rereaders approached the book of Jonah in the light of their identification of the character Jonah in the book with the one in Kings—as the implied and likely historical author intended to, they let their knowledge of the text of Kings inform their understanding of the book of Jonah.[21]

Certainly, it would seem that the book of Kings reached its 'final form' during the exilic period,[22] and would therefore have been available as 'source material' to both the 'writer' and first readers of Jonah, provided the latter book was either contemporaneous with Kings, or else written subsequent to Kings. On this last point, however, Sasson is undecided, but favors the post-exilic period for the composition of Jonah on the basis of its literary and linguistic features.[23] Despite the significant support for a late exilic or post-exilic dating of Jonah the complete absence of datable information within the text ensures that the actual composition of the book is simply not datable "except within the broadest boundaries (*ca* 750–250 B.C.)."[24] On balance, however, a significant body of scholarly opinion would nevertheless place the composition of Jonah in the late exilic or more probably the post-exilic period.[25]

The identification of the prophet in the book of Jonah with the Jonah ben Amittai in Kings has implications for the temporal sequence of two sets of events (i.e. Jeroboam's campaigns vs. the mission to Nineveh), and those implications depend upon "the significance of this identification (which) is not made explicit."[26] In the view of Simon that significance depends on "how one understands the story in the first place,"[27] rather than the isolation of any particular, linking factor(s). Arguing from the basis that Jonah was composed later than the book of Kings, Ben Zvi is moved to "ponder whether some kind

---

21. Ben Zvi, *Signs of Jonah*, 51.

22. Howard argues for a date after 561 BC (Howard Jr., *Introduction to the Old Testament Historical Books*, 171). Landes sets Kings within the wider context of the "final redaction of the Deuteronomic History ca. 550 BCE" (Landes, "Case for the Sixth-Century BCE Dating," 112).

23. Sasson, *Jonah*, 27.

24. Stuart, *Hosea–Jonah*, 432.

25. Limburg provides a representative listing of scholars supporting a range of dates of composition from the eighth to the third century BCE (Limburg, *Jonah*, 28).

26. Simon, *JPS Bible Commentary: Jonah*, xxxvi. The historicity or otherwise of a physical journey to Nineveh by Jonah will be discussed within the fuller discussion of *Jonah* chapter 3 following.

27. Simon, *JPS Bible Commentary: Jonah*, xxxvi

of 'seed' of the narrative in Jonah is to be found in the account in Kings?"[28] He is nevertheless obliged to conclude: "neither the basic narrative of the two accounts, nor their details, nor their respective languages, point to any such 'trigger' or 'seed.'"[29] If, however, it proved possible to isolate such a 'seed' and demonstrate its continued growth through the book of Jonah, then this might confirm the Nineveh mission as temporally posterior to the activities of Jonah ben Amittai recorded in 2 Kings 14:25. It will not, however, be necessary (at least for the purposes of this study) to show that the two Jonahs are one and the same, only that the 'seed' or idea germinated in Kings continues to grow and develop when transplanted into Jonah. In this regard Ben Zvi regards the opening words of Jonah (ויהי דבר־יהוה אל—Jonah 1:1) as being "*in medias res*,"[30] and Sasson maintains that this expression "is found only when contexts and circumstances regarding the prophet and his mission are already established in previous statements."[31]

Consequently, it behoves the would-be exegete of the book of Jonah to digress at this point (Jonah 1:1), and engage in an excursus into precisely what information, if any, is conveyed by the single verse, 2 Kings 14:25. Even a cursory examination of this verse reveals that Jonah seems to have been an accepted prophet at the court of king Jeroboam II (a king who "did what was evil in the sight of the LORD," 2 Kgs 14:24), or at the least his prophesying was accepted there.[32] Although Jonah is not explicitly implicated in or associated with the 'evil' of king Jeroboam by the text, neither is he exonerated. Typically, English translations of 2 Kings 14:25 speak of the expansion of Israel's frontiers to their erstwhile Davidic extent, "according to the word of the LORD, the God of Israel, which he spoke by his servant Jonah son of Amittai, the prophet, who was from Gath-hepher" (NRSV). But translating אשר דבר ביר עבדו as "which he spoke by his servant," fails to convey the full impact of this expression—especially when interpreted using insights from shamanism. In point of fact this expression is more properly rendered by the KJV translation as "which he spake by the hand of his servant . . . ," but even in this form it still fails to convey the full

---

28. Ben Zvi, *Signs of Jonah*, 55.
29. Ben Zvi, *Signs of Jonah*, 56.
30. Ben Zvi, *Signs of Jonah*, 46.

31. Sasson, *Jonah*, 67. Sasson does, however, considers it "farfetched" to connect "the *waw* in *way(ye)hi*" with the Jonah narrative of 2 Kings (Sasson, *Jonah*, 67).

32. In qualification it may be acknowledged that Jonah could have been a 'peripheral prophet' whose prophecy (if only on this occasion) reached the court of king Jeroboam: On 'peripheral prophecy' see Wilson, *Prophecy and Society*. Alternatively a Marian model of lay prophets relaying information to the king via cult personnel at court may be envisaged here (Grabbe, *Priests, Prophets, Diviners, Sages,* 88).

THE MAKING OF A DIVINE MAN—THE BOOK OF JONAH

shamanic import of the phrase. Before evaluating the latter, however, it will be necessary to review the range of concepts conveyed by the components of the construct state expression . . . ביד־עבדו יונה literally translated "by the hand of his servant, Jonah . . ."

Firstly, it is important to recognize the wide semantic range covered by the term עבד (*ebed*, 'slave,' 'servant'). Indeed, the substantive noun עבד fundamentally:

> Refers to a person who is subordinated to someone else. This subordination can manifest itself in various ways, however, and *ebed* accordingly can have different meanings: slave, servant, subject, official, vassal, or "servant" or follower of a particular god.[33]

At this point in the discussion it may be noted that the expression ביד־עבדו appears only five times in the Old Testament (1 Kgs 14:18; 15:29; 2 Kgs 9:36; 10:10; 14:25), and is as a result a much rarer expression than for example עבד־יהוה (servant of the LORD) or עבדי הנבאים (my servants the prophets). It is used not only of Elijah (2 Kgs 9:36; 10:10) and Jonah (2 Kgs 14:25), but also of the less well known prophet, Ahijah the Shilonite (1 Kgs 14:18; 15:29), and there appears to be something of a divergence in status between the three if they are assessed, albeit simplistically, in relation to the amount of text devoted to them within the books of Kings. Indeed, in terms of 'prophetic stature' the widest divergence appears to be between Elijah who uses עבד as a self-referent (1 Kgs 18:36), and who has been equated with Moses,[34] and Jonah, the prophet who has the briefest of appearances of the three within the text. This apparent divergence in status should alert the exegete to the possibility that עבד may not always be being used in any honorific or Mosaic sense,[35] and may in fact refer to "unfree work imposed by YHWH on the servant,"[36] that is, work obtained by the application of non-negotiable compulsion. Given the semantic range of עבד in biblical Hebrew it is important to try to discover whether the intended meaning is 'servant' or 'slave,' since:

> Underlying both meanings is "dependency"; the one bearing the title *ebed* is to a greater or lesser degree, perceived

---

33. Ringgren, "עֶבֶד," 387.

34. See for example, White, *Elijah Legends*, 7.

35. Ringgren observes that *ebed YHWH* is an honorific title used to refer to the special status of Moses' relationship with God (Ringgren, "עֶבֶד," 394).

36. Ben Zvi, *Signs of Jonah*, 68. It is important to accept with Ben Zvi that "in biblical Hebrew and other Semitic languages the same word denotes both servant and slave" (Ben Zvi, *Signs of Jonah*, 68).

to be dependent on someone else. The determination of the degree of dependency, that is whether we are to render ʿ*ebed* as "servant" or "slave," rests solely upon the context in which the word appears.³⁷

Thus, the greatest objections to an interpretation of עבד (in the expression ביד־עבדו) as 'slave' in its fullest, most coercive sense are the two references to Elijah (2 Kgs 9:36; 10:10), where YHWH's imposition of unfree work on to Elijah seems inconsistent with the prophet's otherwise willing, albeit sometimes dispirited, service in all other references to him. The references to Elijah in 2 Kings 9 and 10 could have arisen for any number of reasons ranging from the narrator's recording of a simple error or misunderstanding on Jehu's part, to perhaps the recall of a time before Elijah became the willing servant of YHWH.³⁸ Thus, it would appear at least possible in these two instances for עבד to be considered in the fullest, most coercive sense of 'slave,' rather than in any titular, honorific or Mosaic sense.

Secondly, it is important to note that the first component of this construct state expression is יד (hand), which is the most common term for hand found in the Old Testament. It is not the only term, however, and the noun כף is a frequent though much less common expression found in the texts and tending normally, but not exclusively, to "denote the open hand, ready to receive something."³⁹ In contrast יד is commonly used of the 'holding' or 'grasping' functions of the hand, which lend themselves naturally to an extension of the range of meaning to include "possession and control."⁴⁰ It would appear from the context of 2 Kings 14, where 'prophetic' control/power (v. 25) is found adjacent to military control/power (v. 27), that the latter usage is intended. In such usage, "a specialized and related use (of יד) appears in the prepositional form *bᵉyad*, used frequently to designate the agent through whom a particular action is performed."⁴¹ Thus, the emphasis of ביד in this construct state expression should more properly fall on the exercise of power, control or mastery, and when ביד is translated from a military context into the realm of the shaman-prophet the control and mastery of soldiers, territory or vassals becomes equated with the control

---

37. Ratner, "Jonah, Runaway Slave," 293.

38. Cogan and Tadmor consider that Elijah's oracle in 2 Kings 9:36 is a rendition often considered "more original" than the version recorded in 1 Kings 21:23 (Cogan, and Tadmor, *II Kings*, 112). The version of the oracle found in 1 Kings 21:23 is itself considered by some as "possibly a fragment of an earlier tradition concerning Elijah" unrelated to the pericope in which it is found (Gray, *I & II Kings*, 436).

39. Ackroyd, "יָד," 403.

40. Ackroyd, "יָד," 409.

41. Ackroyd, "יָד," 410.

or mastery of spiritual entities/beings,[42] in the extended reality. Applying these insights to the expression ביד־עבדו would suggest that YHWH has spoken his word by controlling and manipulating the human slave's mastery over other spiritual beings—who themselves are YHWH's slaves, for it is the whole agent-client relationship that is under control.[43] Indeed, the coercive emphasis will equally rest upon these lesser spiritual beings, with "unfree work" expected by YHWH of both Jonah and Jonah's power relationships—where these may be considered to comprise a single spiritual complex. On this interpretation, the phrase "Jonah son of Amittai, the prophet, who was from Gath-hepher" functions as an adjectival expression to designate the particular prophet-spirit complex involved, that is, Jonah.

The discussion so far has emphasized the fact of YHWH's control of Jonah's 'power,' but it is perhaps pertinent to provide further support for the second contention made above that Jonah's 'power' equates to "mastery over other spiritual beings." In this regard, it has already been argued that Elijah on Mount Carmel (1 Kgs 18:42-44) was depicted in a conjuring or adjuring pose (v. 42), and that consequently his subsequent conversations (vv. 43-44) were with a spirit-servant/slave.[44] Moreover, a number of commentators have remarked on the similarities between the accounts of Elijah and Jonah,[45] but it is posited here that it is in their relationships with spirit helpers that the fundamental point of comparison lies. It must be acknowledged, however, that there appears to be no explicit mention of (the control of) spirit servants/helpers in *Jonah*, and this fundamental feature of the shamanic vocation must depend upon a demonstration in Jonah 1 and 2 of that other defining aspect of shamanism—the three modes of shamanic flight. Notwithstanding the latter caveat the foregoing argument has drawn attention to the possibility that both Elijah (2 Kgs 9:36; 10:10) and Jonah (2 Kgs 14:25) are being shown as co-opted into YHWH's service against their will. Moreover, and as previously contended, the narrator of 1 Kings 18 describes an Elijah who, it appears, never relinquished his power relationships with spirit subordinates even though he had become YHWH's

---

42. This is in accordance with the classical picture of the shaman who is "in control of spirits and demons." (Winkelman, *Shamanism*, 61).

43. Designating the first noun in the construct state expression 'A' and the second one 'B,' Gibson notes that "in the subjective usages a personal B "possesses" A" (Gibson, *Davidson's Introductory Hebrew*, 30).

44. See discussion in chapter 4.

45. This is usually in the context of the miraculous qualities of the text of *Jonah*, especially chapter 4 (Sasson, *Jonah*, 285; Van Wijk-Bos, "No Small Thing," 222). But the Lacocques also make extensive psychological comparisons between the two prophets (Lacocque and Lacocque, *Jonah*, 147-54).

willing servant (1 Kgs 18:36), and was "a man of God" (1 Kgs 17:18, 24). If further intertextual support were needed to establish "mastery over other spiritual beings" as foundational in the lives of shaman-prophets, then this may be adduced from the pericope at the end of Genesis 32, in which Jacob struggles with an unknown assailant. The first point to note about this passage (Gen 32:23–33) is that the encounter takes place at, or more likely, all through the night[46] reaching its zenith just before dawn (the dawn/sunrise as a datum point is mentioned three times in the text—vv. 25, 27, 32), and this is of significance because this is the time when the longest period of REM sleep/dreaming takes place.[47] This night time setting and the emphasis upon the dawn suggest the possibility that the entire encounter takes place within an altered state of consciousness, that is, a dream or sequence of dreams. Secondly, there is a body of opinion which holds variously that the 'man' (someone) who attacked Jacob at the river Jabbok (v. 25) was in fact a spirit, demon or local deity.[48] Thirdly, and significantly, Jacob is said to 'prevail' (v. 29) over his supernatural adversary, receiving from him a 'blessing' (some supernatural attribute or "power"[49]), but failing to retain permanent control/mastery over him. Indeed, in v. 30:

> Jacob (asks) the name of the opponent whom he still holds. Here too there is an animistic notion in the background: if one knows the name of a spirit, one can call it. But the unknown opponent does not give his name: it would be dangerous for him.[50]

On this point, Westermann insists that Jacob's question makes "no sense if he knew that his opponent was God,"[51] since Jacob had already called upon

46. Von Rad translates: "a man wrestled with him until the breaking of the dawn" (Von Rad, *Genesis*, 319).

47. Of the (typically) four periods of REM/dreaming sleep during a normal night's sleep, the final period (just before waking) remains the longest in both depressive and non-depressive dreamers. See chapter 3.

48. Westermann offers a cogent argument for considering Jacob's opponent to be "a hostile demon or an evil spirit" (Westermann, *Genesis 12–36*, 516). In an earlier study, Skinner observes: "the god was probably not Yahwe originally, but a local deity, a night-spirit who fears the dawn and refuses to disclose his name," but it is difficult here to reconcile Skinner's understanding of the opponent as a "night-spirit," with his belief that the episode was a "real physical encounter" (Skinner, *Critical and Exegetical Commentary*, 411). According to Davidson "the unidentified man may originally have been the river spirit of the Jabbok," and he notes that river spirits are an animistic feature of the stories of many cultures, which usually require the river spirit "to be placated or defeated before he will allow the traveller to cross" (Davidson, *Genesis 12–50*, 185).

49. Westermann, *Genesis 12–36*, 521.

50. Westermann, *Genesis 12–36*, 518.

51. Westermann, *Genesis 12–36*, 519.

the 'God of his father' in v. 12, and as a consequence Westermann appears to be endorsing the potential for permanent "mastery over other spiritual beings" as the salient point of v. 30.[52] Whether this passage is understood as "a legend, originating at a low level of religion,"[53] a legacy from a "crude, heathen past"[54] or a text bearing the "common mark of the fairy tale,"[55] it should be acknowledged that it (originally) depicts a man's successful mastery of a spiritual being whose subordination would have become permanent had he surrendered his name.

Application of these insights to the Jonah ben Amittai depicted in 1 Kings 14:25 would suggest that YHWH's control of Jonah's spirit helpers places Jonah in an untenable position *vis-à-vis* Jeroboam leaving him with only two options: The first option would be to remain silent—a course of action that would publicly deny a significant part of his vocation as a foreteller in circumstances where the nation (Israel) sought guidance before going into battle.[56] Secondly, compelled by *force majeure* he could convey the word of YHWH (the only information he has access to), but this requires him to acknowledge and display his subservience to YHWH publicly (on this occasion at least), thus denying his *raison d'être* as a master of spirits. In following the second option it is not necessary for Jonah personally to acknowledge an allegiance to YHWH, and consequently it remains a possibility that he continued to harbor resentment towards YHWH for placing him in this predicament.[57] It is suggested here, therefore, that it is the concept of an unwilling Jonah presented with 'Hobson's choice' in the reference in Kings that seeds and initiates the book of Jonah. Indeed, Jonah (or even another Jonah with a similar disposition towards YHWH) is now placed in a one-to-one situation with YHWH (Jonah 1:1)—a situation that at first sight seems to have options. This private, encounter is one in which Jonah ostensibly has the option to refuse any (new?) instruction from YHWH without risk of publicly appearing incompetent, foolish or subservient to others. If he chose to disobey such an instruction, Jonah would not only avoid exposure to the

---

52. Westermann, *Genesis 12–36*, 518–21. But see Curtis on the use of old traditions to account for the formation of person/place names such as 'Peniel' or 'Israel' (etymological aetiology), with the implication that stories may have been "produced or preserved" precisely to account for the existence of those names (Curtis, "Aetiology," 8–9).

53. Skinner, *Critical and Exegetical Commentary*, 411.

54. Von Rad, *Genesis*, 324.

55. Westermann, *Genesis 12–36*, 516.

56. Compare 1 Kings 22.

57. This would be especially so if Jonah was already suffering from a bad reputation and was "known as 'the false prophet'" (as one Midrashic tradition has it) following a similar word from YHWH which did not transpire (Ginzberg, *Legends of the Jews*, 247).

potential for further embarrassment, but would be asserting command of his craft—thereby continuing to deny a personal and willing subservience to YHWH. Moreover, his shamanic skills would enable him simply to withdraw from the encounter with YHWH.

Fleeing the Presence of the LORD: The Descent from Transcendence—Jonah 1:2-3

Perhaps the most discussed feature of Jonah 1:2 is the well-attested distinction found in all the Hebrew manuscripts between the preposition על ('al) of 1:2 and the אל ('el) of 3:2. On this point Sasson is at variance with the scholarly consensus that fails to discriminate between the two prepositions. Indeed:

> Most scholars . . . opt to follow the LXX which carries little perceptible distinctions (sic), in the meaning and consequences, between the sentences in which קרא על/אל are to be found. The common contention is that אל and על are basically interchangeable . . . [58]

Sasson argues that קרא על/אל is a fuller concept than either of the prepositions found alone, and that the קרא על of 1:2 carries "the notion of 'imposing an (unpleasant) fate upon something,'"[59] before going on to argue that this remains thoroughly distinct from 3:2b which he translates: *"and deliver to it the proclamation I am about to tell you."*[60] In this way he is suggesting that these two verses are describing completely different (com)missions, and that this is consistent with a change in prophetic status between them.[61] Interestingly, and further to the above discussion on Jonah's 'slave' status, Sasson considers that Jonah's prophetic status in 1:2 "stands in sharp contrast to the occasions in which God shares with Moses (Exodus 32, Numbers 14) and Abraham (Genesis 18)."[62] Moreover, after conducting a singular piece of philological analysis, Sasson can say:

> The Jonah of I:2, as contrasted from the one of III:2, can be regarded neither as a "forth" nor a "fore" teller, charged with a mission to warn or elicit repentance. Rather, he was sent merely to announce an impending disaster. In a way, the role that he

58. Sasson, "On Jonah's Two Missions," 23.
59. Sasson, *Jonah*, 75.
60. Sasson, "On Jonah's Two Missions," 28.
61. Sasson reads Magonet in this light (Magonet, *Form and Meaning*, 25).
62. Sasson, *Jonah*, 75.

fills in *Jonah* I cannot be differentiated from those of the angels sent to Sodom.⁶³

The second of these observations impinges closely on the first, which although alluding to a simpler task, would be quite likely to involve Jonah's sudden and violent demise were he to make a physical appearance in Nineveh—as indeed Sasson suggests. The unequivocal nature of this first announcement of doom for Nineveh is to be contrasted with Jonah's enigmatic and ambivalent announcement in 3:4—"forty days more, and Nineveh shall be overthrown!" Here, the verb "הפך can mean to overthrow (i.e. to destroy) or to *turn around*. . . . God strategically uses a word . . . that . . . can speak simultaneously of forgiveness and disaster."⁶⁴ Thus, it would seem that at some point between *Jonah* 1 and 3, an element of conditionality has entered into Nineveh's fate, because YHWH has apparently altered his stance towards her to one of ambivalence—prior to a final decision on the matter in 3:10. Sasson is, moreover, certain that Jonah's role in 1:2 is indistinguishable from that of the angels sent to Sodom, and although he fails to specify the 'way' in which it compares, his analysis would appear at least capable of suggesting some kind of mystico-spiritual identity, even though the precise nature of the angels in Genesis 18 is moot. The irrevocable nature of the first announcement (1:2) would argue against the mission involving Jonah in a physical journey to Nineveh, especially given the likely response of the Ninevites, and this would therefore seem to indicate that Jonah's first intended mission was to have been supernatural in some way. The argument that Jonah's first mission was to have been in some way immaterial or supernatural in nature is consistent with the view expressed here that Jonah 1 and 2 exhibit all three modes of shamanic flight—flight engaged in during altered states of consciousness—a feature integral to these chapters and expanded upon in what follows.⁶⁵

In order to facilitate this latter understanding it may prove illuminating to look at the meaning of the name 'Jonah' (Dove) from a shamanic viewpoint. As has already been noted,⁶⁶ classic, shamanic/mystical flight can take place in any one of three classic worlds—lower, middle, or upper—but it is the mode of translation that is important here. Essentially:

> The shaman develops relationships with animal spirit helpers, especially birds, which symbolize the magical flight. The

---

63. Sasson, "On Jonah's Two Missions," 27–28.
64. Sherwood, *Biblical Text and Its Afterlives*, 70.
65. See especially the following subsection entitled 'The Storm.'
66. Winkelman, *Shamanism*, 61.

animal spirits are controlled by the shaman and are the vehicle through which the shaman carries out a variety of activities. Animal transformation or soul flight takes the shaman into an ascent into the sky, movement through the earth, and a descent to the lower world.[67]

Application of these insights from shamanism to the opening verses of *Jonah* 1 suggests, therefore, that the reader first comes across Jonah in transcendence, that is, he has ascended "into the sky" in the guise of his spirit helper, the dove. During this ascent he encounters YHWH—whether intentionally or otherwise—and without dialogue[68] meekly receives his orders about Nineveh. Dialogue is precluded because Jonah is directed in a coercive, subordinate (slave) relationship—as quite distinct from one involving mutual interaction—and consequently discussion or debate with YHWH is not an option. Although not told of Jonah's ascent to the 'upper world'—and herein lies the significance of coming to the story *in medias res* (Jonah 1:1)—the reader is made aware of his return journey. In this regard, Hauser[69] and Limburg[70] amongst others have noted the prevalence of a 'descent motif' in the development of *Jonah* 1 and 2, but Hauser fails to answer his self-posed question: "How does this motif of Jonah's . . . descent contribute to the development of the story?"[71] The answer would appear to lie in the shamanic significance of the motif, for Jonah descends several times throughout these first two chapters (1:3, 5; 2:6), but only in 1:3 does the verb appear twice in what effectively forms a parenthesis: מלפני יהוה . . . וירד . . . וירד מלפני יהוה. In essence this is an "intentional repetition meant to accentuate the prophet's vertical flight from his God, who dwells on high."[72] This kind of vertical descent is an activity that YHWH himself mirrors in Micah 1:3 when he descends to tread the "במותי" (high places)[73]—a practice requiring movement along "the *axis mundi*, the 'centre', 'opening', or 'hole' through which the shamans, spirits, and gods descend and

---

67. Winkelman, *Shamanism*, 62.

68. Hauser remarks on the absence of dialogue between Jonah and God in chapter 1. "One would expect Jonah to raise serious objections with God, as do Moses (Exodus 3–4), Gideon (Judges 6), and Jeremiah (Jeremiah 1) when confronted with similarly demanding tasks" (Hauser, "Jonah: In Pursuit," 25).

69. Hauser, "Jonah: In Pursuit," 30.

70. Limburg, *Jonah*, 27.

71. Hauser, "Jonah: In Pursuit," 30.

72. Simon, *JPS Bible Commentary: Jonah*, 6.

73. See Wilson for discussion on yogic ascent/descent and the identity of the central axis of the universe with the spine or back of the individual body (Wilson, "Significance," 227–28).

ascend."[74] Although most scholars treat Jonah 1:1-3 as a discrete unit, vv. 3-5 (and indeed the remainder of chapter one) are intimately bound up together, for v. 3 is the point at which Jonah's mode of flight changes from the vertical to the horizontal in much the same way that Elijah's did in 1 Kings 19:15. Moreover, whereas the latter's translation from vertical to horizontal flight was at YHWH's instigation,[75] we should note that in Jonah's case it was not, and in light of Micah 1:3 be moved to ponder whether the narrator is suggesting that YHWH was even at this point in hot pursuit.

YHWH Controls "The Horizontal" (The Storm)—Jonah 1:4-16

Jonah's return journey from the upper world and subsequent flight to the west (Tarshish) is an attempt to escape from YHWH that "fails completely and from the very beginning."[76] Indeed, Jonah knew well that YHWH controlled the surface of the earth as his confession in v. 9 demonstrates, but might have concluded he could escape apprehension and detention by obscuring himself in, for example, the bowels of a ship, that is "to escape from God's vision by joining a crowd."[77] At the very point (v. 3) where Jonah's vertical passage from the 'upper world' turns into a translation across the face of the earth/sea (middle world), Jonah is thwarted by YHWH. Indeed, Ben Zvi considers that "the chance occurrences that seem to bode well for Jonah's escape in 1.3 are nothing but a 'ploy' by YHWH, who never lost control of the whereabouts of the supposedly running away slave,"[78] and he derives support for his view from Sasson.[79] Thus, "the messengers employed by YHWH to retake him include . . . even the sailors and the (per-

---

74. Winkelman, *Shamanism*, 62. See also Eliade, (Eliada, *Yoga: Immortality and Freedom*, 241-45), and the discussion in Wilson (chapter five), on the seven chakras—the seventh, or highest chakra being a 'centre' located at the top of the skull. This is the entry/exit point from the world/body and it is at this point that the disciple *identifies* with the cosmos, achieves transcendence (rupture of plane) and ultimately union with the divine (Wilson, "Significance," 204-10).

75. See Chapter 4. Although many scholars see elements of the Elijah cycle in Jonah (Stuart, *Hosea-Jonah*, 435; Sasson, *Jonah*, 23; Lacocque and Lacocque, *Jonah*, 147), few make detailed comparisons at this early point in the narrative.

76. Ben Zvi, *Signs of Jonah*, 78.

77. Sasson, *Jonah*, 84. See also Ackerman's comments on v. 5 where the "word play is re-enforcing Jonah's search for a secure hiding place in his flight from YHWH" (Ackerman, "Satire and Symbolism," 230).

78. Ben Zvi, *Signs of Jonah*, 77-78.

79. Sasson considers "the phrase *bāʾâ taršîš* as implying the ship's *return* from a distant port" (Sasson, *Jonah*, 83).

sonified) ship,"[80] and therefore the ship returning from Tarshish could be said to have 'captured' Jonah (who at this point seems unaware of the fact), in much the same way as the fish effectively does in 2:1. It may be objected that a 'flying,' shamanic Jonah in the guise of a dove would have little use for a ship in order to reach Tarshish, but the picture of Jonah hiding from YHWH is encouraged by the narrator's insistence that "he went down" (וירד) into her. Moreover, the picture of a descending Jonah who hides in darkness suggests that the narrator is introducing, albeit subliminally, a subplot about depression to be developed to the full in chapters three and four. The qualities of darkness and hiddenness so suggestive of depression, as arrived at through descent may even at this stage be pointing to the heated argument of *Jonah* chapter four.[81]

In developing her 'ecological thesis' about *Jonah*, Trible states that YHWH pursues Jonah through the "violent extravagance" of the storm at sea,[82] but this is at variance with the idea developed above that Jonah has been 'captured' as early as v. 3.[83] Certainly, there is discontinuity between v. 3 and v. 4, for as Trible points out, the latter verse commences immediately with 'YHWH,' thereby reversing the "usual Hebrew syntax in which verb precedes subject,"[84] and thereby giving the superficial impression that this is the point at which YHWH takes the initiative. But continuity lies in YHWH's control of the situation established at outset in v. 3, as is further indicated by the strange language employed by the narrator when discussing the ship in both these verses. Indeed, on this point Trible acknowledges that "the inanimate ship *thinks* itself about to splinter,"[85] and in this she follows Ackerman who has observed that "nowhere else in the Hebrew Bible are 'fare' (v. 3) and 'thought' (v. 4) used with inanimate objects."[86] Thus, rather than the storm initiating a new phase in YHWH's 'pursuit' of Jonah, vv. 3–4 are all of a piece, at least insofar as they indicate YHWH's control of the situation from the outset. Moreover, if the Hebrew words 'fare' and 'thought' are not normally applied to "inanimate objects," but rather to living, sentient beings, then it becomes possible, indeed probable, that the ship itself is such a being. The (spiritual) ship is, therefore, co-opted as part of a 'scenario'

---

80. Ben Zvi, *Signs of Jonah*, 77.

81. In his discussion of 'anger' Seamands can say that "depression follows unresolved, repressed, or improperly expressed anger" (Seamands, *Healing*, 140).

82. Trible, "Tempest in a Text," 188.

83. Trible considers the wind/storm to be God's first act in the narrative (Trible, "Tempest in a Text," 188).

84. Trible, *Rhetorical Criticism*, 131.

85. Trible, "Tempest in a Text," 188.

86. Ackerman, "Jonah," 236.

constructed[87] by YHWH (albeit based on Jonah's escape plan) even as Jonah begins his descent. Like the classic, 1960s, science fiction TV series, *The Outer Limits*, wherein each episode began with the apparent control of the television's horizontal and vertical hold controls, this scenario is from outset asserting that it is YHWH who controls the middle (horizontal) as well as the upper and lower (vertical) worlds.

YHWH's control of the situation from the outset (v. 3) is further supported by his action upon Jonah, which although recorded in v. 5, may actually have been effected as early as v. 3—an action in which he sends sleep to Jonah (רדם).[88] The point at which Jonah was induced to fall asleep is a matter of dispute, and Stuart amongst others considers that וירדם should be translated as a pluperfect,[89] thereby supporting the view that Jonah went below to sleep well before the storm broke. In Stuart's view, therefore, the transition from the vertical flight down from YHWH to the horizontal flight across the sea is marked by this period of sleep, which separates one period of speech/action involving Jonah (1:1–3) from another much longer one (1:6—2:11). Thus, the whole sequence (Jonah 1:1–3/1:4–5/1:6—2:11) seems familiar and recognizable as the same ASC/dream—deep sleep—ASC/dream pattern already found in Gen 15, 1 Kings 19:2–21, and elsewhere.[90] It may also be noted in passing that the LXX reinforces the fact that this is non-REM/dreaming sleep by describing Jonah as both sleeping and snoring (ρεγχω,), thereby indicating the depth of the sleep as being significantly below the dreaming/waking boundary. Sasson, however, disagrees with Stuart and points out that Jonah was effectively a member of the crew during the voyage,[91] thus placing him alongside the crew as they lightened the ship, at which point he (inexplicably) goes below to sleep without raising so much as a murmur of disapproval from his hard-pressed 'shipmates.' Moreover, this view raises difficulties with Sasson's earlier conclusion that Jonah had hired the entire ship and its crew,[92] for it seems highly unlikely that any

---

87. Ben Zvi would argue that "the text reflects and shapes a theological construction of the entire world—including nature, people and the products of human hands" (Ben Zvi, *Signs of Jonah*, 77). Indeed, Wolff amongst others has suggested a fictional, albeit didactic function for the entire work, which he argues is constructed as a novella (Wolff, *Obadiah and Jonah*, 82).

88. McAlpine, although clear in his understanding of רדם as generally depicting divinely influenced sleep, remains troubled by its use in Jonah 1:5, 6. Nevertheless, he can say that "as in Isaiah 29:10 (*trdmh*), the effect of the (*t*)*rdm*(*h*) is to render Jonah oblivious to YHWH's current action" (McAlpine, *Sleep*, 58, 71, 76).

89. Stuart, *Hosea-Jonah*, 458.

90. See Chapters 3 and 4.

91. Sasson, *Jonah*, 84.

92. Sasson, *Jonah*, 83. Trible seemingly concurs, "he (Jonah) has financed an entire

passenger—especially an inexperienced 'landlubber'—would hire an entire ship's workforce and then proceed to work alongside them. In Sasson's view v. 5 is the nodal point of the whole narrative where "Jonah capitulates and runs away no more,"[93] and this is consistent with his view that the fish of 2:1 is merely a pedagogical agent,[94] rather than YHWH's destroyer or deliverer[95] who brings Jonah to heel at this later point in the story. Sasson also takes issue with McAlpine over the precise use of *rādam* (רדם—be asleep, unconscious) in this verse without addressing the latter's main argument that it is used principally to convey a sense of control by YHWH, rather than the depth or purpose (revelation?) of the sleep.[96]

Although Stuart acknowledges the possibility that Jonah's "special deep sleep" is divinely induced he remains puzzled as to YHWH's motivation for such action, which appears to serve no purpose "in Yahweh's rebuke of Jonah."[97] In addressing this problem it could be argued that one is left with the overall sense that YHWH simply wanted Jonah 'out of the way' until the ship had safely put to sea, but why should this be so? To answer this question it is important firstly to accept with Sasson[98] that Jonah is both fleeing and hiding, and then to recall that Jonah—in the guise of his spirit helper, the dove—although able to fly has (for the moment) chosen to hide. Despite being embarked and at sea, Jonah is still able to flee the ship provided by YHWH[99] at the first sign of difficulty or discovery, and as a consequence must be put to sleep until the storm reaches its height, at which point even as a dove he may be unable to escape. It is at this point, when his one avenue of escape appears to have been closed down that the captain stirs Jonah to his feet, and demands that he "call upon his god" (v. 6)—as each of the sailors had done—for rescue from their common plight. Jonah now knows that escape across the sea is difficult if not impossible, but may still believe that he remains undiscovered, and so quite understandably he does not comply with the captain's order to call upon (YHWH) 'his god.' Unfortunately for Jonah the crew now engage in the procedure

---

ship for disobedience" (Trible, *Rhetorical Criticism*, 130).

93. Sasson, *Jonah*, 102.
94. Sasson, *Jonah*, 149.
95. Ackerman, "Satire and Symbolism," 225.
96. Ackerman notes that this "unusual word in Jonah 1:5 for "deep sleep" can have polar connotations in the Bible," but nevertheless acknowledges that the one *common* feature of its use is that it is "divinely induced sleep" (Ackerman, "Satire and Symbolism," 231).
97. Stuart, *Hosea–Jonah*, 458.
98. Sasson, *Jonah*, 84.
99. Ben Zvi, *Signs of Jonah*, 77.

of 'casting lots' in an attempt to establish the cause of their misfortune—a procedure or "custom of reaching a decision (that) is spread all over the world and has existed at all times."[100] Lindblom suggests that the original 'efficacy' of lot-casting lay in its "magical power"—a power that was inherent in the procedure itself, and which later on developed into the (Israelite) conception of YHWH as instigator of the (outcome of the) procedure.[101] In both of these conceptions, however, the emphasis lies on catching, seizing or capturing an offender,[102] and therefore when the lot falls on Jonah (v. 7b) the prophet can be in no doubt that he is discovered.

The argument developed above has suggested that Jonah was in supernatural or 'soul flight,'[103] that he was hiding as well as fleeing, and that consequently it was essential for him "to escape from God's vision by joining a crowd,"[104] which one might therefore suppose was composed of similar, that is to say, spiritual beings. For the narrator, as indeed also for his audience, the emphasis of the lot-casting lay on Jonah having been "taken" by YHWH,[105] and it is the desire to know the name of the one responsible for this 'taking' that drives the sailors' first question (v. 8a)[106]—a question answered in detail by Jonah in v. 9b.[107] Essentially, this first question by the sailors is about Jonah's (spiritual) 'power' in relation to the one who has effectively just captured him, and from whom Jonah had already told the sailors he was fleeing (v. 10c)—an important question for this group of spirits amongst whom Jonah was hiding. The spiritual context also has significance for the second group of questions (v. 8b), which have variously either been considered aimed at eliciting four "distinct and separate answers,"[108] or else to be partially redundant.[109] Landes posits that vv. 8–9 have a chiastic structure where vv. 8a, 8b, 9a, and 9b equate to A, B, B′, A′ respectively, and from this suggests that "Jonah is responding to the sailor's questions . . . but in chiastic order."[110] Thus, in Landes' view Jonah's answer in v. 9a is a response to all the questions posed in v. 8b. Indeed:

100. Lindblom, "Lot-Casting," 164.
101. Lindblom, "Lot-Casting," 167.
102. Lindblom, "Lot-Casting," 167.
103. Winkelman, *Shamanism*, 62.
104. Sasson, *Jonah*, 84.
105. Lindblom, "Lot-Casting," 167.
106. Landes, "Textual," 279.
107. Landes, "Textual," 280.
108. Sasson, *Jonah*, 113.
109. Bolin, *Freedom Beyond Forgiveness*, 83.
110. Landes, "Textual," 279.

While Jonah's laconic answer in v. 9A seems most directly to answer only the fourth of the sailors' questions in v. 8B, the narrator may well have thought that the predication of a Hebrew identity also implied something about Jonah's mission, purpose, land, and ethnic affiliation.[111]

In a context where Jonah is being interrogated by a group of spirits the two couplets of questions in v. 8b (מה־מלאכתך ומאין תבוא and מה ארצך ואי־מזה עם אתה) appear at least capable of answer by Jonah's terse reply in v. 9a. Writing about v. 8b Sasson notes that "in most of its occurrences *melāʾkâ* (מלאכה) refers to human occupation or trade," but suspects that if the enquiry was about someone's work Hebrew would pose the question "using language... appreciably different from what the sailors use in our passage."[112] Moreover, Sasson's only objection to מלאכה being used to convey a spiritual or religious activity is the absence of another word in close proximity of the same (spiritual) ilk, such as 'holy' or 'temple.' If, however, the entire exchange takes place in the extended reality then this qualification is met. The second part of the first couplet is likewise capable of assimilation to a spiritual context, insofar as the question: "'From where do you come?' does not rule out the possibility that the sailors are enquiring into Jonah's nature, if he is a god or a spirit."[113] Consequently, it may be the case that if the first couplet is intended to establish what kind of spiritual messenger Jonah is, then perhaps the second seeks to establish Jonah's status. In this regard, the first part of the second couplet may carry a cosmological emphasis,[114] in as much as ארץ (*eretz*, 'land') can have a very broad range of meanings, which include 'underworld' as a potential rendition.[115] Finally, it should be noted that the phrase ואי־מזה עם אתה translated by Trible as "and-where from-this

---

111. Landes, "Textual," 280.
112. Sasson, *Jonah*, 114.
113. Bolin, *Freedom Beyond Forgiveness*, 83.
114. Sasson dismisses this possibility affirming that the sailors obviously have only a geographical or political meaning in mind (Sasson, *Jonah*, 115).
115. On this point Dahood drawing on the work of Baumgartner equates ארץ with the Akkadian *erṣitu* in connection with Jeremiah 17:13, noting that "the crux was solved ... by W. Baumgartner who compared *ʾereṣ* with Accadian *erṣitu* 'underworld.' Dahood goes on to note Gunkel's work which "amassed impressive evidence from Accadian, Hebrew, and Aramaic proving that *ʾereṣ* alone could signify 'underworld,'" before presenting other comparisons as evidence of the equivalence of ארץ and the Ugaritic *arṣ* (Dahood, "Value of Ugaritic," 165–6). Latterly, other examples have been offered where ארץ should be translated "underworld" (Holladay, "*ʾEreṣ* 'Underworld,'" 123–24).

(*weʾê mizzeh*) people (are) you?"[116] may in fact be probing for Jonah's rank,[117] and especially so if מן is considered to be locative.[118]

On the interpretation offered here it is Jonah's spiritual nature and status that the sailors attempt to extract from him in v. 8b, and his response of עברי אנכי (a-Hebrew[119] I [am]) in v. 9a tells them he is neither a (spiritual) messenger (*malak*) nor a spirit, demon or deity. Moreover, his status is revealed to be merely a man (albeit a man who is abroad in his extended, ethereal 'body' [נפש, *nephesh*]),[120] and an ordinary man at that whose origin is the 'world' as quite distinct from the '(under)world.' The (spirit) sailors have realized that Jonah is a denizen from another reality.[121] With a single word Jonah describes himself as a lowly mortal in close juxtaposition with a description of YHWH (v. 9b) as the supreme deity ("God-of-the heavens")—a description which may not have previously been made available to the sailors.[122] The narrator has in vv. 8–9 created a contrast between extremes of power; between mortal and immortal, finite and infinite, and it is this contrast that so terrifies the (spirit) sailors in the next verse. Hitherto:

> The somewhat simple minded sailors got the impression . . . that Jonah was a slave who was fleeing from his lord, his master. . . . Not earlier than now the true quality of Jonah's master is revealed to the sailors, and they have in fact all reason to be "exceedingly afraid" . . . This Hebrew man is . . . trying to escape from the mighty God of Heaven.[123]

---

116. Trible, *Rhetorical Criticism*, 140.

117. That rank is being probed for here may be supported by the use of the singular עם to designate an individual (Ex. 22:25) of a particular status within a group. This text has YHWH "using *ʿammî* to refer to a single individual, "one of my people," in apposition to . . . "the poor one with you"" (O'Connell, "עָם," 430).

118. On locative מן see Wilson, "Significance," 149.

119. The LXX at this point has "*doulos kuriou ego eimi*" instead of עברי, and Tov argues that the latter was "probably original," since "Jonah's answers (in the Masoretic text) suit the various questions concerning his origin, whereas according to (the Septuagint), Jonah does not answer these questions" (Tov, *Textual Criticism*, 257).

120. On the delocalisation of the נפש from its normal locus in the body see Chapter 4.

121. Significantly, "in the Old Testament, עברי, "Hebrew," is found especially often on the lips of foreigners, or is used towards foreigners, " who may equally well be cosmological aliens (Wolff, *Obadiah and Jonah*, 114).

122. In this regard, Harvianen suggests that "the narrator leads his audience and/or the readers to imagine that in the port of Jaffa, Jonah told the heathen sailors; 'from the/my lord I am fleeing,'" hence failing to fully disclose YHWH's identity (Harvianen, "Why were the sailors," 80).

123. Harvianen, "Why were the sailors," 80.

"They feared a great fear" (v. 10a) is the narrator's description of the men's response to Jonah's revelations, but does this echo or amplify Jonah's use of the same word (ירא) to describe his current situation *vis-à-vis* YHWH in the previous verse, or does it signify an entirely different usage? The basic meaning of ירא is "to fear," but most later English translations have chosen to interpret this word in v. 9 as "reverence" or "worship"—a choice that is wholly dependent upon the context in which it is found. If that context depicts events in the life of a willing prophet of YHWH then clearly "worship" is the preferred translation, but that will not be the case where an unwilling, vocational prophet-shaman[124] either does not recognize YHWH at all, obeys him only on sufferance or merely acknowledges him as (one of a number of) titular, state deities.

In addition to defining YHWH as the "God-of-the heavens," in v. 9b the narrator also has Jonah describe him as the maker of "the sea and the dry land," which interestingly records a shift in vocabulary from that used by the sailors in v. 8b. Indeed, in Sasson's view "Jonah's language is . . . unusual here in its use of *yabbāšâ* instead of the more common *'ereṣ*," and he goes on to note that "*yabbāšâ* is not commonly used as a synonym for "earth" in the geographical or physical sense, rather, it emphasizes the dryness of a piece of land, *terra firma* itself."[125] Sasson's point would appear to be equally valid for distinguishing between a cosmological ארץ (*eretz*) in the sailors' mouths (v. 8b) and the *terra firma* of Jonah's response. This point is important insofar as the narrator's choice of language (in Jonah's mouth) would appear to be limiting YHWH's power to the heavens, the sea and the dry land, but excluding the underworld. This in turn has implications for the motivation behind Jonah's response (v. 12),[126] when the sailors' put their final question to him (v. 11). At this point the fate of the sailors is intimately embroiled with that of Jonah and the question they put to him in v. 11 is an attempt to achieve 'a parting of their conjoined ways.' Indeed, Jonah acknowledges that their misfortune is entirely down to him (v. 12b), but his suggested remedy; "pick me up and throw me into the sea" (v. 12a) does not appeal to them as an answer to their woes. Jonah has already exhausted two shamanic avenues of escape from YHWH (the upper and middle worlds), and his language in v. 9b appears to indicate a belief that YHWH does not have power or influence over the underworld. It is possible, therefore, that at this point in the story Jonah believes he can make good an escape to the underworld via

---

124. A master of spirit(s), see earlier discussion in chapter four.

125. Sasson, *Jonah*, 119.

126. "What the reader would like to know here is what intention may be imputed to Jonah in asking the sailors to throw him into the sea" (Landes "Textual," 280).

immersion in the sea,[127] and that the (spirit) mariners remain unimpressed by Jonah's suggestion because they also know that Jonah is still seeking to escape from YHWH by descending below the sea,[128] thus continuing to implicate them in his flight from YHWH.[129]

Certainly, it is likely that the sailors would have by now (vv. 11-12) apprehended Jonah[130] on behalf of YHWH, perhaps even restraining him,[131] whilst deliberating over what should be done with him. What is certain is that the narrator in v. 15 "has the sailors ultimately carrying out Jonah's request to be cast overboard (leaving) the reader to conclude that Jonah's offer of himself is designed more to benefit himself than the sailors."[132] Before this takes place, however, the sailors decide to head for land (v. 13),[133] which although it is entirely the wrong thing to do in a storm would seemingly have delivered Jonah safely beyond their 'province,' the sea, and back into the hands of his master, YHWH. Apparently, they fear YHWH much more than the Hebrew who commands[134] them to free him by hurling him

---

127. Some exegetes have seen in v. 12a the expression of a death wish by Jonah (Lacocque and Lacocque, *Jonah: A Psycho-Religious Approach*, 88; Landes "Textual," 281; Stuart, *Hosea–Jonah*, 462). But this understanding in and of itself demands a further level of exposition of Jonah's motivation, which in the views of these scholars range from suicide to altruistic self-sacrifice.

128. Eliade observes that descent to the underworld is symbolised by "immersion in the water," and that "a number of peoples, and more especially . . . maritime peoples situate the beyond in the depths of the sea" (Eliade, *Shamanism*, 234–35).

129. The sailors have now come to "realize that Jonah has made them accessories to his crime by making them harborers of a fugitive" (Ratner, "Jonah, Runaway Slave," 301).

130. Ratner cites Neo-Babylonian documents bearing directly on the legal milieu of the exilic/post-exilic period in which the writer of Jonah worked, and which "establish a single fundamental legal principle with regard to the treatment of fugitives in the ancient Near East: The runaway must be returned to the rightful owner" (Ratner, "Jonah, Runaway Slave," 287).

131. That Jonah was already being tightly held might explain the significance of שאוני, 'lift me up' in v. 12—considered by Sasson to be somewhat redundant (Sasson, *Jonah*, 124).

132. In Landes' view Jonah is seeking his own death as a means of avoiding the mission to Nineveh, i.e. a final self-serving act (Landes "Textual," 282).

133. "To put him ashore was their decision, probably arrived at after further frantic discussion" (Stuart, *Hosea–Jonah*, 463).

134. This is perhaps the strongest interpretation that can be placed on the imperatives נשא and טול. As noted above Landes has Jonah "request" the sailors to throw him overboard (Landes "Textual," 280). So also Ackerman (Ackerman, "Jonah," 236). Sasson considers Jonah to be offering "counsel" or "advice" to the sailors (Sasson, *Jonah*, 131), whilst Trible has Jonah "insist" upon being hurled into the sea (Trible, *Rhetorical Criticism*, 146).

overboard.¹³⁵ That the level of intensity of the storm does not decrease, but on the contrary increases (v. 13b), alerts the crew to the possibility that YHWH—the supreme God who made "the sea and the dry land"—neither likes nor wants their preferred solution.¹³⁶ Indeed, Sasson notes the narrator's subtle re-use of *yabbāšâ* to indicate the futility of the sailors' action in the face of God's creation and control of their intended destination.¹³⁷ As was the case earlier (vv. 3–5), YHWH is controlling the environment—a fact that is acknowledged in the mariners' prayer (v. 14b) as a function of YHWH's unlimited freedom of action which is unrelated to time whether past or future.¹³⁸ Moreover, in view of the apparent incomprehensibility of YHWH's opposition to their rowing this comment may convey some sense of YHWH's inscrutability, which elicits no response from Jonah whilst perhaps providing an advance indication that YHWH is once again one step ahead in Jonah's escape plan.

The sailors' prayer (v. 14) is illuminating in its use of נפש האיש הזה, about which Sasson states "*nepeš ʾîš* is not common to biblical Hebrew, occurring elsewhere only in a brief saying (Prov 13:8)," and he goes on to liken it to the (slightly) more common expression "*nepeš (hā)ʾādām*," before eventually settling on a 'this person' in translation of נפש האיש הזה.¹³⁹ There are, however, problems with this interpretation: firstly, and in contrast to איש, אדם is almost always used in reference to a particular individual,¹⁴⁰ and this is reinforced in this case by the use of the definite article (making the expression נפש האיש unique in biblical Hebrew), which together with the demonstrative הזה makes האיש הזה an adjectival expression pointing to נפש (*nephesh*, 'soul') as the basic concept. This sense is accentuated when ב is translated causally, for "danger threatens בנפש ("because of the *nepheš*") of this man,"¹⁴¹ and is consistent with understanding Jonah's נפש as an intruder in this scene. Secondly, the noun נפש could be removed from this colon without significantly altering its sense and impact, unless this noun—"one of Hebrew scripture's most versatile"¹⁴²—has a special meaning here, that is,

---

135. "The crew . . . did not want to throw Jonah to the sea. That is evident not by their words, but by their actions, succinctly described by the narrator" (Stuart, *Hosea–Jonah*, 463).

136. "Clearly, Jonah's god and master does not desire *this method* of returning the prophet" (Ratner, "Jonah, Runaway Slave," 302).

137. Sasson, *Jonah*, 131.

138. Sasson, *Jonah*, 136.

139. Sasson, *Jonah*, 133.

140. Hamilton, "אָדָם," 266.

141. Wolff, *Obadiah and Jonah*, 119.

142. Sasson, *Jonah*, 133.

the נפשׁ is to be understood synecdochically as extended beyond the locus of the physical 'body.'[143] Such an understanding would not detract from the following colon; "do not make us guilty of innocent blood" (NRSV), since the act of entry into the lower or underworld is known to be more dangerous for the shaman-prophet than journeys in the middle or upper worlds.[144] Allowing Jonah to 'escape' into the world of the dead would involve the very real possibility of his actual, physical death,[145] which would be tantamount to murder[146] and leave them accountable to his master for that loss, since the primary objective of a slave owner was the retrieval of his property.[147] Mere harboring of a fugitive is not the issue here, but rather the possibility that escape into the underworld, would result in the death of Jonah's נפשׁ, which would simultaneously involve Jonah's bodily death, precisely because the נפשׁ is not a disembodied 'soul.'

After their prayer the sailors lift up Jonah (v. 15), whom they presumably still restrain, and cast him into the sea whereupon the sea immediately quietens down, or remains in its place (עמד)—"its movements ... now restricted"[148] by YHWH. The reactions of the sailors in response to the becalming of the sea are now recorded by the narrator in the final verse (v. 16) of chapter one. Because the sea responded (immediately) to Jonah's immersion and "ceased from its raging," (NRSV) the 'cause and effect' relationship impressed itself on the sailors whose first reaction therefore is to fear YHWH. On their second and third reactions, wherein "they sacrificed

---

143. See Chapter 4. Once again it may be emphasised that נפשׁ is not to be considered as 'soul' (although "pre-Platonic usage of *psychē* exhibits striking similarities to OT usage"), "it refers rather to psychic power . . . " (Seebass, "נֶפֶשׁ," 503, 510).

144. Eliade, *Shamanism*, 234. It may also be noted that in the Greek, Orphic myths, Orpheus, descends to the world of the dead in quest of Eurydice—behaviour that is characteristic of a shaman intent on retrieving the soul of a deceased person following death. Eliade considers such behaviour to bear no relationship to the Greek spirituality of the sixth and fifth centuries, but rather reflects the retention of an archaic shamanism (Eliade, *History of Religious Ideas*, 181–82).

145. Utilising concepts of a circular universe current throughout the Eastern Mediteranean (including Syro/Phoenicia), Marinatos develops the concept of an "Orphic Odysseus" engaged upon a "cosmic journey" into the underworld, in which all his men (an entire fleet) die leaving him alone as the sole survivor (Marinatos, "Cosmic Journey," 410–11).

146. Sasson observes that the motive of the sailors' prayer is the neutralisation of "potential blame for murder" (Sasson, *Jonah*, 133).

147. But it should be noted that in the Babylonian literature to which Ratner refers, "no penalty is imposed upon the harborer of the runaway" (Ratner, "Jonah, Runaway Slave," 287).

148. Sasson, *Jonah*, 137.

a sacrifice ... and they vowed vows"[149] there is a significant divergence of opinion, which is exemplified in the respective views of Stuart and Sasson. Stuart considers it unlikely that sacrifice took place on board ship, given the absence of cargo—and therefore presumably animals—but also principally because sacrifice in the ancient Near East had to be conducted at dedicated shrines or temples, since "one could not simply sacrifice wherever one felt like it."[150] Thus, in Stuart's view this scene had to have taken place at a later time, after the sailors had made landfall in Joppa and even following a pilgrimage to Jerusalem—the accredited sanctuary of YHWH. Moreover, Stuart interprets the 'vowing of vows' to be "almost certainly nothing other than promises to bring yet more sacrifices to Yahweh in the future."[151] In support of these (re)actions having taken place before the ship docked, Sasson cites evidence from ancient sea narratives indicating, "that sacrifice could indeed take place aboard ship; *during* sea voyages."[152] On this point one may note the concept of 'sacrifice' understood in Syro-Phoenicia as a divine banquet, that is, a banquet taking place in the extended reality in the presence of the (chief) deity.[153] Despite, the absence of information in the text it remains a possibility that the (spirit) sailors simply held a feast in honor of YHWH,[154] and in this regard it is perhaps reading too much into v. 5 to suggest that the sailors had thrown all their food or wine overboard. Sasson's pleading of a case for 'sacrifice' aboard ship is the first stage in his argument that the 'vowing' was quite separate from, albeit subsequent to the 'sacrificing'. Thus, one may envisage a celebratory, sacral feast (a 'sacrifice') building up to a moment of dedication by each of the (spirit) sailors to YHWH. Indeed, "with the calming of the seas, the sailors are obviously entering into a pledge not under duress but more in thanksgiving"[155]—a pledge affirmed perhaps in a festive toast to YHWH.

---

149. Sasson, *Jonah*, 137.
150. Stuart, *Hosea–Jonah*, 464.
151. Stuart, *Hosea–Jonah*, 465.
152. Sasson, *Jonah*, 139.
153. Wilson, "Significance," 212–13.
154. The idea that one may eat with the gods in a spiritual context is found elsewhere, compare Rev. 3:20.
155. Sasson, *Jonah*, 140.

YHWH Controls "The Vertical" (The Psalm)—Jonah 2:1-11

A basic tenet of this study has been an acceptance that the passage under scrutiny must have 'worked' as a coherent and unitary narrative for the first hearers/readers of the text, and that this was so irrespective of any subsequent redaction. In this regard, it becomes pertinent briefly to record the once prevalent view that the psalm in Jonah (Jon 2:3-10), does not belong in its present situation, that is, within the prose framework of the remainder of the book. Latterly, however, that view has been (successfully) challenged, initially by Landes[156] and later by Trible,[157] although both authors acknowledge that the text as a whole, and chapter 2 in particular, display a number of "dissonances,"[158] which give rise to problems in the elucidation of meaning. It is important at the outset to ascertain the structure of *Jonah* chapter 2, before dealing with the issues of what it achieves and contributes to the story as a whole, and in this regard Trible has much to offer. In her discussion of the structure of the fish/psalm pericope, Trible has defined "a chiasm of narrated discourse,"[159] which forms a parenthetical inclusio consisting of the content of the psalm. This chiasm is of the form A, B, B', A', which correspond to v. 1 (A and B), v. 2 (B') and v. 11 (A'), and Trible remarks upon the way in which the psalm is asymmetrically "locked within the confines of (this) exquisite chiasm," that is, between B' and A'.

---

156. Landes concludes: "Analysis of the structural symmetry of the book, its content, and the development of its thought have shown that the psalm as it now stands is in the proper position, of an appropriate type, and agrees quite harmoniously with the situation of Jonah in the narrative, both in terms of his physical and psychological portrayal" (Landes, "Kerygma," 30).

157. Trible although acknowledging "the inevitable subjectivity of research" attempts to stand somewhat aloof from the pros and cons of both arguments, insisting that rhetorical criticism can help establish "how the psalm functions in the present story, not if the psalm was added to an earlier story" (Trible, *Rhetorical Criticism*, 160-61). See also Christensen who considers the psalm to be "an integral part of the structural design of the book of Jonah as a whole, and not a secondary insertion" (Christensen, "Narrative Poetics," 30).

158. Trible acknowledges that her "study ponders dissonance" (Trible, *Rhetorical Criticism*, 161). Landes also notes after "undertaking a meticulous, close rereading of Jonah's 48 verses . . . no fewer than 63 places in the text where the author's deliberate or inadvertent withholding of information poses at least some interpretive issue for the reader and, in addition, 13 places where narrative features create a dissonance in the logic or coherence of the story" (Landes "Textual," 273-74).

159. Trible, *Rhetorical Criticism*, 157.

The narrated chiasm begins with Jonah being swallowed by the great fish, and swallowing—as both Ackerman[160] and Trible[161] point out—never has a positive connotation in the Hebrew Bible. In Trible's view therefore the fish is (at least initially) a threat to Jonah, which becomes "his abode" and ultimately concludes the descent (1:3, 5, 15) that "bespeaks death."[162] Indeed Trible can say that in general "chapters 1 and 2 of Jonah abound in terror."[163] In an earlier work Landes had maintained an opposing view, namely that the fish is "simply a beneficient (sic) device for returning Jonah to the place where he may resume the commission he had previously abandoned."[164] Fundamental to this conclusion is Landes' belief that "it is clearly *before* Jonah is swallowed by the fish that he is threatened by the sea and in danger of permanent residence in the nether world."[165] As has been demonstrated, however, from a shamanic perspective Jonah was never threatened by the sea, which he willingly entered in the second phase of his escape from YHWH to temporary residence in the nether world. In shamanic terms Jonah's controlled descent to the underworld under his 'own steam' has been subsumed, or more accurately, consumed under YHWH's control. From a shamanic viewpoint, control over this most life-threatening of activities—flight to the underworld—has been stripped away from Jonah, and he is now totally vulnerable to the actions of other (spiritual) entities. Just as the ship was drafted into Jonah's ASC/dream, so the (spiritual) fish is now co-opted as part of the rapidly evolving extended reality construct ('dream scenario'), as YHWH adapts to and prevails over this new phase of Jonah's escape plan. This fresh ensnaring of Jonah by YHWH is the 'cause' which Trible traces through to the 'effect' of his residence in "the belly of the fish," which in turn becomes the 'cause' of his prayer,[166] and therefore in Trible's view "the elusive phrase 'three days and three nights' indicates . . . a long residence for Jonah,"[167] during which he composes the psalm. The menace of Jonah's sojourn in the "belly of the fish,"—a sojourn to the point of 'no return'[168]—is perhaps equaled only by the importance of this phrase

---

160. Ackerman, "Satire and Symbolism," 220.

161. Trible, *Rhetorical Criticism*, 158.

162. Trible, *Rhetorical Criticism*, 159.

163. Trible, "Tempest in a Text," 191.

164. Landes, "'Three Days,'" 449. See also Craig who considers the fish to be "at least from Jonah's perspective, a vehicle of deliverance" (Craig Jr., *Poetics of Jonah*, 86).

165. Landes, "'Three Days,'" 450.

166. Trible, *Rhetorical Criticism*, 158.

167. Trible, *Rhetorical Criticism*, 159.

168. On the 'three days and three nights' motif in v. 1 Wolff can say that "this particular statement of time may undoubtedly have been prompted by myths and sagas."

to the ongoing development of the plot. Indeed, the appearance of the "*me͑ê haddāg(â)* of v. 1 and its repetition in v 2 obviously act as a device to synchronize Jonah's stay within the fish with his composition of the psalm."[169] But is this the sole extent of the usefulness of this phrase at this point in the narrative? Might it not also provide positive links between prose and poetry, sea and underworld, life and death?

An understanding and acceptance of *Jonah* 1 and 2 as a dream-sleep-dream sequence,[170] that is, as (a portion of) a derived hypnogram, has a number of consequences, not least for the freedom of the narrator who is no longer restricted to a 'rational'[171] development of the story. Clearly, a dream is by its very nature a swift progression of (pictorial) ideas (whether written down later or not), which move the autodramatic story forward in a direction and at a pace that would be impossible within 'normal' reality. A grasp of this basic fact allows an attempt to be made at resolving some of the 'dissonances' within Jonah. Application of this 'narrative freedom' to the first three verses of chapter two allows a smooth translation of ideas across the interface between the narrated introduction (vv. 1, 2) and the beginning of the psalm itself (v. 3).[172] Indeed, understanding these events as taking place in an ASC/dream removes from the scene the danger of drowning and hence the necessity of deliverance from drowning, which has inevitable consequences for viewing Jonah's prayer(s?) in chapter two as a petition for salvation from such a fate.[173] It does, moreover, exclude rescue from physical drowning as motivation for the thanksgiving element of the psalm, allowing the reader to contemplate Jonah giving thanks for deliverance from a more terrible fate—permanent incarceration in the realm of the dead.[174]

Indeed, "after so long a period there is hardly any hope of survival (Luke 24:21)" (Wolff, *Obadiah and Jonah*, 133).

169. Sasson, *Jonah*, 154.

170. In this regard it may be noted that "the Qumran scroll of the Twelve Prophets does not recognise any boundary between the sailors' prayers and the arrival of the fish" (Sasson, *Jonah*, 147).

171. Wolff advocates that interpreters of this text should avoid the adoption of a rational approach to the fish's function, despite suggesting on the basis of vv.1 and 11 that the writer was indicating the time taken (i.e. three days and three nights) to travel from an (unknown!) location at sea, to an (unknown!) landfall (Wolff, *Obadiah and Jonah*, 133).

172. It is generally accepted that the psalm comprises vv. 3(b)–10 (Sasson, *Jonah*, 160; Trible, *Rhetorical Criticism*, 160).

173. See for example Craig's exposition of this view (Craig Jr., *Poetics of Jonah*, 86–87).

174. Trible using Melville's words can say that "Jonah saw 'the opening maw of hell with endless pain and sorrows there'" (Trible, "Tempest in a Text," 190).

On this point of thanksgiving, although Wolff considers that 'drowning' is a (potential) feature of the psalm, he goes on to argue that "the great fish, the devouring, and the three days and nights in no way hint at any rescue operation."[175] Indeed, operating on the understanding that the psalm is an interpolation into the book, he derives the idea of Jonah's utter helplessness from the intricate relationships that exist between the first three verses of chapter two—the interface between narrative and psalm:

> That he (the interpolator) did not initially intend it to be understood as a hymn of thanksgiving emerges from the circumstance that in 2b—picking up v. 1b—he explicitly stresses that the prayer was spoken "out of the belly of the fish"; and this indication of place is immediately explained at the beginning of the psalm as meaning that it is the place of "distress," indeed "the belly of the underworld"; ממעי הדגה, "out of the fish-belly," in v. 2 corresponds to מצרה, "out of my distress," and מבטן שאול, "out of the belly (or womb) of Sheol," in v. 3.[176]

The bonds between these three verses quickly allow the scene to move forward by a series of imaginative leaps, which enable the place in which the recaptured Jonah is held (the belly of the fish) to transform itself into something completely different. Thus, Jonah in the voracious male fish belly of v. 1 (במעי הדג) is immediately labeled by the 'three days/nights' motif as being in a place of death, or at least at the point of no return from death. In v. 2 the male fish undergoes a sex change and it is from this female fish belly (ממעי הדגה) with its suggestion of the female reproductive organ that Jonah prays.[177] Sasson thinks that דג/דגה could be used as an obvious focusing device, but does not elaborate on what that 'focus' might be,[178] yet it would appear at least possible that the reader is being asked—even at this stage—to consider that the 'place of death' is also a 'place of (re)generation.' The next verse (v. 3)—which begins the psalm proper—brings these hints and suggestions into a concrete formulation as Jonah is described as having called from the womb of Sheol (מבטן שאול). The prophet's 'place' of abode has been

---

175. Wolff, *Obadiah and Jonah*, 133.

176. Wolff, *Obadiah and Jonah*, 133.

177. Trible notes that "the feminine (*haddāgâ*) . . . suggests a womb-like enclosure. Though traditionally translated here as "belly," the noun *mēʿeh* (plural *mēʿîm* {sic}) designates a variety of internal organs, including the womb" (Trible, *Rhetorical Criticism*, 158).

178. Indeed, Sasson holds that "the shift is a vernacular phenomenon, and cites as support a Mari letter in which 'lion' and 'lioness' are indiscriminately interchanged" (Sasson, *Jonah*, 155). "That he goes so far to find an example speaks to the unlikelihood of the explanation" (Bolin, *Freedom Beyond Forgiveness*, 106–7).

changed into a (re)generative organ within the netherworld, but without the need to move either through time or space—features which significantly are absent from the whole episode.

Jonah's fast-moving dream imagery is being reflected or traced in this great saga by the switch in narrative style, which 'changes up a gear' from this point (v. 3) in the story onwards. Indeed, in Christensen's view the whole book of Jonah "belongs to the category of poetry as this term is normally used in the field of literature . . . (but) moves between narrative and lyric poetry."[179] Moreover:

> The difference in structure between the psalm of Jonah (2.3–10) and its so-called 'prose' narrative context is more a matter of degree in terms of 'heightened language', than it is a distinction between poetry and prose genres as such.[180]

Christensen's analysis leads him to the conclusion that the 'psalm of Jonah' is an integral part of the structure of the book as a whole, which he considers uses "heightened language" to convey the fast-moving, pictorial imagery of the descent to the underworld. Whereas sea, ships and sailors can be described using relatively mundane forms of expression, "at the very point in the narrative where Jonah makes his final descent to the depths of hell itself, the language soars to lyrical heights."[181] The full significance of this use of lyrical poetry to facilitate the 'tracking' of fast-changing dream imagery is further elaborated in the discussion of v. 6 following.

In Trible's view the psalm likewise commences at v. 3 and terminates at v.10 prior to the ejaculation of the prophet from the fish in v. 11, but although this sits well within Trible's overall chiastic structure for chapter two, it does not describe Jonah's prayer, which appears to comprise two fundamental components—summary and main content. Indeed, v. 3 is part of an introduction[182] to, or formulaic[183] summary[184] of Jonah's prayer that precedes the main body of the supplication, which Sasson treats as the rationale[185] for the whole psalm. If this verse does function as a summary of the whole psalm, then it must necessarily begin with Jonah's position before the psalm (distress), and end with what the psalm achieves (his salvation?). But

---

179. Christensen, "Narrative Poetics," 30.
180. Christensen, "Narrative Poetics," 30.
181. Christensen, "Narrative Poetics," 45.
182. Barré, "Jonah 2,9," 242.
183. Bolin, *Freedom Beyond Forgiveness*, 108.
184. Stuart, *Hosea–Jonah*, 475.
185. Sasson, *Jonah*, 168.

v. 3 which ends with שמעת קולי (you heard my voice) appears not to have achieved anything more than a reiteration of a previous colon ויענני (and he answered me). This fact in itself appears to be a reversal of the expected situation "for we are told God 'answers' Jonah's plea and then 'hears his voice,' . . . (when) God should hear his voice *before* he answers his appeal."[186] Examination of ענה, (to answer), however, reveals that the primary meaning of the verb is 'to respond,' and that such a response may be either verbal or non-verbal,[187] which of course begs the question: What would be the nature of a non-verbal response in this context? The answer from Trible's structural analysis appears to be that "cryer and hearer *meet*,"[188] for:

> At every turn, within lines and between lines, Jonah and Yhwh *meet* and crisscross. Subject vies with object, distance with *proximity*, and distress with deliverance.[189]

Consequently, if indeed YHWH's response to Jonah's call is to become present to him (in the womb of Sheol),[190] then this would allow שמעת קולי (you hear my voice), to be the (permanent) outcome of such a meeting, that is, the permanent outcome of the whole psalm. Moreover, in the context of a meeting "you hear my voice" would imply dialogue—dialogue as the lasting and continuing outcome of the encounter—a feature which, as already noted, is conspicuous by its absence from Jonah's first encounter with YHWH in 1:1. Although not an explicit, recorded feature of the psalm itself dialogue is a feature of Jonah's subsequent experiences (chapter 4).

The foregoing argument has made use of the work of Sasson and Trible who both translate the verbs of v. 3 with English present tenses, over and against Stuart and the versions (e.g. KJV, NIV, NRSV) where the English past tense is used. If, however, the past tense is adhered to and ויענני is translated "and he humbled me/brought me low,"[191]—which appears to be an equally viable alternative for the verb in this context[192]—then the

---

186. Sasson, *Jonah*, 168.
187. Allen, "עָנָה," 679.
188. Trible, *Rhetorical Criticism*, 165.
189. Trible, *Rhetorical Criticism*, 166.
190. This appears to presage the second use of אל־היכל קדשך in v. 8 where in Christensen's view "'the House of the Fish' has . . . become a surrogate 'Temple' of YHWH" (Christensen, "Song of Jonah," 227). Indeed, "surely enough, Jonah has Company in the fish's belly" (Lacocque and Lacocque, *Jonah*, 100).
191. "It refers to near-death affliction (Ps 116:10), hardship used by God to drive the psalmist back to God's word (119:67)" (Wegner, "ענה (*'nh* II)," 450).
192. It is noted that the verb is found here pointed in the *qal*—not the *piel*—but an unpointed, pre-Masoretic consonantal text would allow this translation.

THE MAKING OF A DIVINE MAN—THE BOOK OF JONAH 183

first line of v. 3 is capable of summarizing the core of the prayer (vv. 4–5) immediately following. Reading v. 3 in this way resonates particularly well with an asseverative analysis of the particle אך in the last verset of v. 5 signifying a humble gesture. "Given Jonah's desperate situation, the asseverative reading makes sense,"¹⁹³ although Trible regards an adversative reading as equally possible, but bases this on the prior assumption of a "recalcitrant" Jonah—a description that implies that some kind of interactive (reciprocal) relationship with YHWH once existed—a feature which this study regards as unproven. That this particle (אך) in v. 5 "signals the reversal of Jonah's thoughts"¹⁹⁴ is clear, and what follows (vv. 6–7) may be seen to be the effect of the prayer, which may be regarded as summarized in the last verset of v. 3. Translation of ויענני in v. 3 in this way ("and he humbled me") is not suggested as the sole, preferred reading, but is rather offered with the suggestion that the writer may in fact be presenting a double entendre that refers to both the core prayer with its effect (vv. 4–7), and the lasting outcome of the whole experience post v. 11.

Some support for the view that the prayer itself comprises vv. 4–7—presaged by the summary in v. 3—may be found in Cross's suggestion that "vv. 3–7 derive from an old thanksgiving song (or lament) when traditional-oral skills were flourishing."¹⁹⁵ Following on from this suggestion Cross considers vv. 8–10 to be a "stock cultic ending," which "yields on analysis a far less sophisticated and intricate verse," yet he feels unable to assert that "the author of Jonah has spliced together a thanksgiving hymn to fit his purposes."¹⁹⁶ Having reached the possibility that an original, oral prayer (vv. 3–7) may have been supplemented by the addition of three extra verses, Cross dismisses that conclusion because this "stock cultic ending" fails to facilitate a better fit between psalm and narrative than vv. 3–7 alone would. But if Jonah, the vocational prophet-shaman who was unwilling to serve, or perhaps even acknowledge YHWH, is compelled by the circumstances of this dream/ASC experience to swear fealty to YHWH, then Cross's conclusion gains credibility. To begin with, a written version¹⁹⁷ of the supplemented psalm generates a new central phrase (סוף חבוש לראשי) in the psalm as a whole, which is equidistant in terms of word count from both

---

193. Trible, *Rhetorical Criticism*, 167.
194. Trible, *Rhetorical Criticism*, 167.
195. Cross, "Studies in the Structure," 167.
196. Cross, "Studies in the Structure," 166–67.
197. In this regard, Cross is certain that vv. 3–7 and vv. 8–10 do not "stem from the same poet or from the same time," and one suggestion is, therefore, that vv. 8–10 were a written appendage to what was originally an oral tradition (Cross, "Studies in the Structure," 167).

the beginning of v. 3 and the end of v. 10. The ascription of significance to this feature creates the problem that this rather unremarkable phrase has always seemed to be a relatively unimportant embellishment to the scene in v. 4 where (apparently) a real, 'flesh and blood' Jonah is threatened by actual physical drowning—a feature of the story already discussed and dismissed as unlikely. Moreover, there are other links between vv. 4 and 6 such as the repetition of the verb סבב (to encircle) in both verses—a verb that in v. 4 interestingly marks the centre of the entire book.[198] Yet it remains possible to place a different interpretation on v. 6c—as the centre of the psalm. In order to do this, reference may be made once again to Christensen's work at this point in the poem where "the language soars to lyrical heights."[199] Indeed, Christensen endorses the following definition of a poem:

> A composition designed to convey a vivid and imaginative sense of experience, characterized by the use of condensed language, chosen for its sound and suggestive power as well as its meaning, and by the use of such literary techniques as structured meter, natural cadences, rhyme, or metaphor.[200]

Thus, in the view offered here, lyrical poetry is being used in v. 6 to suggest to the hearer/reader's imagination a sense of the dream experience undergone by Jonah expressed in metaphorical terms. But if a metaphor is being employed here one is compelled to ask what it is that is being depicted?

Before attempting an answer it may prove helpful to recap on Jonah's dream situation. Firstly, from v. 1 the 'three days and three nights' motif indicates that Jonah is as good as dead, and is to be counted a resident of שאול (sheol), the realm of the dead, albeit not through physical drowning. Indeed, without conveying any sense of movement through the spatial dimensions the story continues (v. 3) by transforming Jonah's 'place' of confinement into the 'womb of Sheol'—a (re)generative organ—summarizing the entire prayer/psalm in the process. The supplication now follows (commencing with v. 4) in which Jonah acknowledges for the first time that it is YHWH, not he, who controlled the descent into the sea.[201] Moreover, and contra Sasson,[202] this is the point at which Jonah capitulates, ending his struggle to

---

198. Sasson, *Jonah*, 191.

199. Christensen, "Narrative Poetics," 45.

200. Christensen makes reference to *The American Heritage Dictionary of the English Language*. Christensen, "Narrative Poetics," 48.

201. Wolff, *Obadiah and Jonah*, 135. Viewing v. 4 as an acknowledgement by Jonah of YHWH's overall control of the situation overcomes the dissonance, pointed out by Landes, between this verse and 1:12 (Landes "Textual," 283).

202. Sasson, *Jonah*, 102.

maintain mastery of both himself and his vocation, and going so far as to accept that YHWH was in control from the outset (v. 5a), by the further acknowledgement that he did not flee, but was rather expelled from YHWH's presence (נגרשתי מנגד עיניך).[203] Jonah's entreaty reaches its climax in the last verset of v. 5 where, as already noted, an asseverative analysis of the particle אך signifies a humble gesture. In Trible's view the end of v. 5 marks the nodal point (B—B′) in her chiasm of the psalm,[204] and may be seen to map to the point at which Jonah's thoughts reverse[205]—a reversal which apparently precipitates a fresh description (v. 6) of the distress of drowning. But as already discussed, drowning was never an issue for the 'flying' shaman-prophet within his dream/ASC, and therefore v. 6 does not continue "to describe Jonah's plight in the water," and in this regard Trible acknowledges that "the setting of waters, deep, weeds, and mountains hardly fits the belly of a great fish."[206] Clearly, v. 6 although feeding off v. 4 is now suggesting by its (slightly) shifted language a metaphorical description of a completely different yet related scene.

Although the content of Jonah's entreaty (vv. 4–5) is uttered from the belly/womb of the fish/Sheol, the information it contains almost certainly relates to "a presumed gap between the hurling of Jonah into the sea (1:15) and his swallowing by the fish (2:1)."[207] This tentative suggestion by Trible is offered but then dismissed because of the dissonance between narrative (1:12, 15) and poem (2:4) already discussed. The resolution of this dissonance in terms of the methodology applied here allows v. 4 to be viewed as a description of Jonah's continued flight beneath the sea prior to his capture by the fish. It may be that the change of verb from טול (1:15) to שלך (2:4) is intended to suggest to the hearer/reader the shaman's capacity for animal transformation[208] ('shape-shifting'), in Jonah's case from a dove to a diving bird of prey[209] (שָׁלָךְ)—perhaps a cormorant[210]—able to dive deep beneath the waves. Any such suggestion could only be by word association rather than assonance between שָׁלָךְ and וַתַּשְׁלִיכֵנִי.

---

203. This phrase is acknowledged by Wolff as the equivalent of מלפני יהוה in v. 1:3ab (Wolff, *Obadiah and Jonah*, 135). So also Trible (Trible, *Rhetorical Criticism*, 168).

204. Trible, *Rhetorical Criticism*, 164.

205. Trible, *Rhetorical Criticism*, 167.

206. Trible, *Rhetorical Criticism*, 168.

207. Trible, *Rhetorical Criticism*, 167.

208. Winkelman, *Shamanism*, 62.

209. "On his ecstatic journeys the shaman is accompanied by an aquatic bird (gull, grebe), whose symbolism is precisely immersion in the water, that is, a descent to the underworld" (Eliade, *Shamanism*, 234).

210. Austel, "שָׁלָךְ," 929.

In any event, the symbolism conveyed is that of total immersion in "the heart of the seas," (בלבב ימים) and it is this idea that the poet picks up on in v. 6 where Jonah is found completely surrounded (אפף)[211] by the waters (מים). Indeed, Sasson translates אפף as 'envelop,'[212] but fails to explain how Jonah only manages to be enveloped up to his neck (the latter term being Sasson's rendition of נפש in this context),[213] thereby suggesting a confused picture in which Jonah seems (still?) to be bobbing about on the surface. In v. 6 the narrator describes Jonah as fully immersed and enveloped by primeval waters (מים)[214] as quite distinct from the seas (ימים) of v. 4, and in the (re)generative setting of "the womb of Sheol," the poetry may very well be suggesting dream imagery in which the sea has become transformed into the (primeval) waters surrounding a fetus. This fetal picture may be further assisted by a resonance between (the taste of?) the seawater (v. 4) and the primeval waters (v. 6)—the amniotic fluid[215] or isotonic solution of salts in which a baby develops. The parallelism[216] between v. 4 and v. 6 continues into the middle verset where the same expression of encirclement (יסבבני) is used with נהר in the former, and תהום in the latter verse. Both נהר and תהום are often "paired in Hebrew poetry"[217] and used of dynamic situations in which they can depict motion (flood, current or stream),[218] and in this regard סבב is used appropriately "as a verb of movement,"[219] and it is this verb that links v. 6 to all the imagery of v. 4b and c. Moreover, the introduction by the poet of תהום (v. 6b) in association with מים further establishes a picture of creation and darkness[220] (both of which are features of the womb), by recalling the imagery of Genesis 1:2 and thereby perhaps relating the רוח

211. Brown et al., "אפף-surround, encompass," 67.

212. Trumble and Stevenson, "'Envelop'—Surround and touch on all sides, especially so as to conceal," 839.

213. Sasson, *Jonah*, 182. Also Wolff (Wolff, *Obadiah and Jonah*, 136).

214. Associated cosmologically in both v. 6 and Genesis 1:2 with "the deep" (תהום).

215. Amniotic fluid fills the amnion, or inner membrane, inside which the foetus develops.

216. Sasson, *Jonah*, 182.

217. Sasson, *Jonah*, 182. Snijders considers that "'sea' and 'river' are parallel concepts" in the Jonah psalm, and identifies both with "the realm of the dead" (Ringgren et al., "נָהָר," 269).

218. The primary meaning of נהר is 'river' or 'stream,' and can indicate "water currents in the deep sea." (Ross, "נָהָר," 46). Similarly, תהום can indicate "a body of water . . . subterranean waters that burst forth in the flood (Gen 7:11) and that continues to feed waters and streams (Amos 7:4)" (Grisanti, "תְּהוֹם," 277).

219. Lopez, "סָבַב," 129.

220. Grisanti speaks of "the darkness that permeated the תהום" in his discussion of Genesis 1:2 (Grisanti, "תְּהוֹם," 276).

אלהים to this scene also. If, as seems likely, סבב is connecting and continuing the dynamism of v. 4 into the fetal picture presented in v. 6, then the imagery may be suggesting that this is the point at which the waters surrounding the baby begin to seep through the amnion.[221] Jonah, the baby at full term, feels the amniotic fluid pass over his head—expressed metaphorically by the poet in parallel with v. 4 as "all your waves and your billows passed over me." It may be noted that the use of סבב may also carry connotations of protection[222] and in this regard can be used in a maternal setting.[223]

Thus far the poetic imagery may be pointing to gestation and the commencement of labor, and consequently this requires that the last verset (6c) should be capable of interpretation as the 'birth' itself, yet it is precisely at this point that the parallelism between vv. 4 and 6 (last versets) appears to break down. When treated as a metaphor dependent upon the 'sea' imagery of v. 4, however, this last verset (6c)—positioned at the very centre of the psalm[224]—is able to continue the nativity scene by suggesting a pictorial equation between the clinging kelp[225] of the sea, and the bedraggling wet hair of the newly emergent infant.[226] Sasson's suggestion that it is seaweed that festoons Jonah's head may lack support, but the picture proffered by the poet need only depend upon סוף being a water or marsh plant of some

---

221. There may be other associations with תהום here, i.e. the idea of subterranean waters bursting forth–"the fountains of the deep" (Gen 7:11). It should be noted again, however, that as in all dreams there is little to relate the experience to any spatial or temporal movement, and as a consequence, an entire gestation period may be in view here (v. 6) culminating in the (re)birth itself.

222. "The form in Jonah . . . is an imperfect of the *po'el* conjugation. Scriptural attestations indicate that this verbal conjugation conveys a *protective* rather than a threatening act" (Sasson, *Jonah*, 182).

223. In Jeremiah 31:22 סבב may in fact have a sexual meaning where "the woman (= the people) encompasses the man (= Yahweh)," with the suggestion of a new creation (Lopez, "סָבַב," 136). Anderson observes "it is probably true that the verb *těsôbēb* has a sexual—or, better, maternal—meaning: the Woman (Virgin Israel) will enfold a man (a son) as a sign of Yahweh's gracious gift of new life in the land" (Anderson, "Lord Has Created," 476). So also Keown (Keown et al., *Jeremiah 26–52*, 123).

224. Wolff considers vv. 6b–7a to be the "climax" of Jonah's account, albeit that the experience is believed to be one of distress due to real, physical drowning (Wolff, *Obadiah and Jonah*, 136).

225. Sasson translates סוף as seaweed or 'kelp' (Sasson, *Jonah*, 182). Wolff suggests these sea plants could be "huge algae growing in the depths of the sea" (Wolff, *Obadiah and Jonah*, 136).

226. In Christensen's view "it was inside the fish that Jonah was turned around, or 'born again,' as some would choose to put it" (Christensen, "Song of Jonah," 227). Analogously, in the view of the Lacocques Jonah "painfully gives birth to himself" (Lacocque and Lacocque, *Jonah*, 106).

description, whether the term derives from an Egyptian loan-word[227] or a Semitic root[228] common to both Egyptian and Hebrew. Moreover, a picture of Jonah where "reed grass wraps itself around the prophet's head,"[229] permits an easier imaginative leap to the 'wet hair' of a new born baby.

The next Hebrew phrase (לקצבי הרים) may controversially either commence the next verse (v. 7) as per Stuart, Sasson, and Trible,[230] or be appended to the previous verset (v. 6c) as per Landes, Cross, Wolff, and Barré[231]—in order to regularize the poetic meter. In the latter view ל is considered to be locative, and Sasson's main objection to this view is that it is not clear to him:

> What the poet would be implying if Jonah laments, "Seaweed was twisted round my head at the root of the mountains." Is *what* is choking Jonah the reason for his despair? Or is *where* he is choking that is making him lose hope?[232]

It may objected that in a context in which Jonah is believed to be drowning,[233] having him also choke on seaweed would appear to be more than a little bizarre, perhaps even absurd. In the view expressed here, however, 'choking' is an appropriate word to use in a metaphorical description of Jonah's dream experience of (re)birth. Moreover, in terms of the metaphor, Jonah's emerging head is found positioned at the extremity of (the womb of) Sheol, that is, at the very base of the birth canal, and maintaining the poetic meter such that this 'birth' takes place "at the roots of the mountains" also has cosmological implications. Sasson, following Talmon, notes that the latter expression is a cosmological concept—an axis point at which the "three components of the universe: the earth, the seas, and the underworld" were conjoined.[234] Thus, it follows that this term may be describing the point at which it is possible to effect entry into and exit from these 'realms,'[235] and may be depicting

227. Ottosson and Lamberty-Zielinski, "סוּף," 191.

228. Ward, "Semitic," 348.

229. Ottosson and Lamberty-Zielinski, "סוּף," 192.

230. Stuart, *Hosea–Jonah*, 468; Sasson, *Jonah*, 167. Trible, whilst separating vv. 6c and 7a does, however, allocate them to a single strophe (Trible, *Rhetorical Criticism*, 164).

231. Landes, "Kerygma," 7; Cross, "Studies in the Structure," 164; Barré, "Jonah 2,9," 242. Wolff notes that the first two words of v. 7 should be added to the previous verset "in order to complete the five stress line" (Wolff, *Obadiah and Jonah*, 126–7).

232. Sasson, *Jonah*, 186. Author's emphasis.

233. Sasson, *Jonah*, 176.

234. Sasson, *Jonah*, 187.

235. The LXX's use of σχισμας ορεων may be appropriate here since it can describe both the 'birth' and the axis point in terms of a break, fissure or discontinuity.

Jonah's emergence from both a 'real womb,' and the actual core of Sheol, since had he remained in either place, he would surely have died. At this point Jonah has reached the nether end of the netherworld having escaped confinement in the womb of Sheol through YHWH's deliverance,[236] and in Wolff's estimation has avoided the potential for perpetual incarceration in Sheol. He translates v. 7bc as the recollection of an avoided fate:

> I had descended into the land which (was to close) its bars behind me forever. And yet you have brought my life out of the grave, Yahweh my God![237]

Christensen considers that הארץ (the land)[238] marks the point at which Jonah begins his ascent,[239] and "the shift in direction occurs precisely at the structural centre of the book of Jonah from a metrical point of view."[240] This is consistent with the 'birth' analogy suggested here, insofar as Jonah's ascent can be described as 'a bringing up from the grave[241] alive'[242]—a possible counterpoint to the womb as the potential 'grave' from which an 'infant' could be stillborn.[243] Finally, it may be noted that v. 7 concludes with the first acknowledgement from Jonah's own mouth that YHWH is his God, other than the summary of the psalm in vv. 2–3, and it is not until this point that he 'owns' YHWH as his God.[244]

---

236. Lacocque makes reference to the universality of stories in which a hero is swallowed by a water monster while on a journey. "The water plays a very important symbolic role in the tales, for it represents the maternal depths and the place of (re) birth. It also symbolizes the unconscious. . . . The descent into the belly of a monster of the underworld is always an *ambivalent venture*" (Lacocque, "Fear of Engulfment," 226). It may, however, be appropriate to point out the difficulty of describing Jonah as a "hero," as this term is conventionally understood.

237. Wolff, *Obadiah and Jonah*, 126.

238. הארץ is understood here by both Wolff and Sasson as the 'underworld' or 'netherworld. (Wolff, *Obadiah and Jonah*, 36; Sasson, *Jonah*, 188).

239. Christensen, "Song of Jonah," 223.

240. Christensen, "Narrative Poetics," 44. Moreover, "verse 7 is the psychological centre of the psalm . . . (and) this line's critical role is greater when appraised within the full narrative concerning Jonah" (Sasson, *Jonah*, 182).

241. Wolff observes that שחת is "the usual word for the grave as in Ps. 16:10; 49:9; 103:4; Isa 38:17 and frequently elsewhere" (Wolff, *Obadiah and Jonah*, 137). It should be noted, however, that קבר is a common Hebrew word for grave or tomb occuring "67x in the OT" (Alexander, "קבר," 867).

242. A number of scholars translate חיים as 'alive' (Sasson, *Jonah*, 167; Christensen, "Song of Jonah," 224).

243. The use of חיים in such an analogy would convey a sense of life "as an abstract idea . . . the state of being alive as opposite to being dead" (Smick, "חָיָה," 281).

244. Wolff seems disconcerted by the expression (v. 2a) "Yahweh his God . . . since

The theme of recollection of an avoided fate begun in v. 7bc is now continued as a more general recollection in v. 8, but reflecting here the wider context of the entire dream experience. Indeed "in a similar way to v. 3, the whole path of distress, prayer, and the granting of the petition is traced once more."[245] Recollection of the whole experience would be entirely appropriate here if, as Cross suggests, vv. 8–10 are "welded on to the older traditional verses,"[246] thus creating an almost seamless expansion of that briefer, older theme. Within this expanded recollection, however, lies reference to v. 5[247] where, as already noted, Jonah made humble supplication, with the result that "his rescue was effected as soon as his lips uttered prayers to God,"[248] and the expansion in v. 8ab consists in the manner of Jonah's supplication. The poet, in his use of זכר combines the senses of remembrance and invocation[249] to describe that manner, recalling the stronger sense of invocation conveyed by the call/answer (קרא/ענה) sequence in the psalm summary of v. 3, and signifying how YHWH, on being invoked, becomes present to Jonah in the belly of the fish. The psalmist goes further, however, when in v. 8cd he draws some degree of equivalence between 'YHWH' and 'his holy temple,' for "here the temple is simply a "B" word in the elements of synonymous parallelism to the "A" word "you.""[250] Significantly, the use of such a parallel would be appropriate to Jonah's humility in v. 5, since a now-willing servant desires to look with (lowered?) deferential eyes only in the general direction of his new masters' environs, and it may be posited that such a humble entreaty effectively comprises the pledge or vow referred to in v. 10. In sum, v. 8 sits as a recollectory counterbalance to the introductory prayer-summary of v. 3, with the supplication itself (vv. 4–5) and its consequences (vv. 6–7) parenthetically enclosed between them.

Expansion and explanation continue into v. 9 as the poet moves from the particular (the recollection of Jonah's own personal experience) to the general, but if from the outset this story has been about the nature of prophecy, then this must raise the question: In what precisely does that 'general' situation comprise? Interestingly, this verse is the cause of much consternation amongst commentators. Landes, for example, considers that it fits "least

---

there is nothing comparable in the rest of the story" (Wolff, *Obadiah and Jonah*, 130).

245. Wolff, *Obadiah and Jonah*, 137. So also Sasson (Sasson, *Jonah*, 191).

246. Cross, "Studies in the Structure," 167.

247. Sasson, *Jonah*, 191–2.

248. Sasson, *Jonah*, 191. This is certainly the nodal point (B—B') in Trible's chiastic structure of the psalm (Trible, *Rhetorical Criticism*, 164).

249. "The verb *zākar* merges the notions of "remembering" and "orally invoking" something or someone (Sasson, *Jonah*, 193).

250. Stuart, *Hosea–Jonah*, 478.

well within the book as a whole,"[251] while Trible thinks that it "lies uneasy in the psalm,"[252] and Sasson simply reserves judgment recommending "*caveat emptor*" on a larger than normal range of options.[253] In terms of the methodology applied in this study, however, it may be stated that so far as the phenomenon of prophecy is concerned this verse is probably the central tenet of the book of Jonah in particular, and the Hebrew Bible in general. In defense of the latter position it may firstly be agreed with Wolff that Jonah is included[254] amongst 'those' (משמרים) of v. 9a and has, moreover, moved from one antithetical position[255] to the other. This antithesis has often been seen as a contrast between idol worship and covenant loyalty to YHWH (חסד, *ḥesed*),[256] and those who hold this view, where הבלי־שוא is translated as 'worthless idols,'[257] 'empty idols'[258] or 'empty nothings'[259] are perhaps giving overmuch credence to the physical representation (figurines) of what are at base spiritual realities. In this regard, Sasson urges caution when he reminds his readers that for the ancients "cultic figurines" were merely "a tangible way by which a deity communicated with worshippers."[260] Much, it appears, depends upon context and it might be inappropriate to translate הבלי־שוא as worthless 'figurines' or 'idols' in the (non-cultic) context of the fish/Sheol experience—where the only participants have been Jonah and YHWH, in what is arguably part of an ASC/dream sequence. In such a context it may be agreed with Barré that הבלי־שוא—where שוא adds to the concept by emphasizing the ineffectiveness[261] of these entities—"is probably

---

251. Landes, "Kerygma," 30.

252. Trible, *Rhetorical Criticism*, 170.

253. Sasson, *Jonah*, 199.

254. Although Wolff considers that the entire psalm is an interpolation, and that Jonah is merely a backsliden prophet of YHWH, he believes the verse "shows readers of the book of Jonah the repulsive picture of the old Jonah over against a new picture" (Wolff, *Obadiah and Jonah*, 138).

255. "Grammatically, two verbal forms surround two nominal forms; thematically, two contrasting attitudes . . . surround two contrasting allegiances" (Trible, *Rhetorical Criticism*, 170). See also Sasson (Sasson, *Jonah*, 199) and Barré who observes that the participle and verb in v. 9 are "always related as opposites" where they appear together elsewhere in the MT (Barré, "Jonah 2,9," 239).

256. Stuart, *Hosea-Jonah*, 478 and Barré, "Jonah 2,9," 240. Wolff goes so far as to suggest that חסד is a synonym for God in this context (Wolff, *Obadiah and Jonah*, 138).

257. Wolff, *Obadiah and Jonah*, 127.

258. Trible, *Rhetorical Criticism*, 164.

259. Stuart, *Hosea-Jonah*, 478.

260. Sasson, *Jonah*, 197.

261. Shepherd, "שָׁוְא," 53.

some kind of parody of *ḥesed*."²⁶² Consequently, if the view is taken that in Jonah 2:9 "*ḥesed* stands for God himself,"²⁶³ it follows that the antithetical concept הבלי־שוא must refer to spiritual beings of some (inferior) kind. Moreover, it is Jonah's (now abandoned) relationship with הבלי־שוא that is contrasted with his new חסד relationship,²⁶⁴ which YHWH just inaugurated "in terms of a new creation."²⁶⁵ In a sense, חסד here has an 'inaugural'²⁶⁶ aspect to it, which enables the verse to be anchored firmly to the preceding prayer, cause/effect experience. Significantly Jonah, the vocational prophet-shaman, has abandoned his erstwhile הבלי־שוא, which in one sense may be seen with Barré as "faithless practices,"²⁶⁷ and has ceased to trust the spirits (slaves) he used to keep (שמר).²⁶⁸ Certainly, this is the import of הבלי־שוא where it appears in Psalm 31:7 in opposition to בטח (trust) in YHWH, thus it would seem to be Jonah's change of orientation (position or stance) with respect to trusting in YHWH that is being recollected and generalized in Jonah 2:9. Extrapolating this understanding from the particular (Jonah) to the general would appear to indicate that this verse is directed at those of a similar ilk to Jonah, rather than to faithless²⁶⁹ Israelites²⁷⁰ as a whole.

Jonah's dream now moves swiftly to its conclusion (v. 10) as the poet returns once more from the general to the particular, recording Jonah's thanksgiving for his (re)generation and his affirmation that he will sacrifice to YHWH—the one who has in effect just begotten him. That זבח is here indicating future, cultic²⁷¹ sacrifices possibly at the temple²⁷² in Jerusalem is moot, but the salient point is that Jonah's vow consists solely in his (re) orientation from הבלי־שוא towards YHWH²⁷³ (the nodal point of which oc-

---

262. Barré is, however, firmly of the opinion that הבלי־שוא does not refer to deities. Barré, "Jonah 2,9," 241.

263. Zobel, "חֶסֶד *ḥesed*," 62. So also Wolff, *Obadiah and Jonah*, 138, and Ackerman, "Jonah," 237.

264. "We may . . . conclude quite generally that *ḥesed* is a relational concept" (Zobel, "חֶסֶד *ḥesed*," 49).

265. Christensen, "Song of Jonah," 226.

266. "This interpersonal relationship can be defined . . . as the relationship . . . between two parties, inaugurated by an unusual act of kindness on the part of one" (Zobel, "חֶסֶד *ḥesed*," 46–47).

267. Barré, "Jonah 2,9," 241.

268. Sasson renders v. 9a as "those who *maintain* empty faiths" (Sasson, *Jonah*, 199).

269. Barré, "Jonah 2,9," 248.

270. Wolff, *Obadiah and Jonah*, 138.

271. Trible, *Rhetorical Criticism*, 171.

272. Stuart, *Hosea–Jonah*, 478.

273. Contra Sasson who affirms that "we do not know what Jonah vowed to God"

curs in v. 5b)—as quite distinct from any specific task-related vow (e.g. a mission to Nineveh). It follows that Jonah is affirming his intention (v. 10b) to remain true to that vow.[274] The psalm closes with the emphatic statement that salvation—such as that Jonah has just experienced—belongs to YHWH "in contrast to . . . coming from any other source."[275]

Thus far, with the end of Jonah's poem the account has traced out three components (dream/sleep/dream) of Jonah's derived hypnogram before arriving at v. 11—a verse that is separated in the Masoretic text from both the preceding story and all that follows by scribal marks (ס and פ respectively) instructing copyists to insert empty lines or breaks in the account. Sasson takes such breaks in the text seriously following the threefold, Masoretic division of Jonah's narrative, which because of its duplication at Qumran suggests to him a textual tradition that antedates the second century BC.[276] In Sasson's view the first division of the Jonah narrative (1:1—2:10) corresponds with a downward movement, the second division (2:11—4:3) being horizontal and the third having "no spatial movement,"[277] but this view fails to fully account for what is effectively the isolation of 2:11 within the narrative. If, however, v. 11 is viewed as the conclusion to Jonah's hypnogram, then both the *setûmā'* (ס) and the *petûḥa'* (פ) may be accounted for satisfactorily, and this may be expressed graphically as in figure 9.

Thus, the first division of the Jonah narrative (1:1—2:10)—the dream/sleep/dream sequence—concludes with a further period of sleep, before Jonah enters into a brief and final hypnopompic[278] altered state of consciousness, within which the dream imagery instantly translates Jonah back into the insides of a male fish. In the ejaculation of v. 11 Jonah is in fact undergoing the process of waking up, and one may imagine him jerking awake in a cold sweat following his harrowing experiences of the night, before becoming free to undertake his new mission commencing at 3:1 in 'normal,' waking reality. Viewing v. 11 as the conclusion of a night time hypnogram that traces the events of Jonah 1:1—2:10 is in agreement with Ancient Near Eastern cosmology, in so far as Jonah visits all the points on what may be regarded as a circular cosmos.

(Sasson, *Jonah*, 201).

274. Wolff hints at the non-specific nature of the vow when he observes that "the vow may promise . . . lasting trust" in YHWH (Wolff, *Obadiah and Jonah*, 138).

275. Stuart, *Hosea–Jonah*, 478.

276. Sasson, *Jonah*, 270–71.

277. Sasson, *Jonah*, 271.

278. Hypnopompia–semiconsciousness preceding waking.

APPENDIX

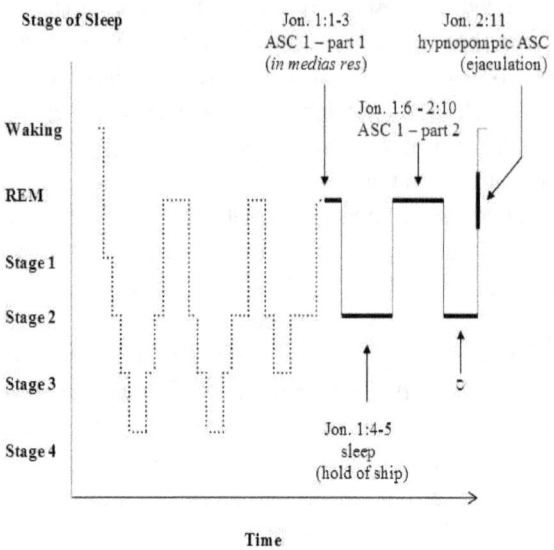

Fig. 9 'Derived Etic' Hypnogram of Jonah 1:1 – 2:11

Marinatos draws on Keel's earlier work on Psalm 139:8–10[279] to show that:

> Complementary bipolar concepts operate in this biblical text. On the one hand, there is an antithesis between up and down, "heaven-underworld"; on the other, East and West are juxtaposed . . . Thus the vertical and horizontal planes are complementary and oftentimes used side by side.[280]

Marinatos amalgamates these biblical concepts with similar models found in other Ancient Near Eastern traditions to produce a composite, circular,[281] Eastern Mediterranean view of the cosmos. In this portrayal, East and the West should be understood as "cosmic junctures"—points that symbolize the normal transitions from night to day (East) and day to night (West), or in Lacocque's view symbols of consciousness and unconsciousness respectively.[282] Marinatos schematizes the composite whole in figure 10, and in his

---

279. Keel, *Symbolism*, 23.
280. Marinatos, "Cosmic Journey," 390.
281. Marinatos, "Cosmic Journey," 395.
282. Lacocque reviews a number of stories from cultures across the world, in many of which "the hero is swallowed by a water monster while on a journey going east (symbol of consciousness). The engulfment typically takes place in the west (symbol of unconsciousness), at the antipode of the planned destination" (Lacocque, "Fear of

view "archaic thought utilizes the concepts of path and gate,"[283] where the paths of the day and night are represented by the upper and lower hemispheres of figure 10,[284] with these paths meeting at the cosmic junctures—the East and the West respectively.[285] If the recorded portion of Jonah's dream or vision quest/journey is mapped to this circular cosmos it will be found to commence at the zenith of the upper hemisphere, before proceeding westwards and downwards (anticlockwise) into the lower hemisphere ('night'), and when Jonah emerges he does so at 'dawn' in the East. On this latter point it may be noted that Jonah makes landfall on *terra firma* (v. 11, יבשה)—to use Sasson's term[286]—the same term used by the sailors when they attempted to row back (to the East?) in 1:13 following Jonah's own use of it in 1:9, and the question that naturally arises is: Were the spirit sailors trying to extricate themselves from their predicament by simply waking Jonah up? In any event, Jonah is finally ejected from his cosmic journey upwards and eastwards to a point corresponding with dawn in the Ancient Near Eastern concept of the cosmos, and coincident with him waking up at the end of a night's sleep traced in part by a characteristic hypnogram. Contra Sasson[287] the first third of the book of Jonah records his almost complete circuit[288] of the Ancient Near Eastern cosmos in both the horizontal and vertical planes, and at no point did YHWH lose control of either.

Engulfment," 219).

283. Sasson commenting on the reference to 'bars' in Jonah 2:7 notes that elsewhere in scripture they commonly secure gates—including the gates of Sheol (Sasson, *Jonah*, 189–90).

284. The arrows track the course of the sun—the cosmic cycle of day and night—from its rising in the east to its setting in the west. Reproduced from Marinatos, "Cosmic Journey," 391.

285. Marinatos, "Cosmic Journey," 396.

286. Sasson, *Jonah*, 119.

287. Sasson argues that the direction of the first segment of Jonah (1:1—2:10) is (exclusively?) downward. (Sasson, *Jonah*, 271).

288. It may be noted that the almost complete circuit (beginning in the upper world) corresponds with the part hypnogram (beginning in mid-dream) likewise recorded in the text.

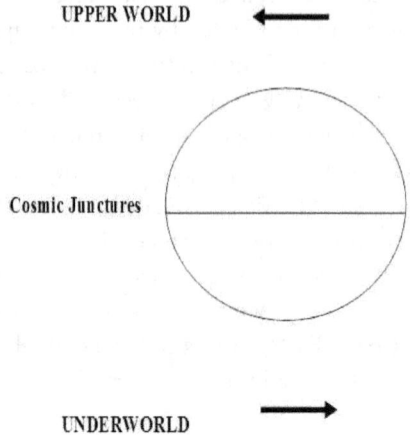

Fig. 10 Eastern Mediterranean View of the Cosmos

Nineveh—Jonah 3:1–4:3

The foregoing demonstration of the isolation of 2:11 within the narrative—as part and parcel of the characteristic rear portion of a hypnogram—makes it virtually certain that when "the word of the LORD came to Jonah a second time" (3:1, NRSV) Jonah was both alive and 'awake.' Jonah has willingly chosen to abandon his previous trust in הבלי־שוא in order to serve YHWH in a new חסד relationship, as a lasting result of his experience in "the belly of Sheol" where YHWH "hears his voice." YHWH hears Jonah in the meeting between them summarized in 2:3, and this has been held to imply Jonah's access to lasting and continuing dialogue with YHWH, for this is certainly what transpires later on in chapter 4. Jonah has, moreover, undergone a 're-birth' experience and has become a "new creation,"[289] and the reader may therefore have a right to expect to see other features of Jonah's new 'condition' in all that now follows, commencing with 3:1.

289. Christensen, "Song of Jonah," 226.

The Second Mission—Jonah 3:1–5a

Some scholars regard 3:1 as a simple resumption of the commission given to Jonah in 1:1, and commensurately allocate little space to its elaboration,[290] and although most remark on the replacement of Jonah's patronym with שנית ("a second time" or "once more"), few ascribe much significance to it. Sasson, however, continues at length in his discussion of this term observing that it is curious "that whenever scripture uses *šēnît* to replay divine messages, only a brief interval separates the two occasions (Gen 22:15;[291] Jer 1:13, 13:3; probably also Jer 33:1 and Zech 4:12)."[292] It is interesting to note that Sasson cites Jeremiah 1:13 as one example of this 'observation,' since an application of the methodology derived in this thesis to the whole of Jeremiah 1 after the opening preface[293] (Jer 1:1–3) suggests that this text is depicting the first portion of a hypnogram. In particular, Jeremiah 1:4–19 commences with ויהי דבר־יהוה אלי ("and the word of the LORD came to me") and is punctuated by two further repetitions of ויהי דבר־יהוה אלי (Jer 1:11, 13) breaking the text up into three periods of speech/action. Each of these periods (Jer 1:4–10; 11–12; and 13–19[294]) appears to bear the same relationship (ratio) to the others—in terms of relative length of text—as exists between the first three periods of REM/dreaming sleep found in the

---

290. See for example Wolff, *Obadiah and Jonah*, 139. Indeed, Stuart can say "the hearer/reader finds in vv. 1–3a a wording which largely repeats and therefore consciously echoes the wording of 1:1–3" (Stuart, *Hosea-Jonah*, 481–82).

291. It may be noted that there is disagreement over whether Genesis 22:15–18 comprise an interpolation into the text—as favoured by von Rad and Westermann (Von Rad, *Genesis*, 242; Westermann, *Genesis 12–36*, 355.), or remain integral to the narrative as maintained by Wenham (Wenham, *Genesis 16–50*, 101–2.). The salient point, however, consists in the fact that the speech/action portrayed in the received narrative (whether redacted or not) is indicating that only a brief period of time separates v. 11 and v. 15.

292. Sasson, *Jonah*, 226. It must be stated that this observation finds little support in the attested usage of the term, although Koehler and Baumgartner suggest an element of immediacy for 2) והשנית Samuel 16:19) where it describes the second point made during a (human) debate/argument, before going on to note the similar usage of an Akkadian analogue (Koehler and Baumgartner, "שֵׁנִי," 1604–5).

293. Craigie et al., *Jeremiah 1–25*, 1. It may be noted that the Masoretic text concludes v. 3 with a *setûmāʾ* (ס) to indicate a vacant space in the text, and thereby the closure of a discrete section of the book.

294. The Masoretic text reinforces this understanding by indicating with a *petûḥāʾ* (פ) that a juncture had been reached after vv. 10 and 12 respectively. It may be further noted, however, that although discontinuities are appropriately indicated by scribal marks after vv. 3, 10, 12 and at the end of the chapter, it is not immediately apparent why another such juncture has been inserted after v. 6—save possibly to indicate the effective nodal point of this 'call narrative' pericope.

hypnogram of a depressive.²⁹⁵ In Chapter 4, Fig. 6, it was demonstrated that the relative duration of the speech/action sequences (1 Kgs 19:2–21) interspersed with sleep periods of varying depth and duration when represented graphically displayed the form of a hypnogram, and moreover, the hypnogram that is characteristic for depression. Jeremiah 1:4–19 could therefore be seen as comprising a highly condensed (and stylized) 'fingerprint' of the first portion of a hypnogram, but without the intervening non-REM sleep periods. The use of שנית in Jeremiah 1:13 would therefore of necessity imply the passage of only a short period of time (1–2 hours) between the commencement of discrete dreams in a sequence of dreams, that is, between v. 11a and v. 13a, and it may be observed that this is the second (visual!) point in YHWH's argument. In this regard, it may be observed that שנית is used specifically to denote the second dream in a sequence of dreams on the same night in Genesis 41:5, where Pharaoh dreams about the seven good and bad years about to befall Egypt.

Although Sasson appears convinced about this usage of שנית as an indicator of the brevity of the intervening periods between such divine messages, he remains puzzled by its interesting implications for the book of Jonah. In particular:

> The storm scene and the three-day psalmodizing within the fish make it difficult, of course, to believe that God is entrusting Jonah with two messages on the selfsame day.²⁹⁶

If, however, Jonah 1:1—2:10 is understood as a dream sequence that leads on to a hypnopompic ASC (i.e. Jonah wakes up, 2:11), then this would allow the two 'words of the LORD' to be separated by a matter of (perhaps 2–4) hours, and give credence to Sasson's intuitive reading of the significance of שנית. More importantly, שנית directs the (ancient) hearer/reader's attention to the differences between the two scenes, insofar as the second word is apparently being received within 'normal' consciousness as quite distinct from a dream.

The content of the "word of the LORD" comprises the whole of v. 2, and immediately—indeed abruptly, the hearer/reader is made aware by vv. 1–2 that Jonah, like Samuel (when walking through town, 1 Sam 9:17) can hear YHWH speak to him. Consequently, the reader is compelled to acknowledge the unavoidable implication that Jonah's intrinsic consciousness²⁹⁷ has become like that of Samuel—capable of accessing both the nor-

---

295. See Chapter 3.
296. Craigie et al., *Jeremiah 1–25*, 1.
297. See Wilson, "Significance," 211.

THE MAKING OF A DIVINE MAN—THE BOOK OF JONAH 199

mal and extended realities simultaneously. Moreover, the narrator "is in the habit of meticulously selecting exact phrasing from the 'Kings corpus,'"[298] directing the hearer/reader's attention to the phrase ויהי דבר־יהוה אליו in 1 Kings 17:2–10, the only alteration in Jonah 3:1 being the replacement of the third person pronominal suffix by the proper name 'Jonah.' Comparison with Elijah is thereby also invited and Jonah, like Samuel and Elijah, is seen to be in receipt of auditions during 'normal waking' reality. The narrator could therefore be suggesting that Jonah too is (now) an Avatar, or Man of God (איש אלהים),[299] and this is consistent with the change in prophetic status hinted at by Sasson following Magonet[300] in their deliberations on *Jonah* 1:2 vis-à-vis 3:2. The reader might, however, reasonably expect to see further support for such a contention in what follows.

Having received a new or second commission (שנית "does not necessarily imply repetition of the previously received message"[301]) perhaps within hours of waking, Jonah rises and goes to Nineveh "according to the word of the LORD." If Sasson is correct the phrase כדבר יהוה "may be purposefully placed here to sharpen recall of that other narrative about Jonah in 2 Kings 14:25"[302]—and as a consequence the narrator could be introducing the reader/hearer to a lesson in relative geography. The latter reference in Kings concludes by noting Jonah's provenance, that is, Jonah hails from Gath-Hepher in Galilee, and it is thus conceivable that the narrator is suggesting that Gath-Hepher is where Jonah wakes up (2:11), rises and leaves (3:3) for Nineveh. Certainly, this understanding is consistent with v. 3b, which in Sasson's view is a parenthetical inclusio[303] in a sequence of activities spanning vv. 2–4—a sequence that should not in his view be arrested or disturbed.[304] The first of the two couplets in this inclusio tends to be treated by some scholars as an indication of the size[305] or importance[306] of Nineveh, but Sasson again suggests another alternative:

---

298. Ferguson, "Who Was the King," 302.

299. See Wilson and the discussion on I Samuel 9:6–11 concerning prophecy, where the terms 'prophet/seer' and 'man of God' are differentiated from each other (Wilson, "Significance," 198–200).

300. Sasson reads Magonet in this light (Magonet, *Form and Meaning*, 25).

301. Sasson, *Jonah*, 225.

302. Sasson, *Jonah*, 227.

303. Wiseman, "Jonah's Nineveh," 36.

304. Sasson, *Jonah*, 228.

305. Marcus thinks a superlative is in play here, which may render עיר־גדולה לאלהים as "an exceptionally big city" or more colloquially as "a godawfully big city" (Marcus, *From Balaam to Jonah*, 101–2).

306. Stuart argues that the phrase indicates Nineveh's importance to God (Stuart,

> I do favor treating ʿîr gedôlâ lēʾ lō hîm as a circumlocution whereby "the large city" is said to "belong" to God. . . . It may be superfluous for us (and very likely for the ancient Hebrews) to be reminded of God's dominion over the staunchest of Israel's foes. Nevertheless, . . . it explains why the Ninevites readily follow Jonah's directives . . .[307]

Certainly, this seems to be a continuation of "Jonah's old argument (1:9), that God is dominant everywhere on earth,"[308] that is, on 'dry land' (יבשה) as well as on the sea, and "invests the statement (v. 3ba) with a spiritual dimension,"[309] which may be indicative of the receptivity of the Ninevites. Moreover, Wiseman observes "it is not impossible that here the author is stressing the polytheism of Nineveh with its worship of many gods,"[310] which may be a long hand way of saying that the narrator considers the Ninevites to be 'very religious.' Both Sasson and Wiseman seem to be observing—in their different ways—the possibility that the narrator is directing attention to the spiritual/religious sensitivity of the Ninevites.

The second of the two couplets within the parenthesis (מהלך שלשת ימים) is the more difficult to interpret, and most commentators consider it refers in some way to the dimensions of Nineveh, either the city's diameter,[311] circumference,[312] or layout.[313] Stuart, following Wiseman favors the view that "a walk of three days" refers to the total duration of Jonah's visit to Nineveh, and includes one day each for arrival, purpose/business, and departure.[314] It is probably correct to accept with Sasson that the latter, minority view has "no merit," whilst noting that Sasson still finds common ground with Stuart on the nature of מהלך (journey) as a measure of duration or

---

Hosea–Jonah, 483).

307. Sasson, Jonah, 229.

308. Sasson, Jonah, 230.

309. Sasson, Jonah, 229.

310. Wiseman, "Jonah's Nineveh," 36.

311. Both Wolff and Sasson translate in this way (Wolff, Obadiah and Jonah, 143; Sasson, Jonah, 224).

312. A typical day's walk of about 17 miles gives a circumference for the city of over 50 miles—a figure wholly inconsistent with Sennacherib's enlargement (assumed to give a circumference of 7.5 miles). Moreover, Wiseman observes; "I do not know of any description of the size of an ancient city by the circuit of its walls" (Wiseman, "Jonah's Nineveh," 37).

313. Simon exemplifies the view that מהלך שלשת ימים refers to the duration required to cross the city street by street repeating the proclamation of v. 4, which implies that Jonah "proclaimed his message in only one third of the city" (Simon, JPS Bible Commentary: Jonah, 28).

314. Stuart, Hosea–Jonah, 487.

THE MAKING OF A DIVINE MAN—THE BOOK OF JONAH   201

time, observing that "*mahalak* is not a standard linear measure."³¹⁵ Thus far, the narration has indicated Jonah's compliance with YHWH's instruction (v. 3a)—perhaps locating the prophet in Gath-Hepher at the beginning of his journey,³¹⁶ followed by a brief parenthetical excursus on the nature of Nineveh and some 'measure' of duration or time associated with it (v. 3b). This appears to be followed by Jonah's actual transit to, and entry into Nineveh (v. 4a), since the expression "began to enter the city" (ויחל יונה לבוא בעיר) normally connotes arrival³¹⁷—in this case Jonah's. The content of the parenthesis (v. 3b), therefore, appears to be providing a reference point with which Jonah's subsequent behavior (vv. 4–5) may be compared—the reader being invited initially to compare the normal transit time to Nineveh (v. 3b) with Jonah's ability to "cover this great distance "lickety split" in an exceptionally short amount of time"³¹⁸ (v. 4a). To put it a little more succinctly the reader is being invited to draw a comparison between a long transit time and a short transit time, where the phrases "a three days' walk" and "a one day's walk" are here being used "figuratively,"³¹⁹ that is, in a general or non-quantitative manner.³²⁰

In Marcus' view *Jonah* is written as a satire and the import of Jonah's fast transit to Nineveh lies in it being a "parodic emulation" of Elijah's³²¹ run from Mount Carmel to Jezreel—a distance of eighteen miles. It may be recalled, however, that Elijah's feat has been explained in terms of *lung gom pa*³²² running, where the subject takes "extraordinarily long tramps with amazing rapidity," but which consist in "wonderful endurance rather than

---

315. Sasson, *Jonah*, 230.

316. David Marcus notes "The language indicating Jonah's compliance is formulated precisely like that of the command (קוּם לֵךְ אֶל־נִינְוֵה v. 3; כִּדְבַר יְהוָה v. 1 // דְּבַר־יְהוָה v. 2 // וַיָּקָם יוֹנָה וַיֵּלֶךְ אֶל־נִינְוֵה v. 3). The force of this statement of Jonah's departure to Nineveh is that of an anticipatory exposition common with descriptions of departure elsewhere in the Bible (e.g. Gen 22:3; 24:10; 28:5; 1 Kgs 17:10). These verses describe reports of departures to a place before the individual arrives there" (Marcus, "Nineveh's "Three Days' Walk," 48–49).

317. Marcus, "Nineveh's "Three Days' Walk," 44.

318. Marcus, "Nineveh's "Three Days' Walk," 47.

319. Marcus, "Nineveh's "Three Days' Walk," 45.

320. M. Sæbø acknowledges that the plural (ימים), which is introduced in the parenthesis (v. 3b) before the singular of v. 4a, can "move in the direction of a general (and abstract) notion of time" (Sæbø, "יוֹם," 22). If it is accepted that a notion of 'time' in a general sense is intended here (v. 3b), then it could be seen to be qualified in construct with שלש relative to the phrase immediately after it (מהלך יום אחד) in v. 4a.

321. Marcus, "Nineveh's "Three Days' Walk," 47.

322. See chapter 4.

... momentary extreme fleetness."[323] Such 'trance' runs[324] are invariably undertaken in a state of possession wherein the subject tramps "at a rapid pace and without stopping during several successive days and nights."[325] Clearly, an immense distance could be covered in this manner, and even the distance between Gath-Hepher and Nineveh (approximately 500–600 miles) could be accomplished in a single such session. Jonah's arrival in Nineveh at the end of a 'trance' run might be seen by the 'religious' Ninevites as a sign of his possession—a sign giving divine authority to any subsequent utterances. On this point, it may be significant that New Testament sources (Matthew 12:38–42, Luke 11:29–32) make reference to "the sign of Jonah," and "the text of Lk. 11.30a at its face value, . . . would seem to convey that Jonah himself, in his own person and presence, was a sign to the Ninevites."[326] The sudden appearance of Jonah 'running' towards the city walls in an altered state of consciousness—the very essence of a (visibly) possessed Divine Man (איש אלהים)[327]—helps to explain the otherwise curious efficacy of his brief announcement; "Forty days more, and Nineveh shall be overthrown!" Wiseman observes that it would not be unusual for men from one city-state to visit another whether alone or in groups for political, medical, or religious purposes, and "there is therefore no difficulty in a prophet being received by the leaders of the city (3:5), though he would probably have had to establish his bona fides first."[328]

A "trance run" of such proportions would without doubt have been sufficient to establish Jonah's *bona fides*[329] not merely as a prophet, but as 'God' himself—embodied and present in(side) the person of Jonah. As a result,

323. David-Neel, *Magic and Mystery*, 184.

324. See chapter 4.

325. David-Neel, *Magic and Mystery*, 185.

326. Landes, "Jonah in Luke," 141. On this point it may be noted that "the word 'sign' in the Synoptic Gospels is not the usual word for "miracle," . . . (and) by itself usually means a unique signal" (Smith, "Sign of Jonah," 755).

327. "Someone endowed with superhuman, divine qualities and powers: possessing something of the nature of the divinity" (Hallevy, "Man of God," 237).

328. Wiseman, "Jonah's Nineveh," 44.

329. Wiseman lists a number of scenarios including foreign invasion, total, solar eclipse, famine, plague and flood that may have (apocalyptically) sensitised the Ninevites to a suitably authenticated prophet. He refers in particular to an "attested solar eclipse, which has since become the earliest astronomically fixed date in Assyrian history, (and which) occurred in 763 BC, significantly during the reign of Jeroboam II of Israel (782–753) and the lifetime of Jonah ben Amittai" (Wiseman, "Jonah's Nineveh," 46). Moreover, Ferguson evidently considers "that the people of Nineveh at this time are ready for a prophetic message and will react positively to it" (Ferguson, "Who Was the King of Nineveh," 309).

the people of Nineveh believe in God—not Jonah (the man), or even God's word,[330] and this leads directly to the narrator's statement; ויאמינו אנשי נינוה באלהים (literally: "and the people of Nineveh [were caused to, hiphil] believe in God," v. 5a), which immediately follows Jonah's utterance, עוד ארבעים יום ונינוה נהפכת ("Forty days more, and Nineveh shall be overthrown," v. 4b). Indeed, the brevity of Jonah's proclamation causes some commentators to note "the ease with which Jonah's message convinces Assyrians to forsake their evil way,"[331] but this is to miss the narrator's point entirely. The narrator is most probably here recording the superhuman qualities (Divinity) of the messenger, which caused the Ninevites to be certain (אמן) about God as personified in Jonah. Contra Sasson "the prevalence of ʾelōhîm in chapter 3," which commences at this point (v. 5a) is not indicating the "power of a divine being" or "the might of the unique God of Israel,"[332] but rather the power of Divine Being—as a visible, qualitative feature of the man, Jonah.[333] Sasson deliberates at length on Jonah's ability to speak "the local Nineveh patois of Assyrian,"[334] but a suitably validated 'ambassador' would presumably have had little difficulty in having his message translated in such a large cosmopolitan metropolis. Alternatively, Jonah's proclamation may have been simply another occasion (the first?) where *xenolalia* is recorded as one of the characteristic features of the divinely possessed.[335]

The Proclamation of a Fast—Jonah 3:5b–4:3

Jonah's second mission appears to reach its conclusion once his 'prophecy' has been delivered, and from this point (v. 5b) onward the narrator recounts the reactions of the Ninevites. The first of those reactions appears to be the spontaneous calling by "the whole population"[336] for a fast—an activity that has nuanced significance for the commentators; Sasson finds penance

330. "We are not told that the Ninevites believed 'the word'" (Wolff, *Obadiah and Jonah*, 150).

331. Sasson, *Jonah*, 236. Trible argues that the absence of a Yahwistic formula (e.g. "thus says Yhwh") "may challenge the authenticity of the utterance" (Trible, *Rhetorical Criticism*, 180). This discussion, however, argues that the authenticity derives from Jonah's recorded behaviour as quite distinct from formulaic pronouncements.

332. Sasson, *Jonah*, 244.

333. Contra Trible who maintains that Jonah never gives the Ninevites "his credentials" (Trible, *Rhetorical Criticism*, 182). Rather, Jonah's demonstrated 'Divinity' is the validation that explains his words.

334. Sasson, *Jonah*, 232.

335. Compare Acts 2:1–12.

336. Sasson, *Jonah*, 246.

(punishment?) and self-denial[337] in fasting, whilst for Wolff it signifies mourning and repentance[338] with Stuart reading faith and penitence[339] into the practice. On hearing the news (v. 6) the king likewise donned the outward signs of 'mourning and repentance,' and this "immediate response shows clearly that the (apocalyptic?) message was taken as affecting not only the city of Nineveh, . . . but also the king and his position."[340] This latter point is significant if one accepts with Ferguson that the 'king' of Nineveh was one of a number of provincial governors "paying lip service to the Assyrian king," in a politically unstable period (781–745 BC) during which the "Assyrian empire almost passed out of existence."[341] Ferguson relies upon a direct, archaeologically-demonstrated[342] equivalence between "the north-west Semitic word for 'king' (*mlk*)" and "the Assyrian word *šakin* which means 'governor,'"[343] and concludes that the leader in Jonah 3 should more properly be considered as a provincial governor who ruled in close consultation with his "provincial and municipal nobles"[344] (cf. v. 7a). Certainly, this is an explanation of the title 'king of Nineveh,' which neither attempts to name this leader as a known, historical king of Assyria,[345] nor uses the title (as most modern commentators do) as 'evidence' that *Jonah* "does not treat a historical event."[346]

In conditions of dire political instability joint decrees by ruling local 'juntas' would have a twofold effect; firstly they would reassure the populace that effective government was continuing, whilst secondly distributing the responsibility for the action taken over all the local nobles. Thus, in the event of a resurgence of central power and authority the 'king' could deflect 'individual' responsibility. In this case the 'king's' decree (v. 7) could be viewed as

337. Sasson, *Jonah*, 245–46.

338. Wolff, *Obadiah and Jonah*, 151.

339. Stuart, *Hosea–Jonah*, 489.

340. Wiseman, "Jonah's Nineveh," 44.

341. Ferguson, "Who Was the King of Nineveh," 311. See also Lemanski in stating: "this (772–745 B.C.) was a period of local autonomy in Assyrian regions as well as in Babylonia" (Lemanski, "Jonah's Nineveh," 46).

342. Ferguson, "Who Was the King of Nineveh," 303.

343. On this point Ferguson highlights recent work in comparative Semitics suggesting that certain "linguistic oddities" in the book of Jonah might betray a northern Israelite dialect (Ferguson, "Who Was the King of Nineveh," 303).

344. Ferguson, "Who Was the King of Nineveh," 313.

345. Stuart leans towards Wiseman's suggestion that the king in question could be Aššur-Dān III (773–756 BC), (Stuart, *Hosea–Jonah*, 492).

346. Sasson appears to favour this interpretation considering the "foundation" of the Wiseman–Stuart position to be "pretty rickety" Sasson, *Jonah*, 248.

THE MAKING OF A DIVINE MAN—THE BOOK OF JONAH   205

an example of "hyperbole," with the whole episode (vv. 6–9) appearing to be a "subsequent explication of v. 5."³⁴⁷ But Sasson favors treating the passage (vv. 5–9) as "sequential:"

> Thus, in v. 5, the response is individual and probably spontaneous, . . . Only after tidings reach the palace is there a more formal and official response.³⁴⁸

Sasson's inclination (he later raises a potential objection) is to see these verses as sequential, and this makes good 'political' sense,³⁴⁹ insofar as the authority or 'grandness' of the decree (and thereby its issuers) is considerably enhanced. The inclusion of some animals (i.e. those of "herd and flock," v. 7) in the king's decree would appear at first sight to be another factor lending support to the idea that *Jonah* is fiction (a novella³⁵⁰), insofar as it strains (modern) credulity to imagine animals included in an actual royal decree. But the prohibition of v. 7 uses two verbs טעם and רעה to refer to humans and animals respectively,³⁵¹ and to enable the animals to 'graze'³⁵² (רעה) requires various actions on the part of their human owners, including leading and protecting them, and stalling them at night. In short, the prohibition is effectively a ban on animal husbandry in its entirety—the cessation/suspension of the whole farming economy. In this respect, the king had led by example, for when he stepped down from the throne and took off his robe (v. 6); he effectively suspended all state business for the duration of the fast. Accordingly, it may be agreed with Sasson that the use of sackcloth to clothe animals during penance (v. 8) is not "an absurdist touch,"³⁵³ especially since such a visible sign on the backs of the (stalled?) animals would signify to all a household's compliance with the king's decree. This issue of ostensible, communal compliance wherein stalled animals are expected to display the outward signs of their owner's compliance continues in v. 8b with the further injunction; ויקראו אל-אלהים בחזקה. Here, as Sasson points out, the noun חזקה is added to the imperfect (jussive) form of the idiom קרא אל for the first and only time in Jonah functioning as a further compliance indicator, and moreover, "as a device by which to gauge the depth of a

---

347. Wolff, *Obadiah and Jonah*, 151–52.

348. Sasson, *Jonah*, 247.

349. "The king's decree adds impetus and official sanction" to a popular action, in order possibly "not to be seen as opposing the populace" (Stuart, *Hosea–Jonah*, 493).

350. Wolff, *Obadiah and Jonah*, 85.

351. Sasson, *Jonah*, 255.

352. Brown et al., "רעה," 944–45.

353. Sasson, *Jonah*, 257.

worshippers *conviction*."[354] The last (two) of the king's imperatives (v. 8cd) give instruction concerning the content of the mighty (חזקה) cry to God: "and let them turn back each from his evil way, and from the violence that {is} in their hands."[355] Following closely upon the cessation/suspension of 'normal (economic) life,' that is, the functions of state (v. 6bc) and the pursuits of animal husbandry (v. 7b), these imperatives imply that רעה and חמס were endemic components of everyday practice and experience.

From the narrator's viewpoint the sequential expansion of the term used in v. 5 (איש) to the more inclusive, generic/collective term (אדם, v. 7) for humankind might be expected to do two things. Firstly, it would elevate the whole passage (vv. 5b–10a—a discussion of the fasting and its outcome) to prominence, as the dominant 'topic' of chapter 3. Secondly, the extension of the popular and spontaneous fast of the men of Nineveh to include foreigners, women and domestic animals would be bound to include Jonah, because the decree would apply the force of law to what was hitherto a voluntary matter for local men only.[356] From this point forward (vv. 7–8) Jonah would be compelled to pursue a fast along with everybody else. After the specifics of his edict the king now expresses (v. 9) the hope that God will relent (שוב)—a hope apparently founded on the completeness of "the 'faith' of the men of Nineveh in God (v. 5a),"[357] following Jonah's arrival in the city. In the next verse (v. 10) the narrator provides the hearer/reader with God's positive response to this 'faith.'

The first thing to note about chapter 4 (v. 1) is the reintroduction of Jonah to the story; he has not been mentioned since 3:4 and presumably therefore has remained in Nineveh throughout the events described in the intervening verses. Certainly, the reader is not told otherwise and must assume that Jonah (who is אדם! 3:7–8) has himself lived through those events including the fast as proclaimed by the king. Thus, it is reasonable to suppose that Jonah is in a fasted condition when he again takes 'centre stage.' This is an important point because the unstated 'it' of v. 1 has usually been taken to refer specifically to YHWH's action in 3:10b, rather than the entire sequence of events since Jonah was last mentioned. Indeed, as Davies argues:

---

354. Sasson, *Jonah*, 258. Author's emphasis.

355. Young's Literal Translation.

356. It may be noted with Dozeman in passing that "the king's proclamation in Jonah 3:6–9 does not function as a call to repentance in its present narrative context, since the people of Nineveh have already repented with fasting and sackcloth in the previous verse (Jonah 3:5)" (Dozeman, "Inner-Biblical Interpretation," 215).

357. Wolff, *Obadiah and Jonah*, 154.

It is quite common for R^c Qal to be used without an explicit subject, and that in such cases the subject is generally a pronoun "it", which refers to the action or situation just described. . . . The subject of *wayyēraʿ* is "it" referring to Yahweh's action described in iii 10b.[358]

Davies' argument is developed to refute Wolff's claim that רעע in v. 1 denotes 'wickedness' on the part of Jonah, but in developing that argument he draws upon the use of מרעתו in v. 6 where he believes it refers to physical discomfort caused in this case by "direct exposure to the sun."[359] This raises the possibility that רעע is likewise referring to some form of physical discomfort[360] in v. 1, and although Sasson believes the latter to be no more than a "feeling of unhappiness" he nevertheless considers it to be something that "Jonah *endures* rather than *initiates*,"[361] and this suggests that the 'it' in v. 1 was a fairly well established condition. Other instances where רעע in the qal (וַיֵּרַע, 'and 'it' was bad/evil/grievous/distressing') is used to refer collectively to the events of the previous several verses include Genesis 38:10—the refusal of Onan to consummate his Levirate marriage, and 1 Chronicles 21:7—David's efforts at census-taking. Thus, it would seem appropriate for וירע to refer collectively to the effect of the events at Nineveh—recounted in the previous five verses, that is, Jonah's condition after enduring (forty?) days of fasting. In short, the narrator having returned to Jonah simply records the 'way' he is now—that is, in a distressed condition—following the whole of the events of 3:5–10.

Verse 1 concludes with ויחר לו and this has traditionally been taken to mean "and he became angry,"[362] but there are other nuances to the verb חרה, which include 'grief' ("and he was grieved"[363]) with its connotations of the reactive depression associated with mourning. Sasson maintains that חרה can denote "depression, chagrin, annoyance" in circumstances where its subject "remains impersonal or unstated,"[364] and he cites a number of

---

358. Davies, "Uses of R^c Qal," 107.

359. Davies, "Uses of R^c Qal," 108.

360. "The semantic spectrum of r^c and its derivatives . . . largely coincides with the range of semantic parallels in other Semitic languages, such as Akk. *lemēnu* and Aram. *bʾš*. Each of these terms covers the most varied aspects of everything not good or negative; they do not make a distinction between "bad" and "evil," and so the exact meaning of r^c in each instance can be determined only from contextual clues" (Dohmen, "רעע," 562).

361. Sasson, *Jonah*, 273. Author's emphasis.

362. Wolff, *Obadiah and Jonah*, 159. Stuart, *Hosea-Jonah*, 498.

363. Bolin, *Freedom Beyond Forgiveness*, 151.

364. Sasson, *Jonah*, 274.

scriptures to underpin this view including Genesis 4:5–6, which would seem to support such a translation by adding פניו נפלו (v. 5) where this phrase is typically translated "and his countenance fell." This latter description of Cain's face (פנים) appears to be portraying his whole demeanor as crestfallen, for in addition to denoting the front side—specifically the head of a living being—"a human face can also reflect the inner feelings."[365] Sasson also draws on Gruber's analysis of Jonah 4:1 where ויחר לו "is to be rendered 'he was depressed,'"[366] and which is based on a parallelism (וירע/ויחר לו) appearing also in 1 Samuel 18:8, although the order of the expressions is reversed in the latter passage. Earlier work by Cohen had likewise suggested חרה shared the dual meaning of anger and despondency with כעס. Indeed:

> The dual meaning of these words is not fortuitous. It indicates that in Biblical times there was an intuition of an important finding of modern dynamic psychology, that depression involves, or resembles, anger turned inwardly, against oneself. It was not beyond Biblical man to make such an observation.[367]

Moreover, the idea of depression as 'anger turned inwardly' is not dissimilar to the central concept of the expression חרה ל ("it was kindled for him"[368]), where this concerns the use of kindling introduced into the very heart of an (as yet) unlit fire.

The characterization of חרה, whether directly as depression or as 'anger'—an (emotional) symptom of depression[369]—is reinforced by v. 3 where Jonah is articulating his "desire to harm self,"[370] or more particularly the desire "not to live."[371] Indeed:

> Wanting to end your life is a very active, aggressive idea which requires energy. It's not very often that people in the very depths of a major clinical depression will have the energy to kill themselves.[372]

---

365. Van Rooy, "פנים," 637.

366. Gruber, *Aspects of Non-verbal Communication*, 373.

367. Cohen, "Tragedy of Jonah," 171.

368. Brown et al., "חרה ל," 354.

369. Gilbert lists groups of symptoms that are categorised under four different aspects of human functioning: a) motivation, b) emotional, c) cognitive and d) biological (Gilbert, *Counselling*, 1–2).

370. Gilbert remarks on suicidality as a measure/marker of depression. Gilbert, *Counselling*, 5. See also Kaplan (Kaplan, "Jonah versus Narcissus," 150).

371. Barnes, *Dealing with Depression*, 114.

372. Barnes, *Dealing with Depression*, 114.

These two depression markers or motifs—'anger' and 'suicidality'—straddle the intervening verse in which Jonah recites "the ancient confession of divine attributes as a complaint."[373] Clearly, if Jonah is depressed both before and after this confession he must seemingly be depressed throughout the confession, that is, his depressed condition must inform any reading of the confession. Moreover, since in Cohen's view "God's compassion, in itself, (v. 2) cannot possibly be the cause of this feeling, we are led to understand that some extension of it is," and because "that extension is not defined in these verses,"[374] the question which then arises is: What could a depressed Jonah be complaining about which was as true when he fled to Tarshish as it is now in Nineveh, and which appears to have survived the life-changing experiences within the fish/Sheol? The answer may lie—as already alluded to[375]—in YHWH's perceived unpredictability[376] and unreliability[377] in Jonah's eyes, both of which have special significance for depressives within the 'self psychology' view of depression. This theory of depression was developed and articulated by Kohut (a contemporary of Freud), and is an interpersonal/relational theory in which the identity of the 'self' is partially constructed from the input of (significant) others. It is posited that there are three components of intrapsychic structure of which the most important is:

> Representation of interaction (i.e. the experience of the interaction [with others] as loving, giving, fun, soothing, or hostile and withholding). It is the "experienced interaction" that is internally stored and important. This "stored representation of interaction" may or may not be an accurate reflection of actual characteristics of the other.[378]

Depression on this view "is nearly always secondary to a painful sense of disappointment . . . that others are not as . . . reliable as was hoped,"[379] and therefore, it is not YHWH's reprieve of the Ninevites that is at issue here, so much as YHWH's perceived characteristic of unreliability in Jonah's eyes. Thus, Jonah's interaction with YHWH (before his experience in the fish/Sheol) appears to have been a significant factor in the formation of endog-

---

373. Trible, "Divine Incongruities," 205. It may be noted, however, that "only in Joel 2:14 and Jonah 4:2 does the motif of divine repentance occur in connection with the formula of divine mercy" (Krašovec, "Salvation," 64).
374. Cohen, "Tragedy of Jonah," 172.
375. But see Cooper (Cooper, "In Praise of Divine Caprice," 153).
376. Trible, "Divine Incongruities," 204.
377. Cooper, "In Praise of Divine Caprice," 153.
378. Gilbert, *Depression*, 303.
379. Gilbert, *Depression*, 315.

enous depression, which continued to afflict him after his experience in the fish and was exacerbated by the fasting in Nineveh. Certainly, as has already been remarked upon, the narrator seems to have introduced a subliminal, depression theme in chapter one,[380] where "Jonah's behavior represents a clear clinical picture of despair and, more fundamentally, of depression. His 'descent' into the bottom of the ship symbolically conveys this mood."[381] The perception of YHWH's unreliability in the formation of a depressed Jonah is therefore the linking factor between chapters one and four, and this is so irrespective of whether Jonah is master of himself/other spirits or has made the transition to being a servant of YHWH. It is at this point in the narrative (v. 3) that the story reaches another juncture—indicated by the Masoretes with a *setûmā'* (ס)—only the second such break in the entire book.

The Dialogue: Altered State of Consciousness (2)—Jonah 4:4–11

The middle section of the book of Jonah (3:1—4:3) ends with the prophet's request for death (ועתה יהוה קח־נא את־נפשי)—a statement considered by many scholars to be an explicit reference to 1 Kings 19:4 where an almost exactly analogous expression is used by Elijah.[382] The key point, however, is that the sentiment in Jonah 4:3 is not exactly analogous to the sentiment in 1 Kings 19:4, but is introduced only to bring Elijah to the reader's mind—and this at precisely the moment when a juncture/closure of the narration is taking place. Indeed, Jonah's request and YHWH's response straddle the juncture, and because Elijah's death-wish statement takes place within a dream[383] the narrator may well be indicating that Jonah also receives his response from YHWH within a dream. Such a reading would be consistent with both of the junctures in the book (Jonah 2:10; 4:3—marked by the Masoretes with a *setûmā'* [ס])—symbolizing deep, insensible, non-REM sleep. In Jonah 2:10 the *setûmā'* is marking the last such period of sleep within Jonah's first

---

380. See earlier section–'The Storm.'
381. Cohen, "Tragedy of Jonah," 170.
382. See for example Wolff: "There is no mistaking the fact that the narrator is putting words into Jonah's mouth taken from the Elijah tradition (I Kings 19:4bβ . . ." (Wolff, *Obadiah and Jonah*, 168). See also Magonet, *Form and Meaning*, 68–69; Stuart, *Hosea–Jonah*, 503; Salters, *Jonah*, 20; Simon, *JPS Bible Commentary: Jonah*, 38. Moreover, "the correspondence between Elijah and Jonah is the very key to the understanding of Jonah 4 and more generally to many a detail within the narrative" (Lacocque and Lacocque, *Jonah*, 147).
383. See Chapter 4, Fig. 6.

hypnogram, whereas in 4:3 it marks the first period in a second hypnogram suggesting the structure for vv. 3-11 shown in figure 11.

Of course, given that only two portions of this proposed second hypnogram are discernable (i.e. 4:3, 4-11) it might be argued that Jonah is conducting his dialogue with YHWH within his intrinsic consciousness, wherein he can access both the 'normal' and extended realities simultaneously. Significantly, however, Jonah flees (v. 5) in response to YHWH's question, in a manner similar to his flight in chapters 1 and 2, thus providing further support by analogy for the contention that vv. 4-11 take place wholly in the extended reality—since 'soul' flight is of its essence non-corporeal. Moreover, if it is accepted from the foregoing argument that Jonah is depressed, then this first speech/action period (vv. 4-11) is found to be proportionate in terms of duration[384] (despite being unfinished) relative to the final, 21-verse dream in Jonah's first hypnogram (1:6—2:10). This suggests that vv. 4-11 comprise part of the first dream of a second hypnogram. Structurally, the latter dream is a mirror image of the first (recorded) dream of the first hypnogram, insofar as the hearer/reader both meets and takes his leave of Jonah in mid-dream.

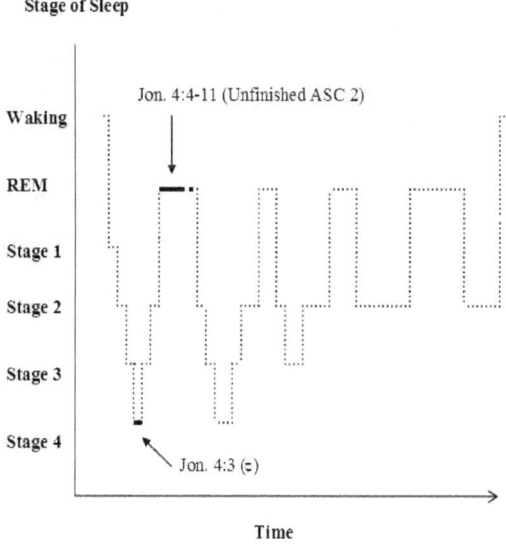

Fig. 11   'Derived Etic' Hypnogram of Jonah 4:3-11

---

384. See Chapter 3, Fig. 3.

In a context of comparison between the first dreams of Jonah and Elijah the hearer/reader is abruptly confronted (v. 4) with the immediacy of YHWH 'in person' *vis-à-vis* the angel in 1 Kings 19:5, for at this point Elijah is still dealing with 'messengers' and far from his final, direct dialogue with YHWH (1 Kgs 19:9–11a). The difference between the two situations would appear to lie in the fact that Jonah—as quite distinct from Elijah—has articulated the 'problem' to YHWH as he perceives it. Jonah's prayer to YHWH in vv. 2–3 results in YHWH's direct response in v. 4, whereas in Elijah's case no complaint about YHWH is made, thus obliging YHWH to adopt a more 'softly, softly' approach to the prophet wherein he progressively draws closer to his prophet over a sequence of dreams. Notwithstanding the protracted nature of the Elijah sequence the result is the same—dialogue, and moreover, dialogue that commences in each case with an open question ("What are you doing here, Elijah?" 1 Kgs 19:9, "Is it right for you to be angry?" Jonah 4:4). "Open questions leave the person to respond in their own way," and are to be preferred over closed questions which do not allow a respondent to "articulate their own meanings."[385] Indeed, Gilbert considers that in terms of counseling skill the employment of open questions comprises "the real bedrock of counseling."[386] In Jonah's case, however, there is no response other than the (silent) 'soul' flight of v. 5, which Magonet maintains is Jonah's answer,[387] but which is in reality the avoidance of an answer. This outcome requires more resourcefulness from YHWH as Jonah now not only flees, but retreats once again into (symbolic?) hiddenness and darkness (cf. Jonah 1:5) by building and entering a booth. Once inside this new refuge Jonah sinks into passivity, withdrawal, and silence—he is manifesting all the features of his earlier sojourn in the bottom of the boat[388] with the exception of sleep and is effectively *ex-communicado*. The voyeurism Jonah now exhibits (v. 5c) is explicable in terms of anxiety reduction through distraction from focusing upon "internal negative ruminations and thoughts," although it has to be said that distraction activity is not usually initiated by the depressive himself.[389] Alternatively, Jonah may

---

385. Gilbert, *Counselling*, 14–15.

386. Gilbert, *Counselling*, 14–15.

387. Magonet resists the view that 4:5 should be placed more appropriately after 3:4 noting that Jonah's response "is not a reply in words but in deeds" (Magonet, *Form and Meaning*, 58).

388. Cohen, "Tragedy of Jonah," 170.

389. Gilbert observes that it is often helpful during counselling with depressives "to use various forms of distraction activity that require their attention to be outwardly directed" (compare Elijah's 'to do list' in 1 Kgs 19:15–18), (Gilbert, *Counselling*, 75–76).

actually be ruminating on the visible, tangible, and current representation (i.e. the city) of YHWH's perceived unreliability.

At this point in the narrative (v. 5) Jonah has effectively refused to take part in 'counseling,' and in order for dialogue to resume YHWH must regain Jonah's attention by the introduction of new features to the dream scenario. The hearer/reader knows that Jonah has once again fled[390] into darkness as he did in 1:1–5 and this suggests that צל is here being used to suggest shadow as distinct from shade, although the word can carry both meanings at the same time.[391] Significantly, it may be noted that a one/two man booth or tent although providing relief from direct sunshine/burn/stroke, does not provide relief from the heat that oppresses occupants of very small tents pitched in the open. This point is crucial to an attempt to understand scholars' puzzlement posed in Sasson's question: "if it (the 'booth' סכה) functioned properly, why would God need to raise a plant over Jonah's head?"[392] The salient point, however, is not an apparent duplication of function, but rather the intrinsic nature of a plant *per se* as distinct from a man-made shelter, since plants are able through transpiration[393] to lower the ambient temperature of their immediate vicinity. Naturally, the air would need to be still to obtain maximum benefit from an effect familiar to all dwellers in the (Ancient) Near East,[394] and we may assume that this was so because we are not told it became windy until v. 8. Moreover, the type of plant is to some extent irrelevant—provided only that it was big enough—although when Robinson concludes that he is "not . . . certain that the author had a specific type of plant or tree in mind at all,"[395] he appears to discount the narrator's use of a proper noun. Following the introduction of the plant (קיקיון) in v. 6 it would seem appropriate to see the צל of the same verse as applying the cooling effect of (specifically) plant shade directly to Jonah's (heated (חרה)?) head,[396] in order to give him deliverance from his distress (מרעתו). This

---

390. Magonet sees structural parallelism between "Jonah's flight to sea" in Chapter 1 and 4:5 (Magonet, *Form and* Meaning, 58).

391. Brown et al., "צל," 853.

392. Sasson, *Jonah*, 290.

393. Transpiration is the evaporation of moisture/water from or through the foliage of plants. Evaporation involves a phase change from liquid to gas which requires the input of the latent heat of vaporisation of water—heat which must be obtained from the immediate environment thereby reducing its temperature.

394. It is a feature of everyday experience, particularly for those living by or near deserts.

395. Robinson, "Jonah's Qiqayon Plant," 402.

396. Wolff notes that this "shade . . . is meant for Jonah's head" (Wolff, *Obadiah and Jonah*, 171). In this regard Cohen suggests that Jonah had himself prepared the booth "to seek some comfort from the heat (symbolically: no less inner than outer)," (Cohen,

reference to מרעתו and allusion to חרה, would appear to indicate that the narrator is employing a *double entendre* in which he "wants this clause to reverse Jonah's condition reported in v. 1,"[397] by means of the surreal dream-constructs of booth and one-day plant.

The reversal of Jonah's condition can only come about through the regaining of Jonah's attention with resultant continuation of dialogue,[398] and this is brought about by God's three 'appointments' (vv. 6–8), which are reminiscent of the appointment of the fish in the last dream of Jonah's first hypnogram. These three interventions into Jonah's 'reality' produce a swing of emotions from the depression of v.6 where the allusion is to the חרה of v. 1, through 'joy' (שמחה) to (suicidal) depression again in v. 8. Indeed, Trible posits three "reactions" by Jonah equivalent to each one of God's interventions:

1. And-delighted Jonah Upon the plant a-delight great (4:6)
2. [and-pitied Jonah the plant, said YHWH] (4:7, 10a)
3. and-he-asked his nepes to-die and-he-said "Better my-death than-my-life" (4:8)[399]

Trible's suggestion is that information about Jonah's middle 'reaction' is supplied later in v. 10 for the hearer/reader to read back into v. 7, and that this reaction to God's action of destroying the plant "lifts Jonah out of himself."[400] Before YHWH can capitalize on the middle reaction (v. 10), however, it is necessary to provoke his prophet into an exaggerated and vociferous rebellion through the removal of both of his protective 'covers,'[401] thus causing him to cover himself up (ויתעלף)[402] with personal clothing in the manner of desert dwellers everywhere. Significantly, 'provocation' to rebellion is also found in modern psychotherapy where counselors find that "it is not unusual that openly helping clients rebel and become asser-

---

"Tragedy of Jonah," 172).

397. Sasson considers this to be "obvious." Sasson, *Jonah*, 292.

398. Trible observes that "Jonah replies to YHWH's question by walking away ... Thereby he breaks off the conversation, sets distance, and shifts attention" (Trible, *Rhetorical Criticism*, 206).

399. Trible, *Rhetorical Criticism*, 222.

400. Trible, *Rhetorical Criticism*, 222.

401. Sasson suggests that the only way the sun could directly bear down on Jonah would be if a powerful wind swept "away the hut (*sukkâ*) that Jonah himself had built outside of Nineveh" (Sasson, *Jonah*, 304).

402. Compare Tamar in Genesis 38:14—much appears to depend on context where עלף can mean either 'cover, enwrap' or 'faint'

tive is an important factor in change."⁴⁰³ It is moreover, "important to help the person articulate their sense of disappointment and to reflect on the sources of this disappointment,"⁴⁰⁴ and this is precisely what God achieves in v. 9. God's second, open question (cf. v. 4) to Jonah is intended to elicit from him an account of his feelings concerning the plant from its 'appointment' to its demise, and succeeds insofar as his response is both vocal and emphatic.⁴⁰⁵ Importantly, the dialogue is finally opened with the plant as the subject of discussion—a subject that has initiated three quite distinct emotional responses in Jonah.

Interestingly, Trible's analysis of these verses (vv. 6–8) in terms of Jonah's "swing from one ... emotional extreme to the other"⁴⁰⁶ resonates well with classifying Jonah's depression under the modern medical category—Bipolar Affective Disorder.⁴⁰⁷ Thus, Jonah, in swinging from the great elation of v. 6 to suicidal depression (v. 8) passes through a nodal point in v. 7, during which he experiences for the first time an unexaggerated, 'normal' emotion (חוס). It is only at this point in Jonah's swing between two extremes of self-absorption that he fastens upon an object external to himself. As Trible puts it: "His delight for the plant (like his anger) is self-serving. . . . His pity, on the other hand, is disinterested compassion."⁴⁰⁸ But this is to suggest that Jonah had choices, when in fact "we can blame Jonah no more than we can blame any individual in the throes of some psychiatric depression."⁴⁰⁹ YHWH continues (v. 10) the dialogue he had provoked in v. 9 by reflecting on Jonah's one normal emotion (חוס), and relating it to his own emotions concerning Nineveh (v. 11) in particular, but also perhaps suggesting a more general characteristic of YHWH *vis-à-vis* humanity (אדם, v. 11) in general. The book of Jonah concludes without resolution; indeed YHWH's "closing question opens the narrative beyond its confines,"⁴¹⁰ suggesting that Jonah continues to participate in debate with (and receipt

---

403. Gilbert, *Counselling*, 120.

404. Gilbert, *Counselling*, 315.

405. Cohen notes that עד־מות "was an ancient way of expressing excess (but) is intended by Jonah in a more literal sense" (Cohen, "Tragedy of Jonah," 172).

406. Trible, *Rhetorical Criticism*, 222.

407. Bipolar Affective Disorder, previously known as Manic Depression, is a form of depression in which the affect swings from 'mania' or extreme elation/excitement to depression. Gilbert suggests that "unipolar depression may in practice be little more than a diagnosis of depression in the absence of a bipolar component" (Gilbert, *Counselling*, 31).

408. Trible, *Rhetorical Criticism*, 222.

409. Cohen, "Tragedy of Jonah," 170.

410. Trible, *Rhetorical Criticism*, 224–5.

of therapy from) YHWH beyond this final verse in the unfinished portion of both this dream, and the remaining REM-sleep/dream periods of the hypnogram. In support of the latter suggestion, it may be observed that the narrator has (painstakingly?) allocated exactly the same number of words to both Jonah and YHWH from Jonah's monologue (vv. 2–3) through to YHWH's final question (vv. 10–11),[411] and there is therefore no reason to suppose that this symmetry will abruptly cease. Clearly the hearer/reader may anticipate an equally robust response from Jonah, even as he expects YHWH ultimately to triumph in "the art of persuasion."[412]

---

411. Sasson, *Jonah*, 317; Trible, *Rhetorical Criticism*, 223–24.
412. Trible, *Rhetorical Criticism*, 225.

Bibliography

Ackerman, James S. "Satire and Symbolism in the Song of Jonah," In *Traditions in Transformation: Turning Points in Biblical Faith.* edited by Baruch Halpern and Jon D. Levenson, 213–46. Winona Lake: Eisenbrauns, 1981.
———. "Jonah," In *The Literary Guide to the Bible.* edited by Robert Alter and Frank Kermode, 234–43. London: Fontana, 1997.
———. "Who Can Stand Before YHWH, This Holy God? A Reading of 1 Samuel 1–15." *Prooftexts* 11 (1991) 1–24.
Ackroyd, P R. "יָד." In *TDOT* 5:393–426.
Alden, Robert L. "אחר." In *TWOT* 1:33–35.
Alexander, T Desmond. "קבר." In *NIDOTTE* 3:865–68.
Allen, Leslie C. *The Books of Joel, Obadiah, Jonah and Micah.* London: Hodder and Stoughton, 1976.
Allen, Ronald B. "ענה." In *TWOT* 2:679–80.
Alvarado, Carlos S. "Sleepwalking and Spontaneous Parapsychological Experiences: A Research Note." *The Journal of Parapsychology* 62 (1998) 349–51.
American Psychiatric Association, *Diagnostic and Statistical Manual of Mental Disorders: DSM IV.* Washington, DC: The American Psychiatric Association, 2000.
Ames, Frank Ritchel. "דבר." In *NIDOTTE* 1:912–15.
Andersen, Arnold E. "Sequencing Treatment Decisions: Cooperation or Conflict Between Therapist and Patient." In *Handbook of Eating Disorders: Theory, Treatment and Research*, edited by George Szmukler, et al., 363–79. Chichester: John Wiley & Sons Ltd., 1995.
Anderson, Bernard W. "'The Lord Has Created Something New' A Stylistic Study of Jer 31:15–22." *CBQ* 40 (1978) 463–78.
Auld, A Graeme. "Prophecy in Books: A Rejoinder." *JSOT* 48 (1990) 31–32.
———. "Prophets and Prophecy in Jeremiah and Kings." *ZAW* 96 (1984) 66–82.
———. "Prophets through the Looking Glass." In *The Prophets,* edited by Philip R. Davies, 22–42. Sheffield: Sheffield Academic Press, 1996.
———. "Prophets through the Looking Glass." *JSOT* 27 (1983) 3–23.
Austel, Hermann J. "שלך." In *TWOT* 2:929–30.
Barnes, Trevor. *Dealing with Depression.* London: Vermillion, 1996.
Barr, James. *The Garden of Eden and the Hope of Immortality.* London: SCM Ltd, 1992.
Barré, Michael L. "Jonah 2,9 and the Structure of Jonah's Prayer." *Biblica* 72 (1991) 237–48.

Bengtsson, H. "Three Sobriquets, their Meaning and Function: The Wicked Priest, Synagogue of Satan, and The Woman Jezebel." In *The Hebrew Bible and Qumran*, edited by James H Charlesworth, 241–73. N. Richland Hills, TX: BIBAL, 2000.

Ben Zvi, Ehud. *Signs of Jonah: Reading and Rereading in Ancient Yehud*. Sheffield: Sheffield Academic Press, 2003.

Bergen, Wesley J. *Elisha and the End of Prophetism*. Sheffield: Sheffield Academic Press, 1999.

Bergman, J., et al. "חֲלוֹם." In *TDOT* 4:421–32.

Berlin, Adele. "A Rejoinder to John A. Miles Jnr., With Some Observations on the Nature of Prophecy." *JQR* 66 (1976) 227–35.

Blenkinsopp, Joseph. *Treasures Old and New: Essays in the Theology of the Pentateuch*. Grand Rapids: Eerdmans, 2004.

Bolin, Thomas M. *Freedom Beyond Forgiveness: The Book of Jonah Re-Examined*. Sheffield: Sheffield Academic Press, 1997.

Borowski, Oded. *Daily Life in Biblical Times*. Atlanta: Society of Biblical Literature, 2003.

Botterweck, G. Johannes. "חֲלוֹם." In *TDOT* 4: 426.

Bourguignon, Erika. *Possession*. San Franscisco: Chandler & Sharp Publishers Inc., 1976.

———. *Religion, Altered States of Consciousness and Social Change*. Columbus: Ohio State University Press, 1973.

———. "World Distribution and Patterns of Possession States." In *Trance and Possession States*, edited by Raymond H. Prince, 3-34. Montreal: Bucke Memorial Society for the Study of Religious Experience, 1968.

Bowie, Fiona. *The Anthropology of Religion: An Introduction*. Oxford: Blackwell Publishers, 2000.

Brinkman, J. A. *A Political History of Post-Kassite Babylonia, 1158-722 B.C.* Roma: Pontificium Institutum Biblicum, 1968.

Bronner, Leah. *The Stories of Elijah and Elisha as Polemics Against Baal Worship*. Leiden: E J Brill, 1968.

Brooke, George J. *The Dead Sea Scrolls and the New Testament: Essays in Mutual Illumination*. London: SPCK, 2005.

Brotzman, Ellis R. "Man and the Meaning of "נֶפֶשׁ." *Bibliotheca Sacra* 145 (1988) 400–409.

Brown, Francis, et al. "חרה ל," In *BDB* 354.

———. "צל." In *BDB* 853.

———. "רעה." In *BDB* 944–45.

Burns, Dan E. "Dream Form in Genesis 2:4b–3:24: Asleep in the Garden." *JSOT* 37 (1987) 3–14.

Bushell, William C. "Psychophysiological and Comparative Analysis of Ascetico-Meditational Discipline: Toward a New Theory of Asceticism." In *Asceticism*, edited by Vincent L. Wimbush and Richard Valantasis, 553–75. New York: Oxford University Press, 1995.

Carr, David. "The Politics of Textual Subversion: A Diachronic Perspective on the Garden of Eden Story." *JBL* 112.4 (1993) 577–95.

Carr, G Lloyd. "עָלָה." In *TWOT* 2:666–70.

Carroll, Robert P. "Whose Prophet? Whose History? Whose Social Reality? Troubling the Interpretative Community Again, Notes Towards a Response to T. W. Overholt's Critique." *JSOT* 48 (1990) 33-49.

Cartwright, Rosalind, et al. "Role of REM Sleep and Dream Affect in Overnight Mood Regulation: A Study of Normal Volunteers." *PR* 81 (1998) 1-8.

Childs, Brevard S. "On Reading the Elijah Narratives." *Interpretation* 34 (1980) 128-37.

Chow, Simon. *The Sign of Jonah Reconsidered: A Study of its Meaning in the Gospel Traditions*. Stockholm: Almqvist & Wiksell, 1995.

Christensen, Duane L. "Narrative Poetics and the Interpretation of the Book of Jonah." In *Directions in Biblical Hebrew Poetry*, edited by Elaine R. Follis, 29-48. Sheffield: Sheffield Academic Press, 1987,

———. "The Song of Jonah: A Metrical Analysis." *JBL* 104 (1985) 217-31.

Claridge, Gordon. "Spiritual Experience: Healthy Psychoticism?" In *Psychosis and Spirituality: Exploring the new Frontier*, edited by Isabel Clarke, 90-106. London: Whurr, 2001,

Clarke, Isabel. "Psychosis and Spirituality: the Discontinuity Model." In *Psychosis and Spirituality: Exploring the new Frontier*, edited by Isabel Clarke, 129-142. London: Whurr, 2001.

Cogan, Mordecai. *1 Kings: A New Translation and Commentary*. New York: Doubleday, 2001.

Cogan, Mordecai, and Hayim Tadmor. *II Kings: A New Translation and Commentary*. New York: Doubleday, 1988.

Cohen, Abraham D. "The Tragedy of Jonah." *Judaism* 21 (1972) 164-75.

Cooper, Alan. "In Praise of Divine Caprice: The Significance of the Book of Jonah." In *Among the Prophets: Language, Image and Structure in the Prophetic Writings*, edited by Philip R. Davies and David J. A. Clines, 144-163. Sheffield: Sheffield Academic Press, 1993.

Cooper, Peter J. "Eating Disorders and Their Relationship to Mood and Anxiety Disorders." In *Eating Disorders and Obesity: A Comprehensive Handbook*, edited by Kelly D. Brounell and Christopher G. Fairburn, 159-64. New York: Guildford, 1995.

Cooper, Zafra. "The Development and Maintenance of Eating Disorders." In *Eating Disorders and Obesity: A Comprehensive Handbook*, edited by Kelly D. Brounell and Christopher G. Fairburn, 199-206. New York: Guildford, 1995.

Coryell, William. "Psychotic Depression." *JCP* 57.3 (1996) 27-31 & 49.

Cox, Stuart, and Emily Finch. "Depression and Substance Misuse." In *Depression and Physical Illness*, edited by M. M. Robertson and C. L. E. Katona, 407-28. Chichester: John Wiley & Sons Ltd., 1997.

Craig, Kenneth M. Jr. *A Poetics of Jonah: Art in the Service of Ideology*. Columbia: University of South Carolina Press, 1993.

Craigie, Peter C., et al. *Jeremiah 1-25 WBC Vol. 26*. Dallas: Word, 1991.

Crespi, Bernard, et al. "Adaptive Evolution of Genes Underlying Schizophrenia." *Proc R Soc Lond [Biol]* 274.1627 (2007) 2801-10.

Cross, Frank M. "Studies in the Structure of Hebrew Verse: The Prosody of the Psalm of Jonah." In *The Quest for the Kingdom of God: Studies in Honor of George E. Mendenhall*, edited by H. B. Huffman, et al., 159-67. Winona Lake: Eisenbrauns, 1983,

Cryer, Frederick H. *Divination in Ancient Israel and its Near Eastern Environment*. Sheffield: JSOT, 1994.
Cullman, Oscar. *Immortality of the Soul or Resurrection of the Dead? The Witness of the New Testament*, London: Epworth, 1958.
Culver, Robert D. "רָאָה." *TWOT* 2: 823–25.
Curtis, Adrian H. W. "Aetiology." In *DBI* 8–10.
———. "Some Observations on 'Bull' Terminology in the Ugaritic Texts and the Old Testament." In *In Quest of the Past: Studies on Israelite Religion, Literature and Prophetism*, edited by A. S. Van der Woude, 17–31. Leiden: E. J. Brill, 1990.
Cytowic, Richard E. *Synesthesia: A Union of the Senses*. Cambridge, Mass.: MIT, 2002.
Dahood, M. "The Value of Ugaritic for Textual Criticism." *Biblica* 40 (1959) 160–70.
Dahood, Mitchell. *Anchor Bible Psalms III (101–150)*. New York: Doubleday, 1970.
Dalley, Stephanie. *Myths from Mesopotamia: Creation, The Flood, Gilgamesh, and Others*. Oxford: Oxford University Press, 1989.
David-Neel, Alexandra. *Magic and Mystery in Tibet*. London. Transworld, 1971.
Davidson, Benjamin. *The Analytical Hebrew and Chaldee Lexicon*. Peabody, Mass.: Hendrickson, 1981.
Davidson, Robert. *Genesis 12–50*. Cambridge: Cambridge University Press, 1979.
Davies, G I. "The Uses of R^c Qal and the Meaning of Jonah IV 1." *VT* 27 (1977) 105–10.
Davila, James R. *Descenders to the Chariot: The People behind the Hekhalot Literature*. Leiden: Brill, 2001.
Dawkins, Richard. *The God Delusion* (London: Bantam, 2006).
Day, John. "Ugarit and the Bible: Do They Presuppose the Same Canaanite Mythology and Religion." In *Ugarit and the Bible: Proceedings of the International Symposium on Ugarit and the Bible, Manchester, September 1992*, edited by George J Brooke et al., 35–52. Münster: Ugarit-Verlag, 1994.
Dennys, N B. *The Folklore of China, and Its Affinities With That of the Aryan and Semitic Races*. London: Trubner & Co., 1876.
DeVries, Simon J. *I Kings WBC*. Waco: Word, 1985.
Dodds, Eric Robertson. *The Greeks and the Irrational*. Berkeley: University of California Press, 1951.
Dohmen, C. "רעע." In *TDOT* 8:560–88.
Dozeman, Thomas B. "Inner-Biblical Interpretation of Yahweh's Gracious and Compassionate Character." *JBL* 108.2 (1989) 207–23.
Dunn, Adrian J. "Psychoneuroimmunology: Introduction and General Perspectives." In *Stress, the Immune System and Psychiatry*, edited by Brian E Leonard and Klara Miller, 1–16. Chichester: John Wiley & Sons, 1995.
Dunn, J. D. G. *Jesus and the Spirit*. London: SCM, 1975.
Eisler, Ivan. "Family Models of Eating Disorders." In *Handbook of Eating Disorders: Theory, Treatment and Research*, edited by George Szmukler et al., 155–76. Chichester: John Wiley & Sons Ltd., 1995.
Eliade, Mircea. "Foreword." In Lacocque, André and Lacocque, Pierre-Emmanuel *Jonah: A Psycho-Religious Approach to the Prophet*, ix-xv. Columbia: University of South Carolina Press, 1990.
———. *A History of Religious Ideas: From Gautama Buddha to the Triumph of Christianity*. Vol 2. London: University of Chicago Press, 1982.
———. *Shamanism: Archaic Techniques of Ecstasy*. New York: Pantheon, 1964.
———. *Yoga: Immortality and Freedom*. London: Routledge & Kegan Paul, 1958.

Eppstein, Victor. "Was Saul Also Among The Prophets." *ZAW* 81.3 (1969) 287–304.
Esler, Philip F. "The Madness of Saul: A Cultural Reading of 1 Samuel 8–31." In *Biblical Studies/Cultural Studies: The Third Sheffield Colloquium*, edited by J. Cheryl Exum and Stephen D. Moore, 220–62. Sheffield: Sheffield Academic Press, 1998.
Evans, Mary J. *1 and 2 Samuel NIBC*. Peabody, MA: Hendrickson, 2000.
———. *Prophets of the Lord*. London: Paternoster, 1992.
Eysenck, H. J. "Schizothymia-Cyclothymia as a Dimension of Personality: II. Experimental." *Journal of Personality* 20 (1952) 345–84.
Eysenck, H. J and S. B. G. Eysenck. *Psychoticism as a Dimension of Personality*. London: Hodder and Stoughton, 1976.
Faber, P. A., et al. "Meditation and Archetypal Content of Nocturnal Dreams." *J Anal Psychol* 23.1 (1978) 1–22.
Fabry, H. J. "חבל." In *TDOT* 4: 172–79.
Fensham, F. C. "A Few Observations on the Polarisation Between Yahweh and Baal in 1 Kings 17–19." *ZAW* 92.2 (1980) 227–36.
Ferguson, Paul. "Who Was the King of Nineveh in Jonah 3:6?" *TynBul* 47.2 (1996) 301–14.
Fichter, M. M., and K. M. Pirke. "Starvation Models and Eating Disorders." In *Handbook of Eating Disorders: Theory, Treatment & Research*, edited by George Szmukler et al., 83–107. Chichester: John Wiley & Sons Ltd., 1995.
Fitzmyer, Joseph A. *The Gospel According to Luke (X–XXIV): Introduction, Translation and Notes*. New York: Doubleday & Co., 1985.
Fleming, Daniel E. "The Etymological Origins of the Hebrew *nābî'*: The One Who Invokes God." *CBQ* 55 (1993) 217–24.
Flood, Gavin. "The Subject, the object, the Path and the Goal: Śaiva Devotion in a Monistic Setting." in *Love Divine: Studies in Bhakti and Devotional Mysticism*, edited by Karel Werner, 173–92. Richmond: Curzon, 1993.
Forster, E. S. *The Works of Aristotle: Problemata. Vol 7*. Oxford: Oxford University Press, 1927.
France, R. T. *The Gospel According to Matthew: An Introduction and Commentary*. Leicester: Inter-Varsity Press, 1985.
Fredericks, Daniel C. "נפש." In *NIDOTTE* 3:133–34.
Freedman, David Noel. "Between God and Man: Prophets in Ancient Israel." In *Prophecy and Prophets*, edited by Yehoshua Gitay, 57–87. Atlanta: Scholars, 1997.
Fritz, Volkmar. *The City in Ancient Israel*. Sheffield: Sheffield Academic Press, 1995.
———. "Monarchy and Re-urbanization: A New Look at Solomon's Kingdom." In *The Origins of the Ancient Israelite States*, edited by Volkmar Fritz and Philip R. Davies, 187–95. Sheffield: Sheffield Academic Press, 1996.
Frolov, Serge, and Vladimir Orel. "A Nameless City." *JBQ* 23 (1995) 252–56.
Gaskell, Deborah. "Weighing in on Slimming Drugs." *Chemistry in Britain* 34.8 (1998) 41–45.
Gibson, J. C. L. *Davidson's Introductory Hebrew Grammar Syntax*. Edinburgh: T & T Clark, 1994.
Gilbert, Paul. *Counselling for Depression*. London: Sage Publications, 1992.
———. *Depression: The Evolution of Powerlessness*. Hove: Lawrence Erlbaum Associates, 1992.
Ginzberg, Louis. *The Legends of the Jews Vol IV*. Philadelphia:The Jewish Publication Society of America, 1913.

Gnuse, Robert. "Dreams in the Night – Scholarly Mirage or Theophanic Formula?: The Dream Report as a Motif of the So-Called Elohist Tradition." *BZ* 39 (1995) 28–53.

———. "A Reconsideration of the Form-Critical Structure of 1 Samuel 3: An Ancient Near Eastern Dream Theophany." *ZAW* 92.3 (1982) 379–90.

Golinger, Ronald C. "Delirium in Surgical Patients Seen at Psychiatric Consultation." *Surg Gynecol Obstet* 163 (1986) 104–6.

Goodhart, Sandor. "Prophecy, Sacrifice and Repentance in the Story of Jonah." *Semeia* 33 (1985) 43–63.

Goodman, Felicitas D. *Ecstasy, Ritual and Alternate Reality: Religion in a Pluralistic World*. Bloomington: Indiana University Press, 1988.

———. "Visions." In *The Encyclopedia of Religion*, edited by Mircea Eliade, 15:282–88. New York: Macmillan, 1987.

Goodman, Neil. "The Serotonergic System and Mysticism: Could LSD and the Nondrug-Induced Mystical Experience Share Common Neural Mechanisms?" *J Psychoactive Drugs* 34.3 (2002) 263–72.

Grabbe, Lester L. "Ancient Near Eastern Prophecy from an Anthropological Perspective." In *Prophecy in its Ancient Near Eastern Context*, edited by Martti Nissenen, 13–32. Atlanta: Society of Biblical Literature, 2000.

———. *Priests, Prophets, Diviners, Sages: A Socio-Historical Study of Religious Specialists in Ancient Israel*. Valley Forge: Trinity, 1995.

Gray, John. *I & II Kings*. London: SCM Press Ltd., 1970, 1977.

Green, Barbara. *How are the Mighty Fallen: A Dialogical Study of King Saul in 1 Samuel*. London: Sheffield Academic Press, 2003.

Greenfield, J. C. "The *Marzēaḥ* as a Social Institution." In *Wirtschaft und Gesellschaft im Alten Vorderasien*, edited by J Harmatta and G. Komoróczy, 451–55. Budapest: Akadémiai Kiadó, 1976.

Greenwell, Bonnie. "Paranormal Abilities: Are They Boons or Obstacles on the Spiritual Path?" *Kundalini and the Paranormal: Annual Conference Papers, Symposium V*. Bloomfield, CT: Academy of Religion and Psychical Research, 1990, 110–22.

Grisanti, Michael A. "תְּהוֹם." In *NIDOTTE* 4: 275–77.

Gruber, Mayer I. *Aspects of Non-verbal Communication in the Ancient Near East. Vol I.* Rome: Biblical Institute, 1980.

Hallevy, Raphael. "Man of God." *JNES* 17 (1958)) 237–44.

Hamayon, Roberte N. "Are 'Trance,' 'Ecstasy' and Similar Concepts Appropriate in the Study of Shamanism?" *Shamanism and Performing Arts, Papers & Abstracts for the Second Conference of the ISSR*. Budapest: Ethnographic Institute Hungarian Academy of Sciences, 1993, 17–34.

Hamilton, Victor P. "אָדָם." In *NIDOTTE* 1: 262–66.

Harman, Allan. "Particles." In *NIDOTTE* 4:1028–42.

Harrington, Daniel J. *The Gospel of Matthew*. Collegeville, Minnesota: Liturgical, 2007.

———. *Wisdom Texts from Qumran*. London: Routledge, 1996.

Hart, Archibald D. *Counselling the Depressed*. Dallas: Word, 1987.

Harvianen, Tapani. "Why were the sailors not afraid of the Lord before verse Jonah 1,10?" *StudOr* 64 (1988) 77–81.

Hasan-Rokem, Galit. "Communication with the Dead in Jewish Dream Culture." In *Dream Cultures: Explorations in the Comparative History of Dreaming*, edited by David Shulman and Guy G. Stroumsa, 213–32. New York: Oxford University Press, 1999.

Hauser, Alan Jon. "Jonah: In Pursuit of the Dove." *JBL* 104.1 (1985) 21–37.
Hauser, Alan J. "Yahweh Versus Death: The Real Struggle in 1 Kings 17–19." In *From Carmel to Horeb: Elijah in Crisis*, edited by Alan J. Hauser, 9–83. Sheffield: Sheffield Academic Press, 1990.
Hess, Richard S. "One Hundred Fifty Years of Comparative Studies on Genesis 1–11." In *I Studied Inscriptions from before the Flood: Ancient Near Eastern, Literary, and Linguistic Approaches to Genesis 1–11*, edited by Richard S. Hess and David Toshio Tsumura, 3–26. Winona Lake, IN: Eisenbrauns, 1994.
Himmelfarb, Martha. "The Practice of Ascent in the Ancient Mediterranean World." In *Death, Ecstasy and Other Worldly Journeys*, edited by John J. Collins and Michael Fishbane, 123–37. New York: State University of New York Press, 1995.
Hobson, J. Allan. *Dreaming: An Introduction to the Science of Sleep*. New York: Oxford University Press, 2002.
———. *Sleep*. New York: Scientific American Library, 1995.
Holden, Constance. "The Origin of Speech." *Science* 303.5662 (2004) 1316–19.
Holladay, William L. "*'Ereṣ* 'Underworld': Two More Suggestions." *VT* 19 (1969) 123–24.
Howard, David M. Jr. *An Introduction to the Old Testament Historical Books*. Chicago: Moody, 1993.
Humphrey, Caroline. "Shamanic Practices and the State in Northern Asia: Views from the Centre and the Periphery." In *Shamanism, History and the State*, edited by Nicholas Thomas and Caroline Humphrey, 191–228. Ann Arbor: University of Michigan Press, 1994.
Humphrey, Caroline, with Urgunge Onon. *Shamans and Elders: Experience, Knowledge and Power among the Daur Mongols*. Oxford: Clarendon, 1996.
Humphreys, W. L. "From Tragic Hero to Villain: A Study of the Figure of Saul and the Development of 1 Samuel." *JSOT* 22 (1982) 95–117.
Idowu, E. Bolaji. *African Traditional Religion: A Definition*. London: SCM Press, 1973.
Irwin, Lee. *The Dream Seekers: Native American Visionary Traditions of the Great Plains*. Norman: University of Oklahoma Press, 1994.
Jacobsen, Thorkild. "The Graven Image." In *Ancient Israelite Religion*, edited by Patrick D. Miller et al., 15–32. Philadelphia: Fortress, 1987.
Jeffers, Ann. *Magic and Divination in Ancient Palestine and Syria*. Leiden: E J Brill, 1996.
Jenks, Alan W. "Eating and Drinking in the Old Testament." In *ABD* 2: 250–54.
Jepsen, A. "חָזָה." In *TDOT* 4:280–90.
Kaiser, Walter C. "לָקַח." In *TWOT* 1:481–82.
Kapelrud, Arvid S. "Shamanistic features in the Old Testament." In *Studies in Shamanism*, edited by Carl-Martin Edsman, 90–96. Stockholm: Almquist & Wiksell, 1967.
Kaplan, Kalman J. "Jonah versus Narcissus: A Biblical Approach to Suicide Prevention." *J Psychol Judaism* 19.2 (1995) 143–51.
Katz, Richard. *Boiling Energy: Community Healing among the Kalahari Kung*. Cambridge, MA.: Harvard University Press, 1982.
Kawashima, Robert S. "A Revisionist Reading Revisited: On the Creation of Adam and then Eve." *VT* 56.1 (2006) 46–57.
Kaye, Walter H. "Neurotransmitters and Anorexia Nervosa." In *Eating Disorders and Obesity: A Comprehensive Handbook*, edited by Kelly D. Brounell and Christopher G. Fairburn, 255–60. New York: Guildford, 1995.

Keel, Othmar. *The Symbolism of the Biblical World: Ancient Near Eastern Iconography and the Book of Psalms*. New York: Seabury, 1978.
Keener, Craig S. *The Gospel of John: A Commentary, Vol. 1*. Peabody: Hendrickson, 2003.
Keown, Gerald L., et al. *Jeremiah 26–52*. WBC Vol 27. Dallas: Word, 1995.
Kessler, R.C., et al. "The U.S. National Comorbidity Survey: Overview and future directions." *Epidemiological Psychiatry Society* 6.1 (1997) 4–16.
Kilborne, B. "Dreams." In *The Encyclopedia of Religion* 4:482–92.
King, Philip J. "The *Marzēaḥ*:. Textual and Archaeological Evidence." *ErIsr* 20 (1989) 98–106.
Kissling, Paul J. *Reliable Characters in the Primary History: Profiles of Moses, Joshua, Elijah and Elisha*. Sheffield: Sheffield Academic Press, 1996.
Kittel, G. "Word and Speech in the New Testament." *TDNT* 4:69–136.
Knibb, M. A. "Martyrdom and Ascension of Isaiah: A New Translation and Introduction." In *The Old Testament Pseudepigrapha*, edited by James H. Charlesworth, 143–76. London: Darton Longman & Todd Ltd., 1985.
Koehler, Ludwig, and Walter Baumgartner. "שְׁנִי." In *HALOT* 4:1604–5.
Kramer, Milton. "The Selective Mood Regulatory Function of Dreaming: An Update and Revision." In *The Functions of Dreaming*, edited by Alan Moffitt et al., 139–95. Albany: State University of New York Press, 1993.
Krašovec, Jože. "Salvation of the Rebellious Prophet Jonah and of the Penitent Heathen Sinners." *Svensk Exegetisk Arsbok* 61 (1996) 53–75.
Lacocque, André, and Pierre-Emmanuel Lacocque. *Jonah: A Psycho-Religious Approach to the Prophet*. Columbia: University of South Carolina Press, 1990.
Lacocque, Pierre E. "Fear of Engulfment and the Problem of Indentity." *JRH* 23 (1984) 218–28.
Landes, George M. "A Case for the Sixth-Century BCE Dating for the Book of Jonah." In *Realia Dei: Essays in Archaeology and Biblical Interpretation in Honor of Edward F. Campbell Jr., at his Retirement*, edited by Prescott H. Williams Jr. and Theodore Hiebert, 100–116. Atlanta: Scholars Press, 1999.
———. "Jonah in Luke: The Hebrew Bible Background to the Interpretation of the 'Sign of Jonah' Pericope in Luke 11.29–32." In *A Gift of God in Due Season: Essays on Scripture and Community in Honor of James A. Sanders*, edited by Richard D. Weis and David M. Carr, 133–63. Sheffield: Sheffield Academic Press, 1996.
———. "The Kerygma of the Book of Jonah: The Contextual Interpretation of the Jonah Psalm." *Interpretation* 21 (1967) 3–31.
———. "The 'Three Days and Three Nights' Motif in Jonah 2:1." *JBL* 86 (1967) 446–50.
———. "Textual 'Information Gaps' and 'Dissonances' in the Interpretation of the Book of Jonah." In *Ki Baruch Hu: Ancient Near Eastern, Biblical, and Judaic Studies in Honor of Baruch A, Levine*, edited by Robert Chazan et al., 273–93. Winona Lake: Eisenbrauns, 1999.
Lau, Daisy, et al. "Psychological Factors Affecting Food Selection." In *Nutrition and Behaviour*, edited by Janina R. Galler, 397–415. New York: Plenum, 1984.
Leeming. David. *The Oxford Companion to World Mythology*. Oxford: Oxford University Press, 2005.
Lemanski, Jay. "Jonah's Nineveh." *CJ* 18 (1992) 40–49.
Leonard, Brian E. *Fundamentals of Psychopharmacology*. Chichester: John Wiley & Sons, 1997.

———. "Stress and the Immune System: Immunological Aspects of Depressive Illness." In *Stress, the Immune System and Psychiatry*, edited by Brian E Leonard and Klara Miller, 113–36. Chichester: John Wiley & Sons, 1995.
Leonard, Brian E., and David Healey. *Differential Effects of Antidepressants*. London: Martin Dunitz Ltd., 1999.
Lewis, I. M. *Ecstatic Religion: An Anthropological Study of Spirit Possession and Shamanism*. Harmondsworth: Penguin, 1971.
———. *Ecstatic Religion: A Study of Shamanism and Spirit Possession*. London: Routledge, 1989.
Lichtenstein, Murray. "Dream Theophany and the E Document." *JANESCU* 1.2 (1969) 45–54.
Lieberman, Philip "The Evolution of Human Speech: Its Anatomical and Neural Bases." *Current Anthropology* 48.1 (2007) 39–66.
Limburg, James. *Jonah: A Commentary*. Louisville: Westminster/John Knox, 1993.
Lindblom, Johannes. "Lot-Casting in the Old Testament." *VT* 12 (1962) 164–78.
———. *Prophecy in Ancient Israel*. Oxford: Basil Blackwell, 1962.
———. "Theophanies in Holy Places in Hebrew Religion." *HUCA* 32 (1961) 91–106.
Lipton, Diana. *Revisions of the Night: Politics and Promises in the Patriarchal Dreams of Genesis*. Sheffield: Sheffield Academic Press, 1999.
Little, Loy D., et al. "Mechanisms of Nutrient Action on Brain Function." In *Nutrition and Behaviour*, edited by Janina R. Galler, 223–65. New York: Plenum, 1984.
Long, V. Philips. *The Reign and Rejection of King Saul: A Case for Literary and Theological Coherence*. Atlanta: Scholars, 1989.
Lopez, Garcia. "סבב." In *TDOT* 10:127–39.
Lynch, Sean. "Chronic Fatigue Syndrome." *Adv Psychiatr Treat* 1 (1994) 33–40.
Magonet, Jonathon. *Form and Meaning: Studies in Literary Techniques in the Book of Jonah*. Frankfurt: Peter Lang, 1976.
Manor, Dale W. "Beer-Sheba." In *ABD* 1:641–45.
Manson, Spero M., et al. "The Depressive Experience in American Indian Communities: A Challenge for Psychiatric Theory and Diagnosis." In *Culture and Depression: Studies in the Anthropology and Cross-Cultural Psychiatry of Affect and Disorder*, edited by Arthur Kleinman and Byron Good, 331–68. Berkeley: University of California Press, 1985.
Marcus, David. *From Balaam to Jonah: Anti-prophetic Satire in the Hebrew Bible*. Atlanta: Scholars, 1995.
———. "Nineveh's 'Three Days' Walk' (Jonah 3:3): Another Interpretation." In *On the Way to Nineveh: Studies in Honour of George M. Landes*, edited by Stephen L. Cook and S. C. Winter, 42–53. Atlanta: Scholars, 1999.
Margalit, Baruch. "The Ugaritic Feast of the Drunken Gods: Another Look at RS 24.258 (KTU 1.114)." *Maarav* 2.1 (1979–80) 65–120.
Marinatos, Nanno. "The Cosmic Journey of Odysseus." *Numen* 48 (2001) 381–416.
Marshall, I. Howard. *The Gospel of Luke: A Commentary on the Greek Text*. Exeter: Paternoster, 1978.
May, Herbert G. (Ed.) *Oxford Bible Atlas*. New York: Oxford University Press, 1984.
McAlpine, Thomas H. *Sleep, Divine & Human, in the Old Testament*. Sheffield: Sheffield Academic Press, 1987.
McCreery, Charles, and Gordon Claridge. "Out-of-Body Experiences and Personality." *JSPR* 60 (1995) 129–48.

McKenzie, Steven L. "The Trouble With Kingship." In *Israel Constructs Its History: Deuteronomistic Historiography in Recent Research*, edited by Albert de Pury et al., 286–314. Sheffield, Sheffield Academic Press, 2000.

McLaughlin, John L. "The *marzeaḥ* at Ugarit: A Textual and Contextual Study." *UF* 23 (1991) 265–81.

Mellars, Paul. "Why did Modern Human Populations Disperse from Africa ca. 60,000 Years Ago? A New Model." *PNAS* 103.25 (2006) 9381–86.

Mendelson, Wallace B. *Human Sleep: Research and Clinical Care*. New York: Plenum, 1987.

Mettinger, Triggve N. D. *The Eden Narrative: A Literary and Religio-historical Study of Genesis 2–3*. Winona Lake, Indiana: Eisenbrauns, 2007.

Michaelsen, P. "Ecstasy and Possession in Ancient Israel: A Review of Some Recent Contributions." *SJOT* (1989) 28–54.

Miller, Klara. "Psychoneurological Aspects of Food Allergy." In *Stress, the Immune System and Psychiatry*, edited by. Brian E Leonard and Klara Miller, 185–206. Chichester: John Wiley & Sons, 1995.

Murphy, Michael, and Steven Donovan. *The Physical and Psychological Effects of Meditation: A Review of Contemporary Research with a Comprehensive Bibliography*. edited by Eugene Taylor. Sausalito, California: Institute of Noetic Sciences, 1997.

Newberg, Andrew, et al. *Why God Won't Go Away: Brain Science and the Biology of Belief*. New York: Ballantine, 2001.

Nicholson, Sarah. *Three Faces of Saul: An Intertextual Approach to Biblical Tragedy*. Sheffield: Sheffield Academic Press, 2002.

Niditch, Susan. *Chaos to Cosmos: Studies in Biblical Patterns of Creation*. Chico, California: Scholars, 1985.

———. *Oral World and Written Word: Ancient Israelite Literature*. London: SPCK, 1997.

Nolland, John. *The Gospel of Matthew: A Commentary on the Greek Text*. Grand Rapids: Eerdmans, 2005.

———. *Luke 9:21—18:34*. WBC Vol. 35b. Dallas: Word, 1993.

O'Connell, Robert H., "עם." *NIDOTTE* 3:429-32.

Oikonomou, E. B. "לין." In *TDOT* 7:543–46.

Oppenheim, A. Leo. "The Interpretation of Dreams in the Ancient Near East. With a Translation of an Assyrian Dream Book." *Transactions of the American Philosophical Society* 46.3 (1956) 179–373.

Ottosson, Magnus. "אֶרֶץ." In *TDOT* I: 388-405.

Ottosson, M., and L. Lamberty-Zielinski. "סוּף." In *TDOT* 10:190–96.

Overholt, Thomas W. *Cultural Anthropology and the Old Testament*. Minneapolis: Fortress, 1996.

———. "Elijah and Elisha in the Context of Israelite Religion." In *Prophets and Paradigms: Essays in Honour of Gene M. Tucker*, edited by Stephen Breck Reid, 94–111. Sheffield: Sheffield Academic Press, 1996.

———. "Jeremiah and the Nature of the Prophetic Process." In *Scripture in History and Theology: Essays in Honour of J. Coert Rylaarsdam*, edited by Arthur L. Merrill and Thomas W. Overholt, 129–50. Pittsburg: Pickwick, 1977.

———. "Prophecy in History: The Social Reality of Intermediation." *JSOT* 48 (1990) 3–29.

———. "Prophecy: The Problem of Cross-Cultural Comparison." In *Anthropological Approaches to the Old Testament*, edited by Bernhard Lang, 60–82. London: SPCK, 1985.
Palagini, Laura, and Rosenlicht Nicholas. "Sleep, Dreaming and Mental Health: A Review of Historical and Neurobiological Perspectives." *Sleep Medicine Reviews* 15 (2011) 179–86.
Parker, K. Langloh. *Australian Legendary Tales*. New York: Viking, 1966.
Parker, Simon B. "Possession Trance and Prophecy in Pre-Exilic Israel." *VT* 28 (1978) 271–85.
Pearson, Raymond F. *In Conversation with Jonah: Conversation Analysis, Literary Criticism and the Book of Jonah*. Sheffield: Sheffield Academic Press, 1996.
Peters, Emmanuelle. "Are Delusions on a Continuum? The Case of Religious and Delusional Beliefs." In *Psychosis and Spirituality: Exploring the new Frontier*, edited by Isabel Clarke, 191–207. London: Whurr, 2001.
Petersen, David L. *The Roles of Israel's Prophets*. Sheffield: JSOT Press, 1981.
Pilch, John J. "Altered States of Consciousness: A 'Kitbashed' Model." *BTB* 26 (1996) 133–38.
———. "Altered States of Consciousness in the Synoptics." In *The Social Setting of Jesus and the Gospels*, edited by Wolfgang Stegemann et al., 103–15. Minneapolis: Fortress, 2002.
———. "The Transfiguration of Jesus: An Experience of Alternate Reality." In *Modelling Early Christianity: Social Scientific Studies of the New Testament in its Context*, edited by Philip F. Esler, 47–64. London: Rouledge, 1995.
———. *Visions and Healing in the Acts of the Apostles: How Early Believers Experienced God*. Collegeville, MN: Liturgical, 2004.
———. "Visions in Revelation and Alternate Consciousness: A Perspective from Cultural Anthropology." *Listening* 28 (1993) 231–44.
Polzin, Robert. "The Monarchy Begins: 1 Samuel 8–10." *SBLSP* 26 (1987) 120–43.
Pope, Marvin H. "The Cult of the Dead at Ugarit." In *Ugarit in Retrospect: Fifty Years of Ugarit and Ugaritic*, edited by Gordon Douglas Young, 159–79. Winona Lake: Eisenbrauns, 1981.
———. "A Divine Banquet at Ugarit." In *The Use of the Old Testament in the New and Other Essays, Studies in Honour of William Franklin Stinespring*, edited by James M. Efird, 170–203. Durham NC: Duke University Press, 1972.
Price, James D. "עיר." In *NIDOTTE* 3:396–99.
Price, J., and A. Stevens. "An Evolutionary Approach to Psychiatric Disorders: Group-Splitting and Schizophrenia." In *Evolution of the Psyche* edited by D. H. Rosen and M. C. Luebbert, 196–207. Westport, CT: Praeger, 1999.
Prince, Raymond H. "Religious Experience and Psychopathology: Cross-Cultural Perspectives." In *Religion and Mental Health*, edited by John F. Schumaker, 281–91. New York: Oxford University Press, 1992.
Procksch, O. "The Word of God in the Old Testament." In *TDNT* 4:92–93.
Pufulete, Maria. "The Voices Within." *Chemistry in Britain* 33.11 (1997) 31–35.
Rasmussen, Morten, et al. "An Aboriginal Australian Genome Reveals Separate Human Dispersals into Asia." *Science* 334.94 (2011) 94–98.
Ratner, Robert J. "Jonah, The Runaway Slave." *Maarav* 5.6 (1990) 281–305.
Reed, H. "Improved Dream Recall Associated with Meditation." *Journal of Clinical Psychology* 34.1 (1978) 150–56.

Reed, Jonathan L. "The Sign of Jonah (Q 11:29–32) and Other Epic Traditions in Q." In *Reimagining Christian Origins: A Colloquium Honoring Burton L. Mack*, edited by. Elizabeth A. Castelli and Hal Taussig, 35–54. Valley Forge: Trinity, 1996.
Rengstorf, K. H. "σημειον in the New Testament." In *TDNT* 7:200.
Ringgren, Helmer. "אֱלֹהִים." In *TDOT* 1:267–84.
———. "עָבַד." In *TDOT* 10:376–90.
Ringgren, H., et al. "נָהַר." In *TDOT* 9:261–70.
Roberts, Alice. *The Incredible Human Journey*. London: Bloomsbury, 2009.
Robinson, Bernard P. "Elijah at Horeb, 1 Kings 19:1–18: A Coherent Narrative?" *RB* 98.4 (1991) 513–36.
———. "Jonah's Qiqayon Plant." *ZAW* 97.3 (1985) 390–403.
Robinson, Margaret G. "Dreams in the Old Testament." PhD diss., University of Manchester, 1987.
Rofé, Alexander. *The Prophetical Stories*. Jerusalem: Magnes, 1988.
Rollin, Sue. "Women and Witchcraft in Ancient Assyria (c. 900–600 BC)." In *Images of Women in Antiquity*, edited by. Averil Cameron and Amélie Kuhrt, 34–45. London: Croom Helm Ltd., 1983.
Ross, Allen P. "נָחַר." In *NIDOTTE* 3:46–51.
Rouget, Gilbert. *Music and Trance: A Theory of the Relations between Music and Possession*. Chicago: University of Chicago Press, 1985.
Rowley, H H. "Elijah on Mount Carmel." *BJRL* 43 (1960) 190–219.
———. *Men of God: Studies in Old Testament History and Prophecy*. London: Thomas Nelson & Sons Ltd., 1963.
Sæbø, M. "יוֹם." In *TDOT* 6:7–32.
Salters, R. B. *Jonah & Lamentations*. Sheffield: Sheffield Academic Press, 1994.
Sanders, Jack T. "When Sacred Canopies Collide: The Reception of the Torah of Moses in the Wisdom Literature of the Second Temple Period." *JSJ* 32.2 (2001) 121–36.
Sannella, Lee. *The Kundalini Experience: Psychosis or Transcendence*. Lower Lake, California: Integral, 1987.
Sarna, Nahum M. "The Interchange of the prepositions *Beth* and *Min* in Biblical Hebrew." *JBL* 78 (1959) 310–16.
Sasson, Jack M. *Jonah: A New Translation with Introduction, Commentary and Interpretation*. New York: Doubleday, 1990.
———. "On Jonah's Two Missions." *Henoch* 6 (1984) 23–30.
Saver, J. L., and J. Rabin. "The Neural Substrates of Religious Experience." *JNCN* 9 (1997) 498–510.
Scafi, Alessandro. *Mapping Paradise: A History of Heaven on Earth* London: The British Library, 2006
Scholem, Gershom. *Major Trends in Jewish Mysticism*. New York: Schocken, 1974.
Schrenk, Gottlob. "δικαιοσύνην." In *TDNT* 2:162–210.
Schunck, K. D. "בָּמָה." In *TDOT* 2:139–45.
Scott, Jack B. "אֵל." In *TWOT* 1: 41.
Seamands, David A. *Healing for Damaged Emotions*. Aylesbury: Alpha, 1986.
Seebass, H. "נֶפֶשׁ." In *TDOT* 9:497–519.
Segall, Marshall H., et al. *Human Behaviour in Global Perspective: An Introduction to Cross-Cultural Psychology*. Boston: Allyn and Bacon, 1990.
Selman, Martin J. "בָּמָה." In *NIDOTTE* 1:670.
Seybold, K. "הֶבֶל *hebhel*." In *TDOT* 3:313–20.

Shepherd, Jerry. "שׁוֹא." In *NIDOTTE* 4:53–55.
Sherwood, Yvonne. *A Biblical Text and Its Afterlives: The Survival of Jonah in Western Culture.* Cambridge: Cambridge University Press, 2000.
———. "Cross-Currents in the Book of Jonah: Some Jewish and Cultural Midrashim on a Traditional Text." *BibInt* 6.1 (1998) 49–79.
Shields, M. A. "Wisdom and Prophecy." In *Dictionary of the Old Testament: Wisdom, Poetry and Writings*, edited by Tremper Longman III and Peter Emms, 876–84. Downers Grove: IVP, 2008.
Simon, Uriel. *The JPS Bible Commentary: Jonah*. Philadelphia: The Jewish Publication Society, 1999.
Skinner, John. *A Critical and Exegetical Commentary on Genesis.* Edinburgh: T &T Clark, 1912.
Smick, Elmer B. "חָיָה." In *TWOT* 1:279–82.
Smith, R. H. "Sign of Jonah." In *DJG* 754–56.
Solomon, Andrew. *The Noonday Demon: An Anatomy of Depression.* London: Chatto & Windus, 2001.
Sparks, Kenton L. "The Problem of Myth in Ancient Historiography." In *Rethinking the Foundations: Historiography in the Ancient World and in the Bible, Essays in Honour of John Van Seters*, edited by Steven L. McKenzie and Thomas Römer in collaboration with Hans Heinrich Schmid, 269–80. Berlin: Walter de Gruyter, 2000.
Stanner, W. H. E. *The Dreaming and Other Essays.* Collingwood: Black Inc, 2009.
Sternberg, Meir. *The Poetics of Biblical Narrative: Ideological Literature and the Drama of Reading.* Bloomington: Indiana University Press, 1987.
Strauss, S. "The Chronic Mononucleosis Syndrome." *Journal of Infectious Diseases* 157.3 (1988) 405–12.
Streete, Gail Corrington. *The Strange Woman: Power and Sex in the Bible.* Louisville, KY: Westminster John Knox, 1997.
Stuart, Douglas. *Hosea-Jonah, WBC Vol 31.* Waco, TX: Word, 1987.
Sussman, Varda. "Lighting the Way Through History: The Evolution of Ancient Oil Lamps." *BARev* 11 (1985) 42–56.
Swetnam, James. "Some Signs of Jonah." *Biblica* 68 (1987) 74–79.
Szmukler, G. I., and G. Patton. "Sociocultural Models of Eating Disorders." In *Handbook of Eating Disorders: Theory, Treatment and Research*, edited by George Szmukler et al., 177–92. Chichester: John Wiley & Sons Ltd., 1995.
Thackeray, H. St. J., and Ralph Marcus. *Josephus: Jewish Antiquities, Vol 5, Books V–VIII.* London: William Heineman Ltd., 1934.
Thalbourne, Michael A., et al. "Transliminality: Its Nature and Correlates." *JSPR* 91 (1997) 305–31.
Tov, Emanuel. *Textual Criticism of the Hebrew Bible.* Minneapolis: Fortress, 2001.
Trevisan, Louis A., et al. "Complications of Alcohol Withdrawal: Pathophysiological Insights." *Alcohol Health & Research World* 22.1 (1998) 61–66.
Trible, Phyllis. "Divine Incongruities in the Book of Jonah." In *God in the Fray: A Tribute to Walter Brueggermann*, edited by Tod Linafelt and Timothy K. Beal, 198–208. Minneapolis: Fortress Press, 1998.
———. "Exegesis for Storytellers and other Strangers." *JBL* 114.1 (1995) 3–19.
———. *God and the Rhetoric of Sexuality.* Philadelphia: Fortress, 1978.

———. *Rhetorical Criticism: Context, Method, and the Book of Jonah*. Minneapolis: Fortress, 1994.

———. "A Tempest in a Text: Ecological Soundings in the Book of Jonah." In *On the Way to Nineveh: Studies in Honour of George M. Landes*, edited by Stephen L. Cook and S. C. Winter, 187–99. Atlanta: Scholars, 1999.

Trumble, William R., and Angus Stevenson, eds. *Shorter Oxford English Dictionary*. 5th ed. 2 vols. Oxford: Oxford University Press, 2002.

Turner, Laurence A. *Genesis*. Sheffield: Sheffield Academic Press, 2000.

Turner, Max *Power from on High: The Spirit in Israel's Restoration and Witness in Luke-Acts*. Sheffield: Sheffield Academic Press, 2000.

Twelftree, G. H. "Temptation of Jesus." In *DJG* 821–27.

Ulrich, Eugene. "From Literature to Scripture: Reflections on the Growth of a Text's Authoritativeness." *DJD* 10 (2003) 3–25.

Van Dam, Cornelis. *The Urim and Thummim*. Winona Lake, Indiana: Eisenbrauns, 1997.

Van der Jagt, Krijn A. "What Did Saul Eat When He First Met Samuel? Light from Anthropology on Biblical Texts." *BT* 47.2 (1996) 226–30.

Van Os, J., et al. "Self-Reported Psychosis-Like Symptoms and the Continuum of Psychosis." *Soc Psych Psych Epid* 34.9 (1999) 459–63.

Van Rooy, Harry F. "פנים." In *NIDOTTE* 3:637–40.

Van Seters, John. *Abraham in History and Tradition*. London: Yale University Press, 1975.

Van Wijk-Bos, Johanna W. H. "No Small Thing: The 'Overturning' of Nineveh in the Third Chapter of Jonah." In *On the Way to Nineveh: Studies in Honour of George M. Landes*, edited by Stephen L. Cook and S. C. Winter, 218–37. Atlanta: Scholars, 1999.

Vaughan, Patrick H. *The Meaning of 'BĀMÂ' in the Old Testament: A Study of Etymological, Textual and Archaeological Evidence*. London: Cambridge University Press, 1974.

Vehse, Charles Ted. "Long Live the King: Historical Fact and Narrative Fiction in 1 Samuel 9–10." In *The Pitcher is Broken: Memorial Essays for Gösta W. Ahlström*, edited by Steven W. Holloway and Lowell K. Handy, 435–44. Sheffield: Sheffield Academic Press, 1995.

Vogel, Gerald W., et al. "Improvement of Depression by REM Sleep Deprivation." *Arch Gen Psychiatry* 37 (1980) 247–53.

Von Rad, Gerhard. *Genesis: A Commentary*. London: SCM Press, 1972.

Wallace, Daniel B. *Greek Grammar Beyond the Basics: An exegetical syntax of the New Testament*. Grand Rapids, Michigan: Zondervan, 1996.

Waltke, Bruce K. *Genesis: A Commentary*. Grand Rapids: Zondervan, 2001.

Ward, William A. "The Semitic Biconsonantal Root *SP* and the Common Origin of Egyptian *ČWF* and Hebrew *SÛP*: 'Marsh(-Plant).'" *VT* 24 (1974) 339–49.

Watson, Wilfred G. E. "The Structure of 1 Sam 3." *BZ* 29.1 (1985) 90–93.

Watts, John D. W. *The Books of Joel, Obadiah, Jonah, Nahum, Habakkuk and Zephaniah*. Cambridge: Cambridge University Press, 1975.

Wegner, Paul "ענה." In *NIDOTTE* 3:449–52.

Wenham, Gordon J. *Genesis 16–50: WBC Vol 2*. Dallas: Word, 1994.

Westerlund, David. "Spiritual Beings as Agents of Illness." In *African Spirituality: Forms, Meanings and Expressions*, edited by Jacob K. Olupona, 152–75. New York: Crossroad, 2000.

Westermann, Claus. *Genesis 1–11: A Continental Commentary*. Minneapolis: Fortress, 1994.

———. *Genesis 12–36: A Commentary*. Minneapolis: Augsburg, 1985.

———. *Isaiah 40–66*. London: SCM Press Ltd., 1969.

Wheeler, Brannon M. *Prophets in the Quran: An Introduction to the Quran and Muslim Exegesis*. London: Continuum, 2002.

White, Marsha C. *The Elijah Legends and Jehu's Coup*. Atlanta: Scholars, 1997.

Whitney, J. T. "'Bamoth' in the Old Testament." *TynBul* 30 (1979) 125–47.

Wiener, Aharon. *The Prophet Elijah in the Development of Judaism: A Depth Psychological Study*. London: Routledge and Kegan Paul, 1978.

Williams, William C. "יָשַׁן." In *NIDOTTE* 2:553–55.

———. "רדם." In *NIDOTTE* 3:1057.

Wilson, David C. "The Significance of Psychophysiological Factors in Prophecy: A Critical Examination of Altered States of Consciousness and Spiritual Encounter in Selected Passages of the Hebrew Bible." PhD diss., University of Manchester, 2006.

Wilson, Robert R. "Prophecy and Ecstasy: A Reexamination." *JBL* 98 (1979) 321–37.

———. *Prophecy and Society in Ancient Israel*. Philadelphia: Fortress, 1980.

Winkelman, Michael. *Shamanism: The Neural Ecology of Consciousness and Healing*. Westport, CT: Bergin & Garvey, 2000.

Winter, Jim. *Depression: A Rescue Plan*. Epsom: Day One Publications, 2000.

Wiseman, D. J. "Jonah's Nineveh." *TynBul* 30(1979) 29–51.

Wiseman, Donald J. *1 & 2 Kings: An Introduction and Commentary*. Leicester: Inter-Varsity Press, 1993.

Wolff, Hans Walter. *Obadiah and Jonah: A Commentary*. Minneapolis: Augsburg, 1986.

Wolpert, Lewis. *Malignant Sadness: The Anatomy of Depression*. London: Faber & Faber, 1999.

Woods, Fred E. *Water and Storm Polemics in the Books of Kings*. New York: P. Lang, 1994.

Wright, Christopher J. H. *Deuteronomy*. Peabody, MA: Hendrickson, 1996.

Wright, N. T. *Jesus and the Victory of God*. London: SPCK, 1996.

Würthwein, Ernst. "Elijah at Horeb: Reflections on 1Kings 19:9–18." In *Proclamation and Presence: Old Testament Essays in Honour of Gwynne Henton Davies*, edited by John I. Durham and J. R. Porter, 152–166. London: SCM, 1970.

Wurtman, Richard J. "Ways That Foods Can Affect the Brain." *Nutr Rev* (Suppl.) 44 (1986) 2–6.

Wyatt, Nick. *Religious Texts from Ugarit:The Words of Ilimilku and His Colleagues*. Sheffield: Sheffield Academic Press, 1998.

Zobel, H. J. "חֶסֶד." In *TDOT* 5:44–64.

Index

Abram, 43–49, 50–51
Adam, 1, 23–24, 26–27, 85–89, 91, 103–4, 106–8, 110–11, 120, 120–23, 126–27, 141, 144, 149
altered state of consciousness, 3, 37, 43n42, 57, 64–67, 73, 100, 116, 133–34, 148, 160, 193, 202
Aristotle, 60, 111, 117, 120
ascent, 53, 62–65, 71–72n101, 164, 189
asexual, 93–94, 96

bipolar disorder, 5, 12, 120, 125–26, 142

carbohydrate, 52, 73, 126
clinical neurology, 43, 85
cross-cultural psychology, xv–xvi, 28, 39, 50, 57, 60, 86

delusional, 37, 115
derived etic hypnogram, xvi, 41–42, 48, 51, 57, 66, 84, 86, 88, 94, 121, 126, 143–45
derived etic view, 28
diaspora, 3, 12, 105
dream theophany, 41–42, 149
dreamform, 11–12, 31–32, 65, 75, 83–86, 88, 104, 111, 120, 124, 126, 142–44
Dreamtime, 12, 88, 142

ecstasy, 57, 63–64, 80, 83
emic, 19, 39–40, 48, 81
endogenous, 116
etic, xv–xvi, 19, 28, 39–44, 48, 51, 57, 66, 71, 84, 86, 88, 94, 121, 126, 143–45

fasting, 34, 36, 51, 62–63, 71, 73, 84, 114–17, 124–26, 128, 204, 206–7, 210
feminist, 18, 24
Freudian, 22, 28

Geschehensbogen, 29

hallucinations, 5, 10, 37
hyperactivity, 51, 54
hypnogram, xvi–xvii, 36, 38–39, 41–42, 44, 48–49, 51, 54–55, 57, 65–66, 83–84, 86, 88, 94, 121, 126, 143–45, 179, 193, 195–98, 211, 214, 216
hypnopompia, 87, 94, 121, 152
hypnopompic, 121–22, 126, 133–34, 145, 193, 198
hypothalamus, 33

immortality, 24, 100–103, 105–9

Jungian, 26–28

Kingdom of Heaven, 116, 119–20

lung gom pa (running), 65, 136, 139, 141, 201

macarism, 112–14, 116–19
Major depressive disorder, 10
meditation, 65, 133–34, 136, 152
Minnesota experiment, 115
mood, 35–36, 52–53, 58, 70, 73, 78, 210
multidisciplinary, 1, 19, 23, 112
mystic(s), 3, 37, 61–64, 71, 79, 133n24

mystical, 3, 37–38, 62–64, 126, 128, 153, 163
myth(s), 1, 6–7, 13, 15–18, 20, 103

nephesh, 22, 31, 70, 74, 84, 90–93, 96, 108–9, 122–23, 171, 174
nocturnal activity, xvi, 39, 41, 57
Non-REM sleep, 34, 87, 198, 210,

pathological, 11
pharmacological, 33–34
possession, 68, 73, 77, 115, 123, 130n8, 136–37, 149, 158, 202
prophetic type(s), 8n33, 10, 60, 111, 117, 125, 144–45, 149
psychiatrist, 37
psychopathic, 9
psychopathology, 8–12
psychosis, 5, 9–12, 58
psychosomatic, 22, 31, 108

reactive, 62, 116, 207
reflexive, 114–15, 117
REM sleep, 34–36, 56–57, 60, 91, 160, 216

schizophrenia, 4–5, 10, 12, 120, 125–26, 142
semi-starvation, 36, 54, 65
serotonin, 33–34, 73, 124, 126

shaman(s), 8–10, 63–64, 67–68, 73–74, 76–77, 114, 123–24, 126, 153–54, 156–60, 162–66, 172–75, 178, 183, 185, 192
social system, 38, 40, 42, 61
soul(s), 22–24, 27, 68, 71, 74, 87, 90, 92–93, 105, 107–9, 114, 122–23, 146, 164, 169, 174–75, 211–12
spiritual encounter, 47, 58, 61, 66, 76, 78, 112
sub-culture of religion, 37
surgical trauma, 34, 58
synesthesia, 38, 43, 79, 122

The Dreaming, 3
theophanic encounter, 23, 27, 29, 30–31, 49, 142, 146
transcendent, 21–23, 30–31, 89, 93, 95, 99, 133, 148
tree of life, 25–26, 31, 100–102, 104, 148–49

vision quest, 64, 66, 70, 74, 81–83, 109–10, 124, 126, 143–44, 195

wilderness, 71, 73–74, 82, 123–24, 126, 140, 143
wisdom, 97, 100–103, 112–13, 117–19, 129–31

www.ingramcontent.com/pod-product-compliance
Lightning Source LLC
Chambersburg PA
CBHW051635230426
43669CB00013B/2306